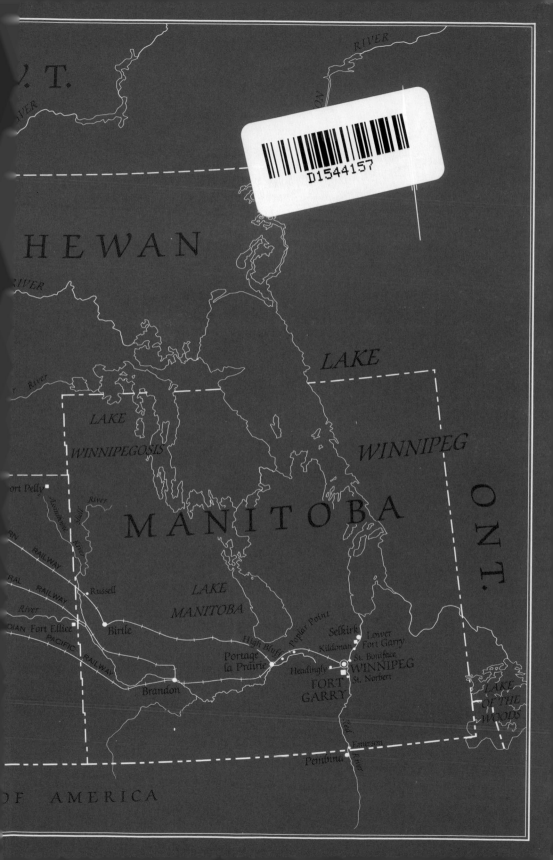

Major Charles Arkoll Boulton

I FOUGHT RIEL

A Military Memoir

Major Charles A. Boulton
Edited by Heather Robertson

A Richard Bonnycastle Book 3

James Lorimer & Company, Publishers
Toronto 1985

DESIGN: Brant Cowie/Artplus Ltd.

The illustrations on pages ii, 10, 19, 116, 149, and 173 are reproduced from the original 1886 edition, *Reminiscences of the North-West Rebellions*. Photography on xiii and xv reproduced courtesy of Manitoba Archives. Endpapers map by Department of Geography, University of Toronto.

CANADIAN CATALOGUING IN PUBLICATION DATA

Boulton, Major, 1841-1899.
 I fought Riel

ISBN 0-88862-935-4

1. Red River Rebellion, 1869–1870 — Personal narratives, Canadian. 2. Riel Rebellion, 1885 — Personal narratives, Canadian. 3. Boulton, Major, 1841 – 1899. 4. Riel, Louis, 1844 – 1885. I. Robertson, Heather, 1942 – II. Title.

FC3215.B68 1985   971.05'1   C85-099405-5
F1060.9.B68 1985

James Lorimer & Company, Publishers
Egerton Ryerson Memorial Building
35 Britain Street
Toronto, Ontario M5A 1R7

Printed and bound in Canada by John Deyell Company

CONTENTS

LIST OF ILLUSTRATIONS

REMINISCENCES

OF THE

North-West Rebellions,

WITH

A RECORD OF THE RAISING OF HER MAJESTY'S
100TH REGIMENT IN CANADA,

AND A CHAPTER ON

CANADIAN SOCIAL & POLITICAL LIFE,

BY

MAJOR BOULTON,

COMMANDING BOULTON'S SCOUTS.

"A restlessness in men's minds to be something they are not, or
to have something they have not, is the root of all
immorality or good."

TORONTO:
PRINTED BY THE GRIP PRINTING AND PUBLISHING CO.
1886.

PREFACE

Heather Robertson

Major Charles A. Boulton's account of his participation in both Riel rebellions, 1869-70 at Red River and 1885 in the North-West Territories, was originally published in 1886 as *Reminiscences of the North-West Rebellions* by Davis & Henderson, Toronto. It was dedicated to "The Officers and Men Composing my Corps during the Campaign of 1885, as a Token of Respect and Esteem for Them."

This edition is a shortened version of the *Reminiscences*. The original included a lengthy appendix listing the names and ranks of the armed forces which suppressed the 1885 rebellion as well as military despatches from the field. Boulton also included chapters on the social and political life of Canada at the time and the history of his early military career. This edition focuses exclusively on Boulton's story of the two rebellions. It has been slightly edited for clarity and continuity, but the spelling and sentence structure reflect Boulton's Victorian prose style.

Charles Boulton had the unusual good fortune to be an active participant in both Métis uprisings, in the first as a young militia officer, in the second as commander of a troop of "irregulars," Boulton's Scouts. He was Riel's opponent and in many ways his eastern Canadian counterpart: brave, combative, proud and an ardent patriot. Boulton was also a Conservative and an imperialist; his attitudes reflect the popular thinking behind the government of Sir John A. Macdonald, whose ruthless expansionist policies precipitated both rebellions. Boulton, however, has no patience with the stupidity and bungling demonstrated by government officials and some of his fellow officers. Apart from his own Scouts he casts a cool eye on all participants and blows his own horn with restraint.

Boulton's view is that of an Upper Canadian, an Anglican, an immigrant, a homesteader and a soldier. To him, Riel was not a revolutionary hero or religious martyr, neither a fool nor a fanatic; he was a powerful adversary, a leader of men, educated and religious, a family man like Boulton himself, prepared, as was Boulton, to fight to the death for his principles and his land. Boulton sincerely believed that the rule of British democracy was best for the North-West; he saw Riel's defiance, especially his violence, as evidence of lawlessness, despotism and American intrigue. This perspective was the conventional wisdom of Boulton's time; today, in the light of Riel's reputation as populist hero and tragic victim, it is unusual and provocative.

I Fought Riel is a personal story, a hair-raising adventure tale of murder and massacre, Indian uprisings, gunfights and guerrilla warfare which plunges into the midst of the action and captures events in vivid detail. I was there, says Major Boulton, and this is what I saw. Straightforward, unsentimental, Boulton's account captures the harshness of a desperate struggle for power in a vast inhospitable wilderness where there seemed to be more than enough room for everyone.

Boulton's own laconic motto on the title page of *Reminiscences* is a fitting epigraph for a cruel conflict which remains in many ways unresolved today:

> A restlessness in men's minds to be something they are not, or to have something they have not, is the root of all immorality, or good.

INTRODUCTION

Heather Robertson

Charles Arkoll Boulton was born into one of Upper Canada's most influential families on September 17, 1841 in Cobourg. He attended Upper Canada College in Toronto and in 1858, at the age of sixteen, decided to join the 100th Prince of Wales Royal Canadian Regiment, which was being recruited in Canada for overseas service.

> Obtaining my parents' consent, and accompanied by my father, I set out for Toronto to wait upon Sir Edmund Head, the Governor-General, with an application for a commission. To my chagrin I learned that all commissions had been given away, but I was relieved at finding that each commission carried with it the responsibility of having to raise a certain number of men. Having received a promise from the Governor-General that, should a vacancy occur, I might obtain it, I immediately returned, determined to raise forty men and trust to the failure of some officer in procuring the required number.
>
> My father supplied me with what necessary funds I wanted, lent me his waggon and a pair of horses, and I engaged a friend who played the bagpipes, the only musical instrument I could procure in the neighbourhood, for recruiting purposes. With an old-fashioned uniform, lent me by an officer who had early settled in the country, I started off to visit the neighbouring villages to recruit; and I need hardly say that I was the envy and admiration of every youth my own age who witnessed my progress through the country. At the end of a fortnight I had got together twenty of as fine, young backwoods fellows as one could wish to see. Great consternation was occasioned in some families who were not accustomed in Canada to have a call from a recruiting-sergeant. One young fellow I had great difficulty in secreting from his mother, who was nearly heartbroken at the prospect

of losing him. He afterwards became a first-class musician, receiving his first training in the band, and never repented of his venture.

My enterprise was successful. As it happened, one of the officers elect dropped out and I obtained a commission as ensign.

After ten years' service in England, Gibraltar and Malta, Boulton returned to Canada with the regiment and took his discharge, determined "to become one of the workers in a country that I am certain is going to be a country to be proud of." He was appointed Major in the East Durham Regiment of Militia, 46th Battalion and in 1869 was one of six young men selected to accompany Col. J.S. Dennis's survey expedition to the North-West Territories.

Major Boulton's account begins when the survey party arrived at Red River in July, 1869 and began to work. However, the formal purchase of the territory from the Hudson's Bay Company had not yet been completed, the Lieutenant-Governor had not arrived, and the residents of Red River – Indians, Scots, and several thousand French-speaking halfbreeds, or Métis – remained in the dark about their rights as Canadians. Colonel Dennis's survey was stopped by an armed force of Métis led by Louis Riel. Riel subsequently occupied the Hudson's Bay Company post at Fort Garry, declared a provisional government, and attempted to negotiate an equitable land settlement for the Métis people.

Major Boulton remained in Red River throughout the Riel regime. In February, 1870, he led a band of settlers from Portage la Prairie in an abortive attack on Fort Garry. Two men were fatally wounded; Boulton and his followers were captured and imprisoned in the fort. Boulton was sentenced to death but reprieved at the last moment; one of his companions, Thomas Scott, was shot instead.

After his release and the collapse of the provisional government, Major Boulton returned to Ontario. He bought a share of a lumber business in Lakefield and in 1874 married Augusta Latter. The lumber business went bankrupt and by 1878 Boulton was dependent on his father's charity. In the winter of

Major Charles Boulton in dress uniform, circa 1885

1880, destitute, with four small children to feed, Charles Boulton returned to the new province of Manitoba intending to homestead on the Shell River about three hundred miles northwest of Winnipeg. He built a small log house and sent for his family to join him. They arrived on November 3, 1880 to find that the house had no roof, no windows, no door, and that there was a man camped in a tent inside.

The next year Boulton bought land fifteen miles south, speculating that the new CPR railway line to the west would pass through his property. It didn't. He moved his house there anyway, log by log, and surveyed the rest into a town site. By the spring of 1885, Boulton's town had two stores, a post office, a town hall and a school. His sixth child, born in 1884, was named Russell after the growing settlement. Boulton's new home, The Manor, built of pressed mud brick, was the grandest in town.

By 1885 the little settlement of Red River had become the boom town of Winnipeg and thousands of homesteaders were pushing the Métis farther and farther west. The Métis had been granted title to their Manitoba lands in the form of scrip, but most sold out for a few dollars. Louis Riel had moved to Montana where he taught school. Once more the Métis of the North-West Territories found themselves landless and threatened by dispossession; they determined to take a stand and once more Riel became their leader. A number of Indian bands joined the Métis in an attempt to resist the encroaching settlements.

When in March, 1885 the North-West Rebellion broke out near Duck Lake, three hundred miles northwest of Russell, Major Boulton offered his services to Gen. Frederick Middleton, commander of the Canadian expedition dispatched to quell the uprising. Within a few days, Boulton mobilized sixty of his friends and neighbours into Boulton's Scouts, and joined General Middleton's troops in the west.

Each scout was paid seventy-five cents a day. He was supplied with a horse, a Winchester rifle, a brown duck coat, a pair of riding breeches, a helmet, a flannel shirt, moccasins and stock-

Members of Boulton's Scouts during North-West Rebellion of 1885

ings. "The white helmets were criticized as too conspicuous," Boulton said, "but I'm convinced that in the kind of fighting we had to face it is well to be able to distinguish friend from foe. It is a most unpleasant thing to be mistaken for the enemy by your friends when creeping through the bush." (Photographs of Boulton's Scouts suggest that they preferred less conspicuous stetson-style hats, and when Major Boulton dug his own white helmet out of mothballs, he found, to his wife's relief, that it was missing its gleaming brass spike.) Major Boulton, of course, wore a scarlet tunic.

Major Boulton and his Scouts accompanied General Middleton throughout the four-month North-West campaign and played a key role in the battles of Fish Creek and Batoche. Boulton had a great deal of respect for his opponents:

> The enemy we had to contend with were cooler and better shots at short range, more accustomed to taking advantage of cover, and possessed a more perfect knowledge of the country. This is not to be wondered at, for by trapping and hunting most of them live. But they will not stand to face a determined charge, especially if they are opposed to the bayonet.

He was pleased to come out of the campaign with only two men killed and eight wounded.

My men were obedient and plucky and thoroughly entered into the spirit of the campaign. They sacrificed their summer's crop to uphold the laws of their adopted country – some even selling their stock for what it would bring that they might not be compelled to stay home. I cannot praise too highly their bravery, their gallantry, and their powers of endurance, combined with great good humour, which made the four months I had the honour of commanding them pass like a pleasure trip.

Major Boulton had sympathy for the suffering of the Indians and Métis, perceiving clearly that with the disappearance of the buffalo their livelihood had completely vanished; he saw them also, however, as a primitive, barbaric people. For Louis Riel himself, Boulton had only dislike and contempt. He considered Riel a despot, a murderer and a traitor.

Unlike the crowd of fortune hunters, speculators, roustabouts, crooks, and ne'er-do-wells who poured into the North-West from Ontario when the Hudson's Bay Company released its hold, Charles Boulton was an officer and a gentleman. He believed in British justice and the rule of law and became the unofficial leader of the "Canadians" at Red River as much for their own safety as to maintain order. In both rebellions, Boulton feared widespread violence and plunder which could lead to an Indian uprising and a major civil war. He had reason to worry: in 1869, Thomas Scott had already been fined for assault and another Ontarian, the poet Charles Mair, had infuriated the halfbreed wives of prominent Red River merchants by publishing rude remarks about them in eastern newspapers. Boulton's lack of jingoism and his coolness to racist bigotry might explain the apparently total neglect of him by the Macdonald government on his return from Red River in 1870, and his failure to acquire a railway line for his property.

Following Riel's execution in November, 1885, Boulton returned to his home in Russell to write his memoirs. In 1889 he was appointed to the Senate. Until his death ten years later, he campaigned vigorously for Empire free trade and the interests of the western farmer. He remained to the end a political activist and a passionate Canadian.

PART ONE

REBELLION AT RED RIVER,
1869-1870

I

RIEL BLOCKS THE WAY

I arrived in the territory in July, 1869. Colonel Dennis's party journeyed through the United States by rail to St. Paul, a small American frontier town on the Mississippi. At St. Cloud we purchased horses and waggons to convey us across the prairie, four hundred and fifty miles north to Winnipeg. This trail had become the chief highway from the railway terminus on the Mississippi to the Hudson's Bay Territory, and at St. Paul hundreds of Red River carts were assembled to convey stores and supplies into the interior. These carts were of native manufacture, constructed entirely without iron, the transport of such heavy material being too costly to admit of its use. The harness consisted of what is called "shagannappi," being the raw hide of the buffalo dressed for the purpose. The term "shagannappi" came to be applied by the new settlers to everything in connection with a Red River outfit. The journey was a long monotonous one, over a level, treeless prairie, with no habitations, until we reached the small frontier village of Pembina, at the boundary between the two countries. After crossing the boundary line we came to the Hudson's Bay post of Pembina, and a few miles further we reached what appeared to be an old settled country. The changed aspect of things was very marked, and one could not help being impressed by it, in coming upon a comparatively well-cultivated settlement in the heart of an immense region which for two centuries had so little communication with the outer world.

The principal fort, or depot, of the Hudson's Bay Company was Fort Garry, now the site of the flourishing city of Winnipeg. It was situated at the junction of the Assiniboine and Red Rivers. The Red River, which is navigable for about four hundred miles, takes its rise in American territory, and flows northward, through Lake Winnipeg, to Hudson's Bay. The Assiniboine, also navigable, empties into the Red River, about thirty miles from Lake Winnipeg, rising in the west in Canadian territory. For a time the English Government maintained troops at Fort Garry, and some of the rifles, ammunition and stores were retained when the last detachment left.

The hardships the employés of the Hudson's Bay Company had to suffer may be imagined when we state that a year's rations for an officer was one bag of flour, while the men got none, and what is generally considered as necessaries of life they had to do without. Fish, cariboo and wild fowl are the chief articles of diet at these remote posts. The Hudson's Bay officer who occupied the position of the Governor of the Territory in 1869 was Mr. Wm. Mactavish. He was unfortunately prostrated with illness at the time the difficulties arose over the transfer of the country, or he might have wielded a greater influence than he did.

When the surveying party arrived, the first thing done was to send the horses down to Point du Chêne and leave them with those of Mr. John A. Snow, the overseer of the construction of the road to the Lake of the Woods. Some of the party were struck with the beauty of the country in that neighbourhood, and determined upon taking up land. Then and there they selected a tract and staked it out for future occupation. This gave rise to jealousy on the part of the half-breeds in the neighbourhood, who watched their proceedings; and their spokesman, Louis Riel, followed us down to ascertain what our movements were likely to be. It was not difficult for him to persuade the half-breeds that this act was hostile to their interests, and they assembled to intercept us on our way. Riel warned our party that they must not survey the land or take possession of any of it. The words of his argument I have forgotten, but the gist of it was to the effect that the country was theirs, and that we had no right to it and must not survey it. We informed him that we were only employés of the Canadian Government and had no control over our movements. There was no show of violence or hostility in this demonstration, and it did not strike us as being of importance at the time. It was, however, the first scene in the drama that was about to be enacted; and I have no doubt gave the idea to the half-breeds of acting in a similar manner, which resulted in what is known as the "stake claims." The party left their horses and returned to Winnipeg, where Colonel Dennis organized a surveying party with Red River carts and ponies as transport, then returned to Pembina and went west along the boundary line for about ten miles. Under the superintendence of Colonel Dennis, we there commenced to run the principal meridian line straight north, upon which the future surveys were to be based.

We were now out upon the open prairie, far removed from any society, and had no opportunity of knowing what was going on in the settlements. We ran our meridian line north as far as Shoal Lake, on the east side of Lake Manitoba. Further proceedings were stopped by winter, which came upon us suddenly. We read in the papers, which occasionally came to hand, that the Honourable Mr. McDougall had been appointed the first Governor of the North-West Territory, and was on his way up.

The Honourable Mr. McDougall, who had probably taken the most active interest in the acquisition of this territory by Canada, and had urged it upon Parliament by able speeches, and had also, in conjunction with Sir George Cartier, negotiated for the purchase of the Hudson's Bay Company's rights with the Imperial Government, had been appointed no doubt as a reward for his services in connection therewith, and as the best fitted to launch the young colony on its new career. We also learned that Major Webb, another surveyor, had been interfered with by Riel and some half-breeds in his surveys, and, awaiting orders, had abandoned his work. Major Webb had apparently been infringing upon the outside two-mile limit which was claimed as hay privilege, and he thought it prudent to desist.

Colonel Dennis, in charge of the surveying parties, felt annoyed at the interference with his work, but found that he was powerless in the matter. He applied to the authorities, the Council of Assiniboia, and asked them to take action; but they expressed themselves as also powerless, and confined themselves to remonstrances. Unfortunately, Archbishop Taché, one of the most influential men in the country, especially with his own people, was absent. The Archbishop had gone to take part in the celebrated Ecumenical Council, at Rome, and on his way thither he called at Ottawa to ascertain from the Dominion Government what were their intentions on acquiring possession of the country. But the Government had already made provision by Act of Parliament for the government of the territory, and no fresh legislation could be obtained before the following session, so Archbishop Taché went on his way to Rome without effecting anything on behalf of his people.

The priest, Père Lestanc, who was left behind in Archbishop Taché's place, was a gentleman apparently with more zeal than discretion in the midst of a difficulty such as the present. He came from France, and was not imbued with the Canadian instincts that most of his clergy possessed. His actions gave rise to the feeling that the Roman Catholic church was in sympathy with the extreme measures enforced by Riel. The attitude of the church seemed more clear, when W. B. O'Donoghue, who at that time was being educated for the priesthood at Saint Boniface, and was a teacher there, saw fit to leave those duties to join Riel and to become his right hand man during the rebellion that immediately followed. With some honourable exceptions, the Americans, of whom there were a few, were hostile, and were fain to fan the flame of discontent, that advantage might possibly accrue to them or their country. The Canadians, who were not numerous, were enthusiastic over the transfer of the territory to the Dominion. Dr. J. C. Schultz, a merchant, undoubtedly represented this feeling at the time, and was most popular among the Canadians. Colonel Dennis advised the Honourable Mr. McDougall, who had just arrived at the boundary line, of the state of affairs that existed at Fort Garry. The Governor unfortunately over-estimated his own power and under-estimated that of the rebels. He had heard rumours on his way from St. Paul of the probability of resistance; and on his arrival at Pembina, on the 21st of October, 1869, he was handed a letter warning him not to enter the country.*

Disregarding this letter, the Governor pushed on to the Hudson's Bay Company's post, about two miles north of the boundary, accompanied by the Honourable Albert Richards as his Attorney-General, Mr. Provencher, Dr. Jakes, and some of his own family. Mr. McDougall deserved the greatest sympathy for the unfortunate position he now found himself placed in. He had travelled by land conveyance four hundred miles from St. Paul in the month of October, and was now advised by Mr. Mactavish to remain at Pembina and await developments, rather than attempt to enter the country. To attempt a return journey at the commencement of a north-west winter seemed to the Governor out of the question. He therefore determined to await the drift of events, trusting that something would turn up to relieve him from the awkwardness of his position. Pembina was a small frontier village where the accommodation was scant and of a very inferior description. It gave great satisfaction to his opponents, of whom there were a number at Pembina, to have at their threshold a Governor who could not further approach his territory; and Mr. McDougall had to suffer many petty indignities, added to the anxiety that he felt over the state of affairs in the country.

---

*A Monsieur W. McDougall

Monsieur, – Le comité national des Métis de la Rivière Rouge intime à Monsieur W. McDougall l'ordre de ne pas entrer sur le territoire du nord ouest, sans une permission spéciale de ce comité.

Par l'ordre du President, John Bruce.

Louis Riel, Secretary.
Daté à St. Norbert, Rivière Rouge,
ce 21e jour d'Octobre, 1869.

Riel began by protests and warnings, but soon he assumed more active measures. By the time the Governor arrived in Pembina he had a small force under his command, at River Sale, where he erected a barricade to guard the entrance into the country. His force at first did not exceed seven men; but being unopposed his followers soon increased. The French half-breeds, from their experience of past excitements, were nothing loth to go in for a little fighting. Riel, finding that the Governor had ignored his warning, forwarded by messenger to Pembina, sent a party to drive him across the line by force, if necessary. Situated as he was, isolated from every friend and support, the Governor could offer no resistance; so he retired across the line, and took up his quarters in Pembina. Probably, had he not dreaded the effects of the winter's journey back across the plains of Minnesota, he would have returned at once to confer with colleagues in Ottawa. Being encouraged by the offers of loyal assistance in the country, he determined, however, to remain; and, as it turned out, it was unfortunate he was so advised, as his presence acted as a red rag to the opposition, even though it was supposed that the country, in a month's time, would be part and parcel of the Dominion. Mr. Provencher and Capt. D. R. Cameron thought that they would try to get in to confer with the legal authorities in the country, in the hope of bringing about a reconciliation of interests. Riel, however, was too cunning to allow anything to interrupt the current of events, which he felt would bring him into importance and satisfy his ambition and vanity. From my knowledge of Riel, at this time, I venture to affirm that his motives were more those of personal ambition and aggrandizement than consideration for the good of his people, and his subsequent action confirms this opinion. He was clever enough to make tools of every one who came in his way, not even excepting the clergy, some of whom were his admiring supporters.

Having succeeded in stopping the surveys, in banishing the new government, and in turning back Captain Cameron and Mr. Provencher, the Governor's emissaries, Riel now felt that he could make a bolder and more determined move. He conceived the idea of taking possession of Fort Garry, seeing, by this time, that the sinews of war were necessary for his complete success. Fort Garry was the central depot of the Hudson's Bay Company, where enormous stores were maintained for the trade of the interior, and where large quantities of furs were made ready for shipment. Riel shrewdly saw that the Fort would prove a rich prize to enable him to carry on his operations, conceived in no illiberal spirit. The settlement was astounded one day by the news that Riel had occupied Fort Garry, although the move had been anticipated by Mulligan, chief of the Company's police, and others. The excuse he offered to the Governor for this act was that he heard an attempt to seize the Fort was about to be made by some other party in the country. Without any warning, Riel marched up about a hundred men from River Sale, entered the Fort, and informed Mr. Mactavish, Governor of the Hudson's Bay Company, that he had come to protect it. Riel, at first, seemed to realize the effect of so bold a move, and for a day or two he permitted no other act. Gradually, however, he became emboldened and he seized the property of the Hudson's Bay Company for his own purposes. He now occupied a very strong position, being protected by the Fort, and surrounded by his own men. The Fort contained the arms and ammunition of the troops which used to be stationed there, together with several cannon and ample ammunition. It also contained everything necessary for the support and pay of a considerable force, with the comfortable quarters of the officers of the Hudson's Bay Company, which Riel was not long in occupying for his own luxury and comfort. Mr. McDougall had taken advantage of the season to have his furniture brought down by the Red River boats, and this Riel also seized and appropriated for his own use. At first he did not attempt to interfere with the officers of the Hudson's Bay Company, but after a while he required the clerks in the store to honour his orders and requisitions. He then regularly employed his men as soldiers at the rate of fifteen to twenty dollars a month, paying

† Spot where Scott was shot.

Alexander & Colcie, Toronto.

Fort Garry in 1869

them by orders on the store. Most of his people Riel found would not act as willing soldiers in the cause he had taken up, and he had to resort to threats and all manner of deception to keep his recruits up to the proper number and to exact due subordination.

There was method in all Riel's plans. He formed a council, putting forward a man named Bruce, a French half-breed, as figurehead. This was previous to the erection of the barricade at River Sale. There did not seem to be any disposition on Riel's part, or that of his people, to oppose the cession of the country to Canada; but the opposition he offered seemed to be confined to the entrance of the Governor or the establishment of the authority of Canada until certain rights, which he and his supporters claimed to be their privilege and to have been granted them as inhabitants of the country, had been conceded. As his successes filled him with vanity and ambition his designs changed, and there is no doubt he conceived the idea of forming an independent government and handing it over to the United States for a good round sum. On Archbishop Taché's return, Taché put Riel off this conceit and brought him to his senses.

Correspondence was meanwhile passing between Mr. McDougall and Governor Mactavish. The former pressed on Mr. Mactavish the necessity of exerting his authority to put down the resistance offered to his entry; but Mr. Mactavish confined his efforts to remonstrances with Riel. He has been blamed for apathy; but, on his behalf, it is fair to say that the negotiations for the transfer of the country seemed there to have been carried on in a loose way, so far as the population existing in the territory at the time was concerned.

Mr. McDougall came up to the country as its future Governor, ahead of his authority. The news of his arrival and his progress was heralded in advance by the press, and Mr. Mactavish was called upon to deal with an insurrection brought about by circumstances which he could not well control, and in an affair over which he had little or no jurisdiction. The responsibility he might incur in dealing with so delicate a matter was greater than he no doubt felt himself able or willing to shoulder. In the light of subsequent events, it is clear that had he attempted to bring in Mr. McDougall by force, he would have assumed a grave responsibility. He even declined the offers of assistance that were made to protect Fort Garry before Riel occupied it, to avoid raising a hostile element in the country. In all of this he must now be judged as having acted wisely; although it was so far fortunate for Canada that this rising occurred before the transfer took place, else she would have had to establish her authority single-handed.

To throw some light upon the deliberations that led to this inaction, I insert an extract from the minutes of a meeting of the Council of Assiniboia, held on the 25th of October, 1869. This Council was the governing body of the territory. There were present on this occasion Judge Black, who, in consequence of the illness of Mr. Mactavish, presided; the Right Reverend, the Lord Bishop of Rupert's Land, Dr. Cowan, Dr. Bird, Messrs. Dease, Sutherland, McBeath, Frazer and Bannatyne. Riel and Bruce, who were known to be the leaders of the insurrectionary movement, had been invited to attend this council meeting and were remonstrated with for taking up arms and the criminality of the proceedings was pointed out to them. The minutes go on to say:

> That Mr. Riel refused to adopt the views of the Council, and persisted in expressing his determination to oppose Mr. McDougall's entrance into the settlement, declining even to press the reasoning and advice of this Council upon his party, although he reluctantly promised to repeat to them what he had just heard, and inform Governor Mactavish of the result by Thursday at 11 o'clock. Mr. Riel and Mr. Bruce having retired, the Council resumed the consideration of the subject before them, and the expediency of calling out an armed force to meet and protect Mr. McDougall was suggested. But as it was seen that it would be from the English-speaking portion of the community that such a force, if forthcoming at all, would be chiefly drawn, the result would evidently be to bring into armed collision sections of the people who, although they had hitherto lived together in comparative harmony, yet differed from each other so widely in

point of race, language, and religion, as well as in general habits, that the commencement of actual hostilities would probably involve not only themselves but the surrounding Indians in a protracted and sanguinary struggle. The Council therefore felt that without a regular military force to fall back upon they could hardly be held justified under the circumstances in resorting to measures so full of possible mischief to the whole country.

The Council, having learned that a number of the most intelligent and influential people among the French were not implicated in the hostile environment against Mr. McDougall, adopted the following resolution, which was moved by Mr. Bannatyne, and seconded by Mr. McBeath, viz.:

That Messrs. Dease and Goulet be appointed to collect immediately as many of the more respectable of the French community as they could, and with them proceed to the camp of the party who intend to intercept Governor McDougall, and endeavour, if possible, to procure their peaceable dispersion; and that Mr. Dease report to Governor Mactavish on or before Thursday next as to their success or otherwise.

This is the reason of the Council's inaction, and that of the Hudson's Bay Company.

Canadians naturally looked upon the act of insurrection as a breach of faith. At much trouble and expense they had completed a bargain with the Hudson's Bay Company, and they felt that it should be carried out and the country be peaceably handed over. Until this was done and peace restored, the Canadian Government temporarily withdrew from the bargain, taking the ground that while Canada had bound herself to pay over the money, the Hudson's Bay Company, on the other hand, was bound to hand the country over to Canada.

II

RIEL IN THE ASCENDANT

Let us now return to matters that were creating an excitement in the Canadian world, and to the delicate position in which the Honourable Mr. McDougall found himself placed. As Canadians on the spot, we beheld with pleasure the advent of the Lieutenant-Governor, and were disposed to judge severely all who were not inclined to view the coming of the Queen's representative in the same light. In this we represented the ambition and hopes of Canada, in having so magnificent a domain added to her boundaries, the value of which, being resident in the country, we thoroughly appreciated. We could not enter into the feelings of those who were about to be subjected to a new order of things, the effect of which no one, at this time, could know. There was, however, a general feeling in the country that a change of government was desirable, otherwise greater opposition might have arisen to its occupation by Canada, which would probably have altered the current of affairs. As things were, the Imperial Government, when it realized that there was opposition to the transfer on the part of the local population, refused to consummate the bargain made, or to send troops to establish the sovereignty of Canada without the people's consent, or rather without a due recognition of their claims.

Riel, about this time, irritated the people by petty acts of tyranny. He seized and opened the mails. He stopped Dr. Schultz's freight and examined it, as he claimed, to see whether there were any arms or ammunition concealed, and to collect the customs duties upon it. He seized the printing press of a local journal, the *Northwester*, belonging to Dr. Bown. On the 6th of November he entered the printing office with about twenty armed men, requiring Dr. Bown to do some printing for him. Bown refused, and was arrested and placed under guard, and while he was under arrest Riel used his office to do the necessary printing. About this time, also, Captain Cameron, with his man-servant, drove from Pembina to the barrier at River Sale, having left his wife – a daughter of Sir Charles Tupper – at Scratching River to await her husband's return. Captain Cameron arrived safely at the barrier, and seeing he could not drive through the obstruction, sitting up in the seat with his arms folded across his breast, he ordered the rebels to remove "that blasted fence." The half-breeds laughed; but liking the pluck of the Captain, they took his horses by the bridles and led him up to Father Ritchot's house, where, it is said, he was invited in, some refreshments were offered, and, after a quiet chat, he was ordered to proceed on his return journey to Pembina. It was Riel's tyrannical acts at this time that prevented the English-speaking portion of the community from working harmoniously with the French half-breeds, in an honest desire to meet the views of the Canadian Commissioners who were sent with full powers to satisfy the people that their rights would be respected. Had Riel not been seeking to gain personal power, the unfortunate results which followed would have been avoided.

Direct communication with Fort Garry having been cut off by the seizure of the mails, Colonel Dennis determined upon going to Pembina to confer personally with the Governor. Accompanied by Mr. Hallet, an intelligent and loyal half-breed, he set out from Fort Garry on the 1st of November for Pembina, crossing the prairie to avoid the main trail. Arrived there, he remained till the 1st of December, when he returned with a commission from the Governor appointing him Lieutenant and Conservator of the Peace. Events now crowded upon one another with rapidity, and Riel's actions became bolder day by day. About Fort Garry he exercised supreme and unquestioned authority.

Being in full possession of the Fort, and feeling the strength of his position, Riel commenced to lay his plans for the assumption of further power. In this he was anxious to have the countenance of the English-speaking part of the population. When he took possession of the printing office of Dr. Bown, he had a proclamation printed, calling a meeting composed of his own council and twelve delegates, who were to be selected from the various English parishes, to discuss the affairs of the country. The English settlers hesitated to countenance in any way the proceedings Riel had initiated; but in the hopes that their counsels might lead to a peaceful solution of the difficulties, they determined to attend the meeting. The convention assembled in the Court-house of the settlement near Fort Garry, on the 16th of November, and was guarded by an armed force. In the meantime Mr. Mactavish had entered a protest against the unlawful acts which had already been committed, and this was read and discussed at the meeting. This protest or proclamation was issued on the 12th of November, upon the demand of a number of influential people, who thought public notice should be taken of the illegal proceedings. Riel expressed his intention of forming a provisional government, and the convention felt it was only invited to carry out his behests and to give the appearance of countenancing them. The members present were not disposed to overturn the lawful authority which at the time existed, and which was only lying dormant in consequence of the authority Riel had usurped. The convention adjourned till the 1st of December. In the interim, there were those at work who still hoped to smooth over the difficulties by allowing authority to revert to its legal channel. They found, however, that Riel was determined to press his own authority. He had prepared what he called a "bill of rights," which, in itself, with the exception of some unconstitutional clauses, contained no disloyal or objectionable features. This was passed by the convention. The English members made an attempt to bring about a conference with the Governor upon this basis, but Riel took a personal stand against this and would not listen to reason. They therefore dispersed, feeling that they could not join in the unreasonable opposition Riel seemed determined upon giving, and which was likely to jeopardize the peace of the settlement. The colony was isolated from the outer world by hundreds of miles of prairie, with an Indian population in their midst, which, it was feared, would take advantage of the excitement to commit depredations.

While matters in the settlements had reached the stage I have related, the Governor still remained at Pembina, awaiting the date upon which it had been arranged that the proclamation should be issued transferring the territory to Canada. Mr. McDougall, no doubt unaware of the altered policy of the Canadian Government, and thinking that the Queen's proclamation, which by pre-arrangement was to issue on the 2nd of December, would duly arrive, and that it had been only delayed in the mails, and being also impatient at his detention in Pembina, he boldly determined upon a *Coup d'Etat*. He issued a proclamation of his own, proclaiming himself Governor of the territory, and crossed the boundary line for the purpose of reading it on Canadian soil and giving it full legal effect. At the same time, by virtue of this proclamation, he commissioned Colonel Dennis to enter the territory and raise a force to quell the insurrection, giving him extended powers in the premises. About the 20th of November, Mr. Newcombe had gone out to Pembina to Mr. McDougall, to see what was to be done about protecting the Government provisions. Mr. McDougall kept him there and sent him back with copies of his proclamation in French and English; and after many adventures Mr. Newcombe arrived on the 30th of November. Colonel Dennis arrived on the following day, by way of St. John's, with a further supply of the proclamation, and handed them to me and others to copy out, and have posted up in conspicuous places, as the printing presses had been seized by Riel. This task we gladly undertook, feeling that a lawful authority now existed which would make itself felt. Colonel Dennis informed us of his intention to raise a force and establish the authority of the Governor; and instructed me and others to follow him to the Stone Fort, which was a post of the

Hudson's Bay Company, thirty miles down the river towards Lake Winnipeg. The proclamation we posted up in various parts of the settlement, and I, with Mr. Hart and others of his surveying parties, followed him to the Stone Fort, Major Webb being sent to Portage la Prairie there to organize four companies. We found that good feeling existed on the part of the English-speaking people, who were desirous that a vigorous and legal authority should be established to deal with the serious aspect of affairs. Colonel Dennis set vigorously to work, called upon the people to support him, and organized a force intending to deal summarily with the usurper Riel, and those who had joined him.

The effect of the proclamation upon the people of Winnipeg was marked. They soon saw that submission to the new authority would become necessary, and that a choice would have to be made between the provisional government, sought to be established by Riel, and the Canadian Government, represented in the person of Colonel Dennis.

At the time, the tone of the people of Winnipeg was decidedly loyal; and, had Mr. McDougall's authority been legal, and had Colonel Dennis remained in Winnipeg to enforce it, it would have been maintained. But after the people had recovered from the first surprise, it began to be whispered about that all was not right; and there were some who felt that if the transfer of the country had actually taken place, they would have been apprised of it. But before these doubts got into circulation, Colonel Dennis had retired to the Stone Fort, and thither all those who wished to join him repaired.

In Dr. Schultz's storehouse was a quantity of Government provisions brought up to supply the surveying parties and the workmen on the Government road during the winter. These provisions were of great importance in the isolated position of the country, for they could not easily be replaced; and as there had been a large addition to the population during the summer, provisions would most likely be scarce. Consequently, a very jealous eye was kept on these stores, especially as Riel fully appreciated their value, and aroused our fears by coming over

Winnipeg in 1869

to Dr. Schultz's place and taking an inventory of the property. Riel attempted to put a guard on the provisions, stating that his reasons for doing so were lest we might take them and he be accused of the theft. To hold on to these provisions, and to protect Dr. Schultz's property, were the reasons which led the Canadians to occupy his premises and defend what they felt to be their food for the coming winter. The Canadians all went down to the Stone Fort, to enrol with Colonel Dennis, and the Colonel sent them back to Winnipeg to remain there and keep together for mutual protection. It was on their return to Winnipeg that they occupied the Doctor's premises. On the 4th of December a memorandum came from Colonel Dennis requesting the Canadians to withdraw from the village; but it was decided, after anxious consultation, to remain, as no better place was offered at the time where the party could keep together for safety and protection. In coming to this decision they were influenced by the natural desire to prevent the provisions, upon which all depended for the winter, from falling into Riel's hands, while at the time no one thought of the probability of an attack.

Colonel Dennis lost no time in taking active measures for the suppression of the rising. He requisitioned and purchased supplies, arms and ammunition, and proceeded to the formation of companies in various parishes, a duty which he entrusted to me. With the first call for loyal support a large number of Christianized Indians from the neighbourhood of Lake Winnipeg, under Chief Prince, came to offer their services. Individual members also flocked in, and Colonel Dennis soon found that he would have a number of men to tax heavily his commissariat. I immediately left for the parishes, for the purpose of enrolling the different companies, appointing their officers, and drilling them. I found a ready response to the call. In each parish I formed a company of fifty, appointed officers and non-commissioned officers, and arranged for their drill. I went to Winnipeg and formed the men who had returned there into a company, with Dr. Lynch as Captain, Mr. Miller, 1st Lieutenant, and Mr. Allan, 2nd Lieutenant. I directed them to remain where they were until further orders; to make no offensive movement; and, if necessary, to defend themselves, but on no account to fire the first shot.

On reaching Kildonan, the parish adjoining Winnipeg, I held a public meeting in the evening, to enrol members of the company, and it was at that meeting I had the first doubts thrown upon the legality of the proceedings which the Governor had taken. I was questioned closely by Mr. William Frazer and one or two others, as to the seal that had been attached to the proclamation, wishing to know if it was under the Queen's seal. I could only reply that I knew nothing about seals, that I was there acting under the orders of my superior officers, and that my duty was simply to enrol men. My explanation was accepted by the majority, who apparently were not anxious to question too closely the authority; and after Judge Black had been consulted as to the legality of the proceedings, I succeeded in enrolling a full company, including Mr. Frazer and those who had been my questioners.

On the following day, about the 6th of December, the company fell in, were formed up, and spent the day drilling. In the evening I intended to pass on to St. James's parish, to enrol a similar company there. But in the afternoon I received a letter from Colonel Dennis telling me he did not wish Dr. Schultz to occupy his buildings any longer; that he could not support him, and that he wished him to retire. I rode to Dr. Schultz's house, arriving there during the night, and found them all assembled in the two houses. I informed the doctor of Colonel Dennis's wishes, and a consultation of a few of the leading men was held. It was agreed that it was too late to evacuate the premises that night, but it should be done on the following day. There were a number of ladies present, and arrangements could not at any earlier moment be properly made for their departure. During the night Riel paraded the town with a number of men and performed a variety of evolutions, and about two o'clock in the morning he returned to the Fort. There was much excitement in the town over the action being taken by Colonel Dennis, and in consequence Riel aroused the spirit of his people and called to his support a large following in the Fort. To their great credit be it said, a strong party of the French, under William Dease, remained aloof, and steadily refused to be drawn into any unlawful or disloyal action. In fact, I think, very few of the French half-breeds were really disloyal, and in other hands would have been open to reason. But Riel, by persuasion, insidious arguments, and promises of reward, which he was enabled to make good from the stores he controlled in Fort Garry, succeeded in gathering a strong force. This, however, we did not know at the time, for Riel's support was drawn from the parishes to the south of the Assiniboine, while the English parishes lay to the north, and little communication was at that time held between them.

Early on the following morning I went on my way to St. James's parish, about three miles to the west of Winnipeg, to enrol a company there. When I left, there were a number of people about and a great deal of excitement. This, however, was the case every morning, and it was expected about noon that Dr. Schultz and those with him would be able to retire without exciting any opposition on the part of Riel. I held a meeting in Rev. Mr. Pinckham's parish about nine o'clock, and, after arranging for the enrolment of a company, I went across the prairie to Kildonan, where I drilled a company during the day, and had provisions and blankets put into a house for the reception of Dr. Schultz's party. About four o'clock in the evening, the party not having arrived, I went up to Winnipeg but was unable to get into the village. I then heard that they had surrendered, in response to negotiations opened by Mr. Snow, who went to the Fort on behalf of the party and the property on the premises. Riel was told that they had only assembled at Dr. Schultz's to protect themselves and their property, and if Riel would guarantee that their lives and property would not be threatened they would retire quietly to their homes. This was answered by a written command to surrender in fifteen minutes, and backed by an additional force of two hundred men. The messenger who brought the message led the party to believe that it would be a mere matter of form, that they would be marched to the Fort and set at liberty, and that all property would be respected. Their hands were tied, by the strict orders that had been issued, that they were on no account to fire the first shot. Of this Riel had heard, and it emboldened him in the action he took. It is fortunate that so much moderation was shown by Dr. Schultz, Dr. Lynch and others, or hostilities might have commenced on that occasion. The whole party, with the exception of the ladies, were made prisoners on reaching Fort Garry. Riel was, no doubt, further emboldened in this action by the knowledge, which had now become almost a certainty with him, that the action taken by the Governor was illegal.

I hastened to return to Colonel Dennis with news of the surrender of Dr. Schultz's party, but was met by a courier with a letter from the Colonel informing me that he had abandoned his project and was leaving the country. He instructed me to go to Portage la Prairie to hold a conference with a tribe there of Sioux, asking them to remain peaceable and loyal to the Queen, and not to interfere in the difficulties that had arisen. These Sioux were the remnants of the tribe that had committed a massacre in Dakota, in 1863, when twelve hundred whites fell victims to their lust of blood. They found protection under the British Government and had lived peaceably in our midst ever since. I was relieved to find that they had no desire to break the peace, as Chief Little Fox assured me.

Before leaving, Colonel Dennis had taken steps to send similar messages to other tribes, with a request to remain at peace. He instructed me at the same time to remain in the country and do my utmost to keep matters quiet. I proceeded at once to High Bluff and Portage la Prairie to carry out his instructions and was nearly made prisoner on my way thither by a party of Riel's men who were encamped in a house about half way to intercept messengers. While there I met Colonel Dennis, who was on his way to Pembina to rejoin Mr. McDougall. I remained at Portage la Prairie during the winter, receiving the hospitality of the Reverend Mr. George and Mr. Alcock.

Disquieting rumours were now the order of the day. The sudden collapse of Colonel Dennis's movement and the capture of fifty prisoners, who were detained in the Fort, gave Riel complete control over the country. He, however, confined his jurisdiction to the neighbourhood of Fort Garry and the town of Winnipeg; but his ambition was greatly stimulated by his success, and his success emboldened some to uphold the authority he had usurped.

III

THE PLOT THICKENS

The Government in the previous session had passed an Act for the administration of affairs in the North-West suitable to a crown colony, and, with the highest motives and in an enterprising spirit, provided for the government of the territory. But finding that, in addition to paying three hundred thousand pounds for the acquisition of the territory, possibly a greater burden might be in store to obtain or enforce possession, the Government withheld the purchase money, and caused a postponement of the proclamation annexing it to Canada.

The Government, however, sent friendly commissioners, in the persons of Vicar-General Thibault, who had spent many years in the country, and Colonel de Salaberry, to assure the people of their good intentions, and also appointed Mr. Donald A. Smith, an officer of the Hudson's Bay Company, a commissioner on behalf of Canada. The two former were sent for the purpose of enlightening the French half-breeds as to the good disposition of the Government towards them, and to reassure the people. The latter was armed with a commission giving him more extended powers. They arrived almost simultaneously. But Riel by this time had so agitated the public mind and acquired such power that his ambition knew no bounds. He was therefore not disposed to allow any influence to be used over his people, which would interfere with the plans maturing in his mind for the founding of an independent state, probably flying the stars and stripes, with himself as dictator, in the full enjoyment of all the honours and emoluments of the position. His people, however, were loyal to Canadian connection; so his schemes in that direction were happily frustrated.

Riel was a man of great natural ability. He had been well educated, at the expense of Madame Masson, whose aid had been obtained by the kind interest of Archbishop Taché, who, recognizing the boy's ability, had hoped to educate him for the priesthood. At the time when the political troubles arose in the settlement, Riel was a freighter on the plains between St. Paul and Winnipeg. While so occupied he acquired much knowledge of the half-breed character, and his education, on the other hand, enabled him to exercise considerable influence on the half-breed in return. At this formative period in his life, he drew a great deal of inspiration from American companions and counsellors, of whom there were not a few at the time in the neighbourhood.

Archbishop Taché's acquaintance with Riel will prove of interest to show the latter's early training and career. Had Riel remained under the guidance of this venerable prelate, he might have been a useful citizen of the country to-day; but his depraved, ambitious nature and lack of moral rectitude has brought him to the unerring fate of the criminal. I here insert the following cutting from a newspaper. On being interviewed the Archbishop made this statement:

> Every old settler knows the facts, but I will again go over the simple story in a few words for the benefit of the public. When I returned to the Red River settlement from the far north to resume my episcopal duties, I found then, in the small college attached to my See at St. Boniface, three Métis lads, one French, one German, and one Scotch, viz., Macdougall (since dead), Schmidt, and Riel. I found them studying Latin, and took a great interest in their aptness for study. While in Montreal in 1858 I obtained admission for two of them to the College of Montreal, and for the other at St. Hyacinthe College. They went to college that year, and I returned to my diocese. In 1867, while in Montreal on a visit, I met Riel and told him that now that I had secured an education for him he must begin to look out for himself and endeavour to gain a respectable living. He went to the United

States and remained there until he returned to his mother in the Red River settlement in the fall of 1868. From the time of his return till the outbreak of 1869 I did not see much of him, being a good deal absent in connection with my duties, so, as a matter of fact, I had but a comparatively slight acquaintance with Riel.

Riel's vanity and self-confidence had been immensely puffed up by the success he had gained through a variety of fortuitous circumstances, which had so far helped him. He could not be called a bold man, for he felt his way, bit by bit, but was clever enough to take advantage of the circumstances favouring his schemes.

He did not at first ignore Mr. Donald A. Smith, as a commissioner from the Canadian Government, but admitted him into the Fort, where he was allowed to take up his quarters with his brother officers of the Company. Here, however, he was virtually a prisoner in Riel's hands, and was not allowed to exercise his authority as a commissioner, but remained a spectator of the events daily occurring in and around the Fort. Nor was he able to exercise any influence in obtaining the release of prisoners or in mitigating the severity of the rule which Riel exercised in the vicinity of Fort Garry. Neither was the mission of the Reverend Mr. Thibault or of Colonel de Salaberry productive of results, though they were allowed a greater freedom than was accorded to Mr. Smith, whom Riel regarded with suspicion, as an official of the Canadian Government. On their arrival at Fort Garry, Mr. Thibault and Colonel de Salaberry handed their papers to Riel, who took possession of them, and that was the last that was seen of them. Mr. Donald A. Smith was more wary, and took the precaution of leaving his papers at Pembina, in the care of Mr. Provencher, until he could be assured of bringing them in with safety.

The indignities the prisoners suffered while in close confinement were humiliating in the extreme. They were detained for no offence, but merely that Riel might use them to serve his purpose in any way that seemed to him expedient. Their confinement and poor food were not long in telling on them; but they were unable to get release, or any amelioration of their lot, for Riel was obdurate, and they were closely guarded by a large force. Their sufferings were greater by reason of the inclemency of the weather, it now being the depth of winter; and neither sufficient warmth nor clothing were allowed them. Having been confined for some weeks without any hope of speedy release, nothing having so far been accomplished by the mission of Mr. Smith, some of the prisoners determined to effect their escape. The guards had become careless; and, an opportunity presenting itself, these prisoners made a dash for their liberty. But the difficulties they had to contend with in finding their way across the snow-clad prairies after effecting their escape were greater than they anticipated. Out of twelve who escaped seven were re-taken. One of them, poor Hyman, was badly frozen. Charles Mair, and Thomas Scott, whose life was afterwards taken by Riel, reached Portage la Prairie.

The prisoners had hitherto been confined in the Company's gaol, outside the Fort, which was in rather a dilapidated condition; but after this they were removed to quarters inside the Fort. Their re-incarceration occurred on the 9th of January, 1870. Dr. Schultz was confined in a room by himself; and this act led the doctor to fear that he had been marked out as a special object of Riel's vengeance. But the doctor was not the man quietly to submit to any sinister designs of such a man as Riel. He had a devoted and noble wife, who kept watch and ward, from without the walls of the Fort, over the welfare of the prisoners; and no doubt she managed to keep up some kind of communication with her husband. This we know, at any rate, that, with her assistance, preparations were made for her husband's escape, for towards the latter end of January great excitement was caused by the news that Dr. Schultz had gained his liberty. With the assistance of a gimlet and knife, he contrived to open the windows of his prison, and by cutting his buffalo robe into strips, let himself down to *terra firma*. He then scaled the walls of the Fort, and under the friendly screen of a severe blizzard, finally obtained his freedom. Outside the Fort a cutter was in waiting to convey him a few miles off to the hospitable home of Mr. Macbeth, in the parish of Kildonan, where he was for the time in comparative safety. The chagrin of Riel, when it was discovered the next morning that his most valued prisoner had effected his escape, amused his late comrades. They cheered to the echo on ascertaining that the news was true, despite the consequences that might befall, and in disregard of the abusive epithets Riel heaped upon them.

Doctor Schultz is an able, and in many ways, a remarkable man. Possessed of a magnificent physique and great force of character, he was popular in the cause he espoused, and was a tower of strength to it. No one could help admiring his firmness of purpose, the boldness of his policy, and the skill and judgment with which he achieved his ends. He came to the country a young man of nineteen, having already obtained his diploma as a doctor of medicine at Victoria College, Cobourg. With great ardour he identified himself with the country, intelligently appreciated its circumstances, and did yeoman service in its behalf. He fought with determination against the whole power of the Hudson's Bay Company, defied them on their own ground, and succeeded in holding his own against their attempts to overthrow him. There is no doubt that it was very largely due to Dr. Schultz's boldness in dealing with the Company that the way was prepared for the acquisition of the country by the Dominion, for, with such a determined spirit to deal with, they were beginning to find it difficult to maintain their authority. He possessed the confidence of the people for many years afterwards as their representative in the Dominion Parliament, and upon being defeated, after a hot political contest, was rewarded for his services by being appointed to the Senate.

During this period Mr. Donald A. Smith had not wasted his time. With the assistance of Mr. Mactavish and others he succeeded in weaning some of Riel's councillors and men; and when Riel found defections were taking place, he thought it best to wait upon Mr. Smith to inquire of him in person the object of his visit, and to ascertain what powers had been conferred upon him. Mr. Smith, however, had taken the precaution of leaving his papers at Pembina, to be sure of their safety, and before replying to Riel, he asked permission to send his secretary for them. It was arranged that a public meeting should be held and the papers presented to the people, as Mr. Smith would not recognize Riel or his government. Now commenced a new game of Riel's. He thought he would try to get hold of these papers, as he had got Mr. Thibault's and Colonel de Salaberry's, but Mr. Smith was not to be caught. Smith sent Mr. Hardesty, his secretary, and arranged with him privately that a party would be sent to meet him. Riel kept back Mr. Hardesty without Mr. Smith's knowledge for twenty-four hours, trying to work upon him. He placed a sentry in Mr. Smith's room and one on his door, night and day, while Mr. Hardesty was away. However, a party went to meet the secretary about twenty miles from Fort Garry to escort him in, and as they were returning they were met by some of Riel's men who attempted to get the papers, but a loyal French half-breed drew his revolver and threatened to shoot the first man who interfered with Hardesty, and so the whole party returned to Fort Garry together, and Hardesty was conducted to the council chamber. Mr. Smith came there to receive the papers, and in handing them to Mr. Smith, O'Donoghue, a member of Riel's provisional government, attempted to snatch them, but Mr. Grant drew his revolver and prevented this. The scene, as described to me, was an exciting one. For Riel and his council were anxious to get the papers, so as to deprive Mr. Smith of any authority before the people; and it required a great deal of planning on Mr. Smith's part to get possession of them.

Throughout the whole of these proceedings Mr. Smith showed great diplomatic skill under very trying circumstances, opposed as he was by Riel's tyranny and cunning. At this time Riel was ably assisted by Père Lestanc, with whom he secretly consulted, and who used his influence with the people to aid and support him. Mr. Smith, having obtained possession of his papers, now called a meeting of the people. This meeting, which was attended by upwards of a thousand people, was held in the open air, notwithstanding the fact that the thermometer ranged many degrees below zero. Its deliberations extended over two days. Riel managed to get himself appointed interpreter for the French half-breeds in placing before the people Mr. Smith's statements. This gave him considerable power over the proceedings of the meeting. Judge Black was appointed chairman. The reading of Mr. Smith's commission, the Queen's letter, and every other document was contested with much obstinacy by Riel, but ultimately without effect. According to Mr. Smith's report of the proceedings, the result was the appointment of forty delegates, twenty from either side, to meet on the 25th of January, 1870, "with the object of considering the subject of Mr. Smith's commission and to decide what course would be best to pursue for the welfare of the country." The English, as a body, and a large number of the French declared their entire satisfaction with the explanations given and their desire for union with Canada.

During this period Mr. Smith had been able to retain in the Fort about forty loyal French half-breeds, who assisted him in his efforts at conciliation. Riel, finding that the ground was thus slipping from under his feet, on the 22nd of January had a conference with these loyal supporters, and, with tears in his eyes, told them how earnestly he desired an arrangement with Canada. He further assured them he would lay down his authority immediately on the meeting of the convention. Believing him sincere in this assurance, they agreed to leave the Fort, thinking that ten of their number would be sufficient to remain for its protection. They had hardly gone, however, when Riel resorted to more oppressive measures; and the Hudson's Bay Company stores, which had hitherto been only partially in his hands, were now wholly taken possession of by Riel. It would be tedious to relate the tyrannous influences that Riel sought to wield about this time. On the 25th of January the convention met, and Judge Black was appointed chairman. It sat for nearly fifteen days, and many were the earnest discussions for the welfare of the country. Mr. Smith placed all his documents before the meeting and a "bill of rights" was prepared for submission to the Canadian Government. Riel was anxious to have a Province created and the question was discussed in convention, but, on the 4th of February, a proposition to form a province was negatived by the meeting; and, on the following day, another motion, directed against the Hudson's Bay Company, was vetoed. Riel's language and conduct now became violent in the extreme. He put a guard upon Governor Mactavish, who was then lying dangerously ill, and he took Dr. Cowan prisoner and placed him in confinement with the rest of the captives. Mr. Smith was also put under a strict guard.

The "bill of rights" was prepared and handed to Mr. Smith, who invited the convention to appoint delegates to confer with the Dominion Government, and he assured them that their delegates would have a cordial reception and obtain recognition of their claims. The delegates named were Judge Black, Rev. Mr. Ritchot, and Mr. Alfred H. Scott. The convention terminated on the 10th of February, but, before closing, Riel succeeded in forming a provisional government with himself as president. In this government several delegates who were asked to join it declined to take part. As a condition, in forming his administration, Riel promised that the prisoners should be released, and on the following day he released six or eight of them. Riel had now accomplished the object of his desires; having formed an independent government by the vote of the convention, to which he was himself elected president. If he had been sincere and pacific in his intentions he would have conducted the affairs of the country on a conciliatory basis, and have released all the prisoners. But he would not let go his personal hold, and continued to rule as an autocrat. If he had at once opened the prison doors and let all his unfortunate victims out, and allowed the people, without intimidation, to elect their delegates to the new convention, an honourable career might have been open to him. But this was not his course; and there was a want of moral stamina and a diseased vanity in the man that has proved his ruin.

While these proceedings were going on at Fort Garry, I was in Portage la Prairie, with many others, who had there taken refuge at the commencement of the troubles. Our sources of information were meagre, as all mail communication was stopped, and we knew nothing about the action of the conventions, nor did we know what was going on at the Fort. Some of the people had friends among the prisoners and were anxious about their safety. Rumours came from time to time that they were suffering from close confinement and were ill-treated. Attempts had been made on one or two occasions to organize a party to secure their release, which I discouraged, knowing that commissioners had been appointed by the Canadian Government on a mission of peace. My orders from Colonel Dennis, moreover, were to do my utmost to keep things quiet.

When Scott escaped from his prison he came to Portage la Prairie for safety and was warmly welcomed by the people. He gave graphic accounts of his imprisonment and escape, and once more the question was raised to organize a party to effect the release of the other prisoners. As it was known that I had previously discouraged such attempts, the meetings for the purpose of organization were held secretly and information kept from me. But when I discovered that they were determined to go, I felt it my duty to accompany them, and endeavour to keep them to the legitimate object for which they had organized. This I did, fearing that a rash act might bring trouble upon the country, the consequences of which would be serious, for I had now realized the dangerous position things had assumed. Enthusiastic meetings were held and preparations were made for a start. The plan decided upon was to leave Portage la Prairie so as to arrive at Fort Garry before daybreak and surprise the Fort, which at that hour would probably be little guarded. We were then to release the prisoners and return. Everything being in readiness, on the 12th of February we took our departure, lightly armed, many of the men having only oak clubs. We mustered at one o'clock, sixty strong, and marched off from Portage la Prairie on foot. Mr. Gaddy, an English half-breed, was one of the leaders. I was elected commander.

When one realizes the severity of the North-West climate, the thermometer ranging down to thirty or forty degrees below zero, and the month of February being the most inclement of the year, and that we had undertaken this trying march of sixty miles without transport and without provisions, the boldness of the undertaking will be seen to be great. But the earnestness which actuated the men in their desire to release their friends from a durance so vile, made them all cheerful under the circumstances. The men marched merrily along the frozen snow for about nine hours without rest until they reached Headingly, a settlement eighteen miles from Fort Garry. On the way, two prisoners were taken. I took the precaution to have them detained until we passed on our way, that no information might reach Fort Garry in advance of our movements. The men's blood was up, and some felt that the prisoners we had taken had been too leniently dealt with, and should have been brought with the party; but I did not wish anything done that would arouse a feeling prejudicial to our movement, or that would imperil the safety of peaceable settlers, should reprisals be taken. We picked up detachments at Poplar Point and High Bluff, on our way, and reached Headingly about midnight.

At Headingly, we sought shelter in the houses of settlers for the purpose of resting and preparing for the attack, which we proposed to make on the Fort at dawn. In the short space of an hour a storm arose, which soon turned into a North-West blizzard, during which it is perilous, if not fatal, for travellers to proceed on their way. This necessitated a change of plans. At Headingly all the settlers and half-breeds fully approved of the enterprise, and some joined the party. The blizzard blew for forty-eight hours without intermission, and we had to trust the hospitality of our friends, whose kindness was unbounded.

On the morning following our arrival at Headingly, we assembled in Mr. Taylor's house to hold a meeting. I felt that I had lost the confidence of many of the men, who thought that I was not in earnest, and who knew that I was not in thorough accord with the expedition. At the meeting, feeling that without their confidence I could not proceed, I resigned the position to which they had elected me on leaving Portage la Prairie, explaining my reasons, and proposing that they should re-elect their officers. I was re-nominated, and some one at the meeting got up and asked, before having the motion put, "If Major Boulton meant fight." I answered that if by fighting they meant leading the men on to any rash act or undertaking, irrespective of the consequences, I did not mean fighting; but if I was re-elected I would do my utmost to accomplish the object for which we had left the Portage, if I could see my way to accomplish this without undue risk to the force under my command. This satisfied the party, and I was duly re-elected their commander. I give these details thus minutely as I have always been credited with having raised the force at the Portage. I did not take that position; I felt a responsibility others did not feel, having been left behind with certain instructions; and my anxiety was to carry them out. As I could not alter their determination to attempt to release their friends, I went with them to help to guide them, for, realizing the serious position the settlement was placed in, my anxiety was to avoid any actual outbreak of hostilities. The blizzard interfered with our first plans, and I set about making preparations to accomplish our purpose by a different method.

The knowledge of our adventure was not known to the other settlements friendly to our cause; but rumours, no doubt, had by this time reached Riel's ears, and as soon as the storm abated sufficiently to permit of our travelling, two emissaries were sent to acquaint the friendly settlements of the object we had in view. Mr. Gaddy, with a companion, went to Dease, who was the leader of the loyal party in the French settlement; and Mr. Taylor, afterwards the Honourable John Taylor, went with a companion to the English settlements to the north of Fort Garry, to tell them that a party had come down for the purpose of effecting the release of the prisoners, and that on the following day we proposed to march to Kildonan Church, and there await the arrival of reinforcements from their parishes.

We started from Headingly at eight o'clock on a fine moonlit night to march to the rendezvous, and had to pass close under the walls of the Fort in order to reach it. As we passed the Fort, the sentries saw us and fired a signal of alarm, which we took no notice of, but went on our way without interference. As we passed through the village of Winnipeg, we heard of a house which Riel used continually to visit. Thinking we might make a timely capture, we surrounded the house, and Scott and I entered to search for Riel; but the host assured us he was not there; so we passed on without disturbing the family. Some of the settlers, seeing us arrive at Kildonan, were alarmed at the sudden turn affairs had taken. The action of the convention, they expected, was about to bring a peaceful solution of the difficulties, which they had hoped would be realized; but the appearance of another armed force on the scene cast all their hopes to the wind. Before leaving Portage la Prairie we had, of course, no knowledge of the arrangements that had been made between the commissioners and Riel and the population, a few days before. Riel, we argued, brought this attack on by illegally, unjustly and cruelly keeping forty peaceable citizens in his prison, day after day, and month after month. So we moved on and reached Kildonan Church, where we took up our position as previously arranged, and made the people acquainted with the object we had in view. The news soon spread, and many people flocked to our assistance. The emissaries we had sent down to the lower settlements had returned and reported that a large force was coming up with Dr. Schultz.

It was a fine sight, about three o'clock in the afternoon, to see three or four hundred settlers marching up to our neighbourhood, headed by a small cannon, drawn by four oxen, the whole under the leadership of Dr. Schultz, whose powerful figure stood out boldly as he led them up. They came approving of the course that had been taken, and determined to assist. They were enraged at the insincerity of Riel, who had promised, upon the formation of the new provisional government, to have the prisoners released. He had broken his promise, and they felt that nothing but force would compel him to keep it. The utmost enthusiasm now prevailed, though there were many who felt great anxiety under the new turn of affairs, fearing that a conflict was inevitable, which so far had been happily averted. I shared in this anxiety, but the thought that immediately pressed upon me was how to feed the large gathering. A subscription list was passed round to raise sufficient to purchase some supplies; but beyond a sovereign from Dr. Schultz, who emptied his pockets, and half a sovereign from one or two others, there was no money among the party, so we had to fall back upon the hospitality of the people in the immediate neighbourhood for our evening and morning meals. The Reverend Mr. Black placed his house, stores, and everything that he had at our disposal; and we camped in the church for the night.

Towards dusk, a prisoner, whose name was Parisien, was brought in as a suspected spy. He was taken in charge by the guard, and no more secure place offering, he was imprisoned underneath the pulpit. On the following morning, he asked permission to go out. Leave being granted, he was accompanied by the sergeant of the guard and two men. Around the church were numbers of people, and others constantly arriving; their sleighs and cutters were standing about, and in one of these was a gun lying on the seat. This caught the eye of Parisien, who was as quick as lightning to conceive the idea of escape. He made a bolt from the guard, seized the gun from the cutter, and ran for the banks of the river, only a few yards distant. As he got down the bank there happened to be riding towards the church on the frozen river the son of Mr. (now Senator) Sutherland. He was coming from his father's house to join the force, and without any knowledge of what had occurred, this poor young fellow, about one-and-twenty years of age, was suddenly fired at twice by the prisoner, both shots taking effect.

The ruffianly act was seen by the people on the bank, who had witnessed the attempt to escape, and they immediately began firing on Parisien, who continued his flight. The object he had in view, in shooting young Sutherland, was evidently to seize his horse to assist him to escape, or to prevent Sutherland riding after him. From where I was, inside the church, I heard the firing, and rushed out to ascertain what was going on. When I was informed of the shooting, I ran down the bank and found poor Sutherland lying on the snow still alive. I had him carried into the house of Mr. Black, where Dr. Schultz and another doctor present attended him. The poor young fellow lingered through the day and then died. As soon as I had seen him placed in Mr. Black's house, I went off down the river to ascertain what had taken place in regard to Parisien. I saw about half a mile distant a large crowd. I ran to them and found that they had caught the prisoner and were handling him severely. They were infuriated at the death of Sutherland, and intended showing their captive no mercy. His feet were tied together with a sash, and he was being dragged along the ice by another sash, which was tied around his neck. Before long he would, no doubt, have suffered the consequences of this act. But I interfered, and had him taken in charge and brought back to the church, determined to allow no hasty act or feeling to prejudice our proceedings, as his case was one for a judicial trial. When the force broke up on the following day Parisien was sent down in charge of a guard to the Stone Fort: on his way down he again tried to escape, but was fired upon by the guard, who recaptured him, and about a month after he died of his wounds.

IV

THE DRAMA OF THE REBELLION

In the meantime, a message was sent to Riel demanding the release of the prisoners. We had to act promptly, as we had gathered in great numbers, amid much enthusiasm, but the force was poorly armed, and without provisions or the means of maintaining our position for any length of time. I felt that delay was therefore dangerous. A number of settlers were anxious that no collision should take place which would throw the settlement into convulsions; and messengers bearing counsels of peace passed between Fort Garry and us. These settlers brought pressure to bear upon Riel, who now realized the danger of his position should determined action on our part be taken. The majority of his men were only half-hearted in supporting his arbitrary measures, and it was only by rousing their fears and appealing to their prejudices that he could keep them loyal to himself. Riel saw this, and acted accordingly.

The negotiations resulted in his releasing the prisoners and allowing them all to come down to report themselves to us. They arrived at Kildonan Church about two o'clock in the afternoon, and the question now arose whether the advantages we had already gained by the demonstration should be followed up, to oust Riel from his position in the Fort. The Bishop of Rupert's Land, Archdeacon Maclean, Judge Black, and many others, came down to counsel peace; but I had much difficulty in withstanding the excitement of the assembled force, who thought further action should be pressed. I argued with them that the object for which the expedition had been undertaken was gained, in the release of the prisoners, who had been so long confined. I also cautioned them that while it was a legitimate effort on their part to make, the moment we attempted anything further we were as amenable to the law as were Riel and his followers, and would be responsible for any danger that might threaten the settlement. These counsels prevailed, though an aggressive policy was abandoned with great reluctance by many who thought that we should show more courage in withstanding Riel. This discussion took up some time, but about four o'clock in the afternoon I was able to announce that the object for which we had assembled had been successfully accomplished, and that there was no further need for the services of those who had so loyally come forward to effect the release of the prisoners.

In half an hour the assembly dispersed as quickly as it had come together, the majority at once retiring north to their settlements. Those who had come from Portage la Prairie now made arrangements to return to their homes, but as this could only be done by passing Fort Garry, they kept together and camped for the night in Mr. Boyd's store, at Point Douglas. The following morning a council was held, at which it was determined to return home at once. I knew that to march past the Fort in a body would only tempt Riel to make another attack, so I urged that we should dismiss and accept the hospitality of our friends in the English settlements until the excitement had somewhat quieted down, when we could return singly, and if captured it would have no political significance. An old pensioner, who had been a sergeant-major in the British service, argued that we had come down like brave men and that we should go back like brave men, in a body; and as most of the party were anxious to reach their homes his counsel prevailed, although I rebuked him for taking the responsibility upon himself of recommending so imprudent a course.

Their determination was strengthened by the statement that Riel had sent a message to say that he did not intend taking any more prisoners and that our safety would be assured. If such a message did reach us I knew it was a treacherous message, for I felt that Riel, protected by the walls of the Fort and by a numerous force, collected in expectation of an attack, was not likely to forego the advantage of making an easy capture of new prisoners. Some of my friends urged me not to openly join the returning party, as having been its commander I would, most likely, be the first to suffer; but I determined, whatever happened, to stay with my party, as we had a long way to go to reach home. Having made up our minds to start, I concluded that no time should be lost; so, about nine o'clock in the morning, we made our preparations. As the travelled road would take us within a few hundred yards of Fort Garry, I thought it better to cross the open prairie to St. James's parish, which would keep us about a mile and a half from the Fort, although the difficulty of travelling in the deep snow was very great. In taking this course I was in hopes that Riel would see that we wished to avoid a conflict and to return to our homes peaceably. As we were leaving, news came that Mr. Gaddy, the emissary whom I had sent down to advise Dease and his loyal party of our action, had been captured and hanged that morning. This news did not at all reassure me, but it afterwards turned out that it was only a threat. At last, we started out across the plains in single file, following closely in one another's footsteps, on account of the depth of the snow, which was up to our waists; and in this order we marched until we got opposite the Fort, when we observed a party of men on horseback issuing out of it. They marched towards us, followed about two hundred yards in the rear by some fifty men on foot. We kept steadily on our way, without hesitation, until they approached within a hundred and fifty yards, when some of the men asked for orders, whether we should form up for defence. I gave strict orders that on no account should a shot be fired or any hostility be provoked; and the party on horseback, numbering about fifty, continued to approach us. I sent forward one of the half-breeds to parley, and to inform them that we were quietly returning to our homes – I following him. The party, headed by O'Donoghue and Ambroise Lépine, then came forward, and O'Donoghue asked, "What party is this?" I answered "It is a party of men returning to the Portage." He then asked, "Is Major Boulton here?" I replied that I was the man, at which he expressed pleasure, and informed me that Riel had sent him out from the Fort to meet us, and to invite us to the Fort to hold a parley. I told him that we wished to go on our way without interference.

While this conversation was going on, Lépine went up to one of the men, named Murdoch Macleod, a fine young Scotchman, who belonged to my party. Macleod had his revolver in his hand, and Lépine attempted to wrest it from him. This was an aggressive movement on Lépine's part, and no doubt intended to provoke hostilities. I was afraid that in the struggle the revolver would go off, which would be the signal for a massacre, from which there was no escape. We were not armed; we were up to our waists in snow; and in the presence of double our number, who were well armed, supported by a large force in the Fort near by, and who were excited over the events of the previous day. Under the circumstances I knew that it would be criminal to jeopardize the lives of the settlers who formed the party, many of whom had left large families at home. I therefore ordered Macleod to give up the revolver, and signalled the party to follow me to the Fort. Thither we marched, side by side, on the invitation of Mr. O'Donoghue, although I felt there was treachery in the invitation. In support of this I here quote an extract from a statement made by O'Donoghue, bearing upon these events, which is in possession of his brother:

> During the 15th and 16th several self-constituted delegates of peace and order passed between both armies, but on the morning of the 16th one Norquay was officially sent by the revolters, stating that the English party would not recognize the provisional government. Riel at once cast this commissioner into prison, where he allowed him to remain till the evening of the same day, when he liberated him, and the following letter he handed him for the English party as a reply to their mission:
>
> Fort Garry, Feb. 16th, 1870.
> Fellow-countrymen, – Mr. Norquay came this morning with

a message and even he has been detained. He will reach you time enough to tell you that for my part I understand that war, horrible, civil war, is the destruction of this country. We are ready to meet any party, but peace over British rights we want before all. Gentlemen, the prisoners are out – they have sworn to keep peace. We have taken the responsibility of our past acts. Mr. Wm. Mactavish has asked you for the sake of God to form and complete the provisional government; your representatives have joined us on that ground. Who will now come and destroy the Red River Settlement?

Louis Riel

Accompanying this letter Riel gave a verbal guarantee that should the opposing party disband none of them would be molested on their peaceable return to their homes. Relying on this assurance, both parties disbanded. In violation of this guarantee, Riel ordered out his men to attack them as soon as they came in sight; but the Portage party, confiding in Riel's honour, made no resistance, and they surrendered and were marched prisoners into Fort Garry. I commanded the party to whom the Portage party surrendered, but was in total ignorance of the guarantees Riel had made them the evening previous, and only learned of their existence from one of the party after they were marched into the Fort. Immediately after this I had an interview with Riel and I demanded of him if the statements were true. Riel did not deny the statements, but positively asserted that he alone was responsible for his acts, and, guarantee or no guarantee, those men should remain in prison.

We reached the Fort in about half an hour, and, entering the gates, which were at once closed behind us, we were immediately surrounded by about four hundred men. My party was marched off to quarters assigned them, a house in the centre of the Fort, which had been used by the clerks of the Hudson's Bay Company as a residence. There they were disarmed and everything of value taken from them. I was placed in a room by myself, and the rest of the prisoners, for such we were, about forty in number, were placed in rooms adjoining. In the hall was placed a strong guard of about twenty men, armed with British rifles and fixed bayonets.

About a quarter of an hour after I was placed in my room,

a guard came in and put handcuffs and chains on my legs. I was given an old buffalo robe to lie down on and a pitcher of water and a piece of pemican were placed by my side. Shortly after this I heard the door open and Riel looked in. Without entering, he said, "Major Boulton, you prepare to die to-morrow at twelve o'clock." I answered, "Very well," and he retired. I was now left to my cogitations, which were not of the most pleasant description. By means of a knot-hole which I had knocked out of the wooden partition, I managed to communicate with the prisoners in the next room, and told them what had happened. I then sat down to take off my moccasins and stockings, which were wet through by the snow and perspiration arising from the exertions of our march. When I got them off, I was able to slip the chain from my legs, but the noise aroused the sergeant of the guard, who came in, and thinking I was trying to escape, he alarmed the guard and marched them all in, filling the room. Taking no notice of them, I wrung out my stockings, put them on again, with my leg chains and moccasins, while they gravely looked on. Fearing, however, that my actions meant more than appeared on the surface, the guard was ordered to retire and a sentry was placed inside the room.

The difficulty of the position in which I now found myself was great. I was in a room without heat, the thermometer being many degrees below zero, with nothing but the bare floor to lie upon, and with chains on my hands and feet, and a guard set over me. To add to my depression, I was under the sentence of death by a man who, in order to make a show of his power, I felt was fully prepared to carry out his dark deed. My feelings may therefore be better imagined than described. But I was not going to give up without an effort, and I felt that the first thing I had to do was to acquaint my friends with what had taken place; so I asked the sentry to get me paper and pencil. He had to send to Riel before he dare grant my request. However, I got the paper, and wrote a note to Archdeacon Maclean, now Bishop of Saskatchewan, to inform him of what had occurred, and of my impending fate, and wishing him to come to visit me. My letter was taken to Riel, who in about an hour's time returned with the paper in his hand. He came into the room to question me. He asked me what was my object in coming down with the force. I answered, "For the purpose of releasing the prisoners whom you were unjustly and unlawfully detaining." He further asked me what was the oath we took. I told him, to leave no stone unturned until we had accomplished our purpose. He then asked me what I intended to do when I entered the house where he was supposed to be. I told him, to take him prisoner, and then to exchange him for those of our friends in the Fort. After further questioning, he said, "Very well; you wish to see Archdeacon Maclean? I will allow him to come."

About a couple of hours afterwards Archdeacon Maclean appeared in a state of great excitement and anxiety. After conversing with me, he at once went to remonstrate with Riel in regard to his intentions, but returned in an hour, having effected nothing. He remained with me a couple of hours and then left, promising to return soon. He returned in the evening about eight o'clock, and told me that he had obtained a postponement of my execution for twelve hours later than the following day at twelve o'clock.

The anxiety of the remainder of the prisoners over my threatened execution was great. Occasionally I had a chance of conversing with some of them as we met in the hall going to and fro. The clanging of the long chains attached to my feet had a most ominous sound as I walked about. I conversed a good deal with my guards, and enlisted their sympathy. They, I believe, were by no means a party to the murderous designs contemplated by Riel.

The measures taken by Riel were not justified by any act that had been committed by the English settlers, who had shown no disposition to attack him, their actions having been confined to a demonstration to force him to release the prisoners, which he had previously promised to do. The party taken prisoner with me were quietly returning to their homes, without further designs against him; and the act he was contemplating was for no other purpose than to strike terror to the hearts of the people, and to more firmly fix himself as the autocrat of the country. In this he showed a bloodthirsty spirit, as well as a want of tact, which were repeatedly manifested traits in his character.

That night I slept on the bare floor, without a pillow, covered with my buffalo robe, and with the sentry as my only companion. During the night I was continually disturbed by the sentry, who would come and wake me, go down on his knees and pray and groan. I sent him away repeatedly, but only to return again. He was in great trouble and concern about me, and the next morning, when they unlocked my door, he was found in a state of lunacy. The excitement of being locked up with me had proved too much for him, and his mind was unstrung. I heard afterwards that he was the father of the young man who had shot Sutherland. Another sentry was placed in my room; a tall man, about six feet two inches in height, who lay down all day in the corner. About three o'clock in the afternoon, I was aroused by a peculiar gurgling noise, which caused me to go over to look at my sentry. I found that he was dead. I alarmed the sergeant of the guard, who once more marched his whole squad into the room, sent for Riel, and an inquest was held, which lasted about an hour. It was found that the sentry had died of apoplexy. The dead man was then carried off, but without placing another sentry over me. In fact, I think the guards had become superstitious, and now refused to be locked up with me, which, I need hardly say, was a decided relief.

In the morning Archdeacon Maclean returned and stated that every exertion was being made to obtain a reversal of my sentence. Mrs. Sutherland, while her poor son lay still unburied, came beseeching for my life, with many others. The autocrat himself paid me a visit about ten o'clock in the morning. Riel entered the room in a tragic way, took out his pocket-handkerchief, walked up and down for a while, pretending to weep, and then went out without having spoken a word. About twelve o'clock he returned and entered into conversation with me. He made me this proposition, that if I could get Dr. Schultz to give himself up, or if I could secure his capture, I should obtain my reprieve. I think he also included Mr. Mair, for whom he had no affection. I could not help smiling at his solemn proposal, for I did not think Dr. Schultz's sympathy for me would lead him to offer himself up a willing sacrifice. And with regard to capturing him, I knew that by this time he was making the best of his way to a place of greater safety than the settlements now offered. As Riel's scheme for capturing Dr. Schultz or Mr. Mair by this means resulted in nothing, he made no offer to me of freedom.

Anxiety about my fate continued to increase, and Riel was continually visited by people of all kinds, interceding in my behalf. The impression I had created on the guards was favouring me, and Riel sought to grant some pretext for sparing my life, although he showed no signs of abandoning his purpose. Mr. Smith told me afterwards he knew he would have to give an equivalent in asking for my life. Riel allowed this state of affairs to continue all day, and in the evening Archdeacon Maclean administered the sacrament to me, holding out no hope for reprieve. I wrote a statement, which I gave to him, to the effect that I was about to be foully murdered, without having a trial, and without any reasonable charge being brought against me. About ten o'clock in the evening I was visited by O'Donoghue. He came to ask if he could do anything for me. I thanked him, and told him I had settled all my affairs, if Riel was bent on murdering me; but that I should be glad if he would send me a glass of sherry and a basin of water. In this answer, I was determined to give O'Donoghue no satisfaction from his visit, which was one of pure curiosity. He retired, and about half-past ten Archdeacon Maclean, who had been all day in the Fort, came in and told me that I had been reprieved for a week, and that Riel had consented to spare my life if Mr. Smith would go round and get the English-speaking settlements to elect their representatives and send them once more to meet him in council. This task Mr. Smith willingly undertook, assisted by Archdeacon Maclean, and before the week was out they had held meetings in every parish and obtained the consent of the people to send their representatives. Mr. John MacTavish kindly sent a special message without delay to my friends in Canada to inform them that I was safe.

As soon as Archdeacon Maclean had left, I lay down and went to sleep. I could not have been long asleep when I was suddenly awoken by some one shaking me. I looked up and saw Riel with a lantern. He said, "Major Boulton, I have come to see you. I have come to shake you by the hand, and to make a proposition to you. I perceive that you are a man of ability, that you are a leader. The English people, they have no leader. Will you join my government, and be their leader?" The sudden transition from being under sentence of death to being asked to take a position in Riel's government, struck me as serio-comic; but I collected my wits and replied that his proposition was so startling that I could not give an answer at the moment; but if he would release all the prisoners and allow me to go back to the Portage to consult with my friends, I would consider his proposition seriously. He retired, but I heard no more about joining his government. Riel evidently would not forego the personal advantage the possession of the prisoners gave him. That night the chains were removed from my limbs. The officers of the Hudson's Bay Company asked and obtained permission to supply me with my meals and a bed. The prison discipline was relaxed, and the rest of the prisoners were allowed to have provisions brought them by their friends, which they never neglected, bringing bags of bread and many things that added to the comfort of the prisoners. Riel had no sooner agreed to spare my life than he attempted to capture Dr. Schultz. With that object he took a hundred men and went down through the lower settlement to the Stone Fort, visiting it upon the same evening that Mr. Smith and Archdeacon Maclean reached it. The latter was rudely awakened from his sleep in the middle of the night by having a revolver thrust into his face by Riel, who was searching the rooms; but by this time Dr. Schultz had made his escape. This circumstance shows the determination of Riel to capture some one he could threaten.

The prisoners whiled away the weary hours by singing songs and telling stories; and put in the time with as much hilarity as they could pretend to assume. I could only hear them through the thin wooden partition, or when I met them in the hall, where the guards were, and where we were allowed to bring our pemican to stew it on the stove. The monotony was occasionally relieved by the excitement of bringing in fresh prisoners, who were now getting so numerous that two strangers were placed in the room with me. Some were put to menial work, cleaning out the premises about the Fort, which enraged them greatly. The most important prisoner brought in during our imprisonment was Dr. Cowan, the 2nd officer of the Hudson's Bay Company.

We had little opportunity of obtaining news of what was going on outside; but one day excitement was caused by the information, whispered to me by one of the prisoners, that an attempt was to be made that night to effect our release. The plan, I was informed, was to set the premises on fire, and during the excitement we were to make good our escape. Adjoining the house in which we were imprisoned was the magazine, in which was stored several tons of gunpowder. I was alarmed lest the plot should miscarry, or that the magazine would be blown up and with it all my friends, so I did not sleep that night in my anxiety. However, nothing was attempted.

Things continued in the same monotonous round for about a fortnight, until one day I heard a racket in the guard-room, and recognized Thomas Scott's voice. I heard him say, "I want my pocket-book which you have taken from me." Considerable scuffling ensued, and the door of the room next to me was opened, and Scott was placed inside. I took an early opportunity to go out to ascertain what had been going on; and was told that two men – W.L. Scott, who had been appointed as one of the delegates, and a man named Dan Shea – had visited the prisoners in the room where Scott was, to solicit the suffrage of the prisoners who had come from Portage la Prairie. Shea wanted them to vote for him and asked them to use their influence with their friends at the Portage to secure his election, and in consideration of this he promised to get their release. Thomas Scott had said, "Don't have anything to do with these men, boys." Whereupon Dan Shea said, "I will see whether you'll interfere with me." And he and W. L. Scott retired from the room. The delegates had not yet been elected to form the council summoned by the provisional government, which had been created at the convention on the 10th of February, and in consequence of the visit to the English-speaking settlements, Mr. Smith and Archdeacon Maclean had agreed to send representatives in order to save my life and maintain the peace of the country. Riel was now seeking to obtain as many personal supporters among the English-speaking community as he could, and it was with that view he sent Dan Shea to solicit the suffrage of the prisoners resident at Portage la Prairie. It was this effort on Riel's part that caused Scott to warn the prisoners not to vote for Shea, and which, consequently, enraged Riel against Scott. Later on, Scott asked leave to go outside, and was refused by the guards, which led to an altercation. Riel and O'Donoghue visited the prison once or twice that afternoon and evening, and used violent language towards Scott. A court-martial was convened to try him, composed of Lépine, as president, and some of the guards as members, upon whom Riel no doubt wished, with mock show of legality, to throw the responsibility of taking Scott's life. Feeling anxious about what was going on, I asked the guard's permission to go into Scott's room to see him, and questioned him as to what had taken place. I found that similar questions had been put to him as had been put to me, and the same mode of passing sentence had been passed upon him as was passed upon me. I told Scott to be very careful what he said, as I felt sure that Riel meant mischief and would take his life if he could. I also told him that my life had been spared only in consequence of the exertions that had been made on my behalf. He had sent for Rev. Mr. Young to come to see him, who arrived some time during the night. Riel had got the opportunity he now wanted, which was to commit his people to an act of violence. Heretofore, there had been no violence or resistance to his wrong-doings, but Scott, he thought, had now given sufficient provocation for him to work upon his guards. He represented to his people that Scott was a dangerous man, and if he ever got at large he would take his revenge. So he worked up their feelings to the pitch he desired; at least that is the idea we formed at the time. Riel came into my room about 11 o'clock on the morning of Scott's death. I spoke to him and said, "Don't you think you are doing a most imprudent act for your own safety in shooting Scott; don't you know enough about history to realize that England has never yet left the most remote region unpenetrated, to punish those who take the life of a British subject?" The only answer I got was, "I did not come here to talk to you about that," and he made some passing remark and went away. That was the most effectual appeal that I could think of, to impress upon him the responsibility of the horrible proceedings he contemplated. It was blood that Riel wanted, for the purpose of making the people respect him, and he did not propose to let this opportunity slip. According to Mr. Donald A. Smith's report, at the winding up of the interview, when he went to intercede for Scott's life, Riel said, "I have done three good things since I have commenced; I have spared Boulton's life at your instance, I pardoned Gaddy, and now I shall shoot Scott." A few minutes before the execution took place Rev. Mr. Young came to see Scott for the last time. It now became apparent that in a short time the poor fellow was to be hurled into eternity. Mr. Young, hitherto, had so little realized the task before him, and was so unprepared for it, that he came into my room and borrowed my Bible, which had been left with me by Archdeacon Maclean, returning to Scott's room, where he spent the remainder of the time with him.

About 12 o'clock we heard preparations being made by the guards, and a few minutes afterwards my door opened and Scott came in and said, "Good-bye, Major." He was followed by about twenty guards, and was allowed to go to each room and say, "Good-bye, boys!" He was then marched down the stairs, between the guards with fixed bayonets, his hands tied behind his back, and a white rag tied over his head and hanging down behind ready to throw over his face when the fatal shots were to be fired. We watched his departure and listened to the receding footsteps, and for fifteen minutes a dead silence pervaded the building. Presently we heard the fatal shots fired from beneath the walls of the Fort. A few minutes afterwards, Mr. Young returned to our prison and gave me back my Bible, and his eyes blinded with tears, told me what had happened. Loud and deep were the murmurs of the remaining prisoners. In the evening the servant of the Hudson's Bay Company who brought me my meals gave me an account of the execution, and at the same time told me that Scott had been put into one of the bastions of the Fort, and that he had just been heard to cry out: "My God! put an end to me!" He had lain there for some hours unconscious, and must have come to his senses and called out. How he was finally despatched has never been settled, but in corroboration of the foul and brutal manner in which he was treated, I give the testimony of John Bruce, a French half-breed, who was the first president of Riel's provisional government. Bruce had been appointed by Riel as president, and no doubt accepted the position at the commencement of the outbreak, hoping by constitutional means to obtain a recognition of the rights of the population which existed in the country previous to the transfer. Bruce, however, disappeared from among the active workers when Riel resorted to extreme measures. Bruce says:

> Six soldiers had been chosen to shoot Scott. I have here again to write the name of the man whose behaviour in that circumstance reflects on him the greatest honour. Augustin Parisien, one of the six soldiers, declared openly that he would not shoot at Scott; in fact, he took off the cap from his gun before the word of command "present" was given. Of the five balls remaining, only two hit the poor victim, one on the left shoulder, and the other in the upper part of the chest above the heart. Had the other soldiers missed the mark undesignedly, or had they intentionally aimed away from Riel's victim, it is not known.

However that may be, as the two wounds were not sufficient to cause death, at least sudden death, a man, named Guillemette, stepped forward and discharged the contents of a pistol close to Scott's head while he was lying on the ground. This ball, however, took a wrong direction. It penetrated the upper part of the left cheek and came out somewhere about the cartilage of the nose. Scott was still not dead, but that did not prevent his butchers from placing him, alive and still speaking, in a kind of coffin made of four rough boards. It was nailed and plated in the south-eastern bastion, and an armed soldier was placed at the door. This would seem like a story made at one's ease, if there were not several credible witnesses who, between the hours of five and six in the evening, heard the unfortunate Scott speaking from under the lid of his coffin, and it was known that he had been shot at half-past twelve. What a long and horrible agony, and what ferocious cruelty was this on the part of his butchers! The words heard and understood by the French Métis were only these: "My God! My God!" Some English Métis, and those understanding English, heard distinctly these words: "For God's sake take me out of here or kill me." Towards 11 o'clock – that is, after ten and a half hours of frightful agony – a person, whose name I shall withhold for the present, went into the bastion, and, according to some, gave him the finishing stroke with a butcher's knife, with a pistol, according to others. After having inflicted the last blow on poor Scott, that person said, as he was coming back from the bastion: "He is dead this time!" The corpse was left for a few days in the south-eastern bastion, being guarded by the soldiers, relieving each other in turn.

In addition, I append an extract from a letter of Rev. Mr. Young to Scott's brother, Mr. Hugh Scott, written the day after the murder:

Let me then express my deep sympathy for you and your bereaved family in this sore trouble. As you probably know already, your brother was taken prisoner by Mr. Riel in December last, and made his escape after many weeks' imprisonment, but joining another company of volunteers he was again captured, with forty-seven others. The day before yesterday he was singled out and tried for these offences, as well as for "insulting Mr. Riel and the guards by something he said" – which he positively denied – and was sentenced to be shot at noon *next day*. I was sent for as a minister who had visited the prisoners regularly, and was known by your brother. During the evening I stayed with him, giving instructions and exhortations, and engaging frequently in prayer. He was deeply penitent and earnestly prayerful before God. Next morning I went again and begged personally of Mr. Riel to reprieve your brother, and got Commissioner Smith to do the same. We urged that one day more should be given him to prepare. But, alas! all in vain. I was with him to the end. He prayed frequently, and said it was dreadful to put him to death; but expressed hope of salvation. He was led out a few feet from the walls of Fort Garry, where again he knelt in the snow and prayed, remaining on his knees until the fatal shots were fired. I have begged the body, which Riel intended to bury in the Fort, and I think, through others helping, that we shall get it, when we intend burying it at the Presbyterian churchyard, five miles below this.

That same afternoon some of the prisoners saw preparations for the grave being made, and the coffin made ready. Rev. Mr. Young and the Bishop of Rupert's Land both made a request for the body, but were refused, lest the additional damning evidence of the murdered man should stand against the perpetrators of the bloody tragedy. It was rumoured in the Fort that his body had been buried, but had been exhumed, sewed up in canvas, weighted with cannon balls and sunk beneath the ice at the junction of the Seine with the Red River, near by.

Scott, it ought to be said, was not taken prisoner with arms in his hands. On the first occasion, before the prisoners were captured in Dr. Schultz's house, he had gone boldly down to the Fort to ask Riel to give safe conduct to the ladies and children who were in danger there, and Riel's only answer to his peaceful mission was to thrust him into prison. Nor on the second occasion was he armed; so this murder has no extenuation, and for cold bloodedness and deliberate butchery poor Scott's fate has scarcely a parallel.

Riel had now committed his people to a deed which could not be recalled; and no doubt those who were implicated in it, when they came to realize what had been done, repented of the murderous act. On the following day Riel singled out another man, Murdoch Macleod, from among the prisoners, and put him in chains. We all dreaded that another life would be taken. From my knowledge of Riel at this time, I feared this would have happened; but his people were not prepared to go any further, so no sentence was passed upon him. But, during the remainder of his imprisonment, Murdoch continued to be shackled, and to have indignities heaped upon him.

I had forgotten to mention an interesting reminiscence which should not be overlooked, namely, the visit to Winnipeg, in January, of Mr. John Ross Robertson, of the Toronto *Telegram*, and Mr. Cunningham, of the Toronto *Globe*. They came in search of news, having travelled over the prairie, in the winter time, from St. Paul, and were the only two correspondents who ventured up to the scene of the troubles. I do not know if their enterprise rewarded them; but they were detained by Riel for two days in Fort Garry, and were then allowed to return. Riel at this time kept the strictest censorship over the local press and the mail bags, so that no information could get out not in accord with his plans.

V

THE OVERTURES FOR PEACE

A few days after Scott's tragic death, there were rumours of
Archbishop Taché's proposed visit. The Canadian Goverment,
in their anxiety to use every means to quiet disturbance, and
hearing that Archbishop Taché would return from Rome to
meet the emergencies, telegraphed for him, and he arrived in
Ottawa in the beginning of February.

After conferring with the Government, he was authorized
to assure his people upon the most important points of the
good intentions of the Government, and also to inform the
leaders that if the Company's government was restored there
would be a general amnesty. At the time this conference was
going on between the Dominion Government and the Archbishop, neither of the two sad events, the murder of Scott and
the shooting of young Sutherland, had occurred. Up to that
time Riel and his followers had only committed depredations,
unlawfully detained prisoners, and resisted authority. They
had committed no bloodshed. But in the interval between
Archbishop Taché's leaving Ottawa and his arrival in Winnipeg, or rather at St. Boniface, the tragedies which so stirred
the hearts of the Canadian people had taken place. The journey between Ottawa and St. Boniface, at this period, was a
long and tedious one. As soon as I heard of the arrival of the
Archbishop, I felt that a change would soon take place in the
condition of affairs, as the prelate possessed great influence
over his people, was greatly respected by all who knew him,
and possessed sufficient astuteness to realize the danger his
people incurred by continuing to resist lawful authority. I have

forgotten the precise date of the Archbishop's arrival; but, no doubt, on his coming lengthy negotiations took place between him and Riel, and he must have experienced much difficulty in compelling the usurper to abandon the desperate attitude he had assumed.

Riel had made his first attempts at resistance with the countenance and connivance of many of the priests, who always desired the temporal as well as the spiritual welfare of their people. Up to a certain point, he used them to further his designs; but as soon as he had obtained the prestige and power which his continued success gave him, his vanity and personal ambition led him to cast off the authority of his spiritual advisers, and he would now brook little interference on their part. Such was the opinion I formed at the time of the murder of Scott, and I felt that the influence of the clergy on his behalf, if it was used, would have little avail; for Riel was bloodthirsty and determined to make his personal power felt by the most extreme measures. To show his mood at this time, he even put a guard on the Archbishop's palace, and tried to prevent him from communicating with Mr. Mactavish or with Mr. Smith.

When Archbishop Taché arrived, he found Riel in this position of power, with a considerable personal following within the walls of the Fort to assist him in sustaining it. As the actions of the Archbishop at this period brought about political results which created a great deal of excitement and controversy, and placed the Government in a difficult position, it is necessary to point out, so far as we could judge, how these events were brought about. As I said before, the Archbishop had received authority from the Governor-General to promise a general amnesty to his people, in order to re-establish, as far as possible, law and order in the settlement. Added to that, he had a strong personal sympathy for Riel, and this, no doubt, influenced his actions considerably. However, he was dismayed at the turn affairs had taken, by the second incarceration of the prisoners, and by the murder of Scott, and he was, doubtless, embarrassed as to the course he should pursue. As there was no telegraph, and no means of communication, short of a journey over the four hundred and fifty miles of snow-clad prairie to St. Paul, he had to use his best judgment under the circumstances, and, of course, had to deal with Riel, who held full control of the situation and was not prepared to allow any temporal interference on the Archbishop's part.

Riel held the prisoners as a constant menace to the peace and safety of the settlement, and Archbishop Taché, wishing to obtain their release and restore order, had to choose between leaving the prisoners where they were or to include Riel in the amnesty which he had been empowered to grant. There is no doubt he must have had some difficulty in convincing Riel of the prudence of his accepting an amnesty, though such was not contemplated by the Dominion Government, who were not aware of the altered aspect of affairs since the dark deed had been committed. While Archbishop Taché has been condemned for using the authority conferred upon him, and for extending the amnesty to Riel, he no doubt felt himself justified, under the grave circumstances which threatened the country, to stretch the authority he possessed.

During all this time Mr. Donald Smith had been diligently prosecuting the practical object of his mission, to bring the people into direct communication with the Dominion Government through the delegates that had been appointed, and he was anxious to get them off. He, no doubt, felt it of importance that there should be an evidence of arms being laid down to insure a proper reception for them, though he himself never seems to have consented to an amnesty in any way. On the 16th of March we were made aware of the result of Archbishop Taché's interference by being told that on the following day we were to be released, upon taking an oath that we would not again take up arms in opposition to the provisional government. I advised the prisoners, one and all, not to hesitate to take this oath, thus illegally enforced, before granting our release. The oath was administered to each by Lépine. One half of the prisoners were released one day and the other half on the following day. I remained in the Fort receiving the hospitality of the officers of the Hudson's Bay Company until

I saw that all the prisoners had been released. Unfortunately, for some reason, Riel still retained Murdoch Macleod, who had been confined with the chains on all this time, and I could not leave the Fort until his release was guaranteed.

With the release of the prisoners ended the exciting part of the insurrection organized by Riel. The winter passed over without greater disaster than the death of Senator Sutherland's son, the murder of poor Scott, and the death of the French half-breed, Parisien. Had hostilities been provoked, or the first shot in anger fired, the country in its isolated position would probably have been handed over to a scene of rapine, murder and pillage, fearful to contemplate, through the excitement of the Indian population, whose savage nature cannot be controlled when the opportunity for warfare presents itself. But, fortunately for Canada and fortunately for the Hudson's Bay Company, the critical period passed, and the task of Sir Garnet Wolseley, upon whose shoulders afterward fell the duty of enforcing law and order in this fair heritage of the British Crown, enabled him to march in peacefully and hand over the reins of government to the civil authorities, now constituted by Act of Parliament. To the Bishop of Rupert's Land, Judge Black, Mr. Donald A. Smith, Archdeacon Maclean, and the Reverend Mr. Young, is chiefly due the salvation of the settlement through the winter by the prudence of their policy and the influence of their counsels. There were so many inflammable elements and such a strong feeling against Riel's tyranny, that there was constant danger of another uprising, and only great tact and prudence prevented this further calamity.

In two days I left my prison walls for the English settlements, and upon the advice of friends I at once took my departure for Canada, for the purpose of giving such information to the Government as they might desire. I made the journey across the prairies on sleds, with Judge Black, who was on his way to Ottawa, on the delegation commissioned to confer with the Government. On reaching Ontario, I found the greatest excitement prevailing over the news of Scott's murder, which had sent a thrill of horror through the whole of Upper Canada.

I found that Dr. Schultz had just arrived, having performed the marvellous task of marching on snowshoes through a forest country, from the Stone Fort to Duluth, a distance of about five hundred miles, under the guidance of a faithful half-breed, named Monkman. In the later rebellion a son of the latter was convicted of supporting Riel, and apparently had not inherited the loyal instincts of his brave father. Dr. Schultz's march indicates the great powers of endurance he at that time possessed; for he passed through an immense region, poorly supplied with provisions, through deep snow, in continual danger of losing his way, and with the knowledge that he might be pursued. But he arrived in safety, to be a hero among his countrymen.

On the arrival at Ottawa of Father Ritchot and Alfred Scott, the other two delegates nominated by the convention, they were at once arrested for complicity in the murder of Thomas Scott, whose brother was in Ottawa, and who with the friends of the murdered man secured the delegates' arrest. They were, however, released for want of direct evidence to implicate them. After their release they assumed the official capacity in which they had come to the country, as delegates to arrange the terms by which the interests of their country were to be protected. These negotiations resulted in a Bill being passed by Parliament, creating the Province of Manitoba, the boundary of which was at the time designedly limited by the Act. The half-breeds gained substantial advantages in a grant of one million four hundred thousand acres, to be set apart in reserve for them and all the children belonging to them, at the date of transfer. On computation this was found to be two hundred and forty acres for each child, and one hundred and sixty acres for each head of a family, besides a patent for the homes they occupied.

The new province had a constitution granted it, giving it self-government, based upon the system which prevailed elsewhere in Canada, and giving it representatives in both Houses of Parliament, as well as control over its local affairs.

Although the results gained for the half-breeds by Riel's insurrection appear to be advantageous, yet the half-breeds put very little value on the two hundred and forty acres of scrip that had been issued to each. This land-grant they almost immediately sold for a song, ranging from fifteen dollars upwards. Thus nearly the whole of the one million four hundred thousand acres became the property of non-residents, who in consequence of the cheap rate at which they acquired the property could allow it to remain to accumulate in value with the development of the country. This has been very prejudicial to the interests of that portion of Manitoba which it was designed to benefit; for at Winnipeg, on entering the gateway of the country, the stranger is met on all sides by vast unoccupied tracts of valuable lands which are not only unproductive, but handicap the industry of the population, and retard the progress of the provincial capital. In some respects, however, the Government was wise in yielding to the pressure that was brought to bear upon them; for agitation would have been kept up by interested parties to secure the local advantage of self-government.

Although the delegates appointed by the provisional government had been received at Ottawa, and their terms acceded to, yet the Government was not prepared to take over the country from the Hudson's Bay Company, unless an armed force was sent to support its authority. Otherwise there was nothing to prevent Riel from continuing to exercise the authority he had usurped. Negotiations were therefore opened by the Dominion Government with the view of sending an armed force into the country, which the English Government sanctioned, Canada to pay three-fourths of the cost. But before the English Government would allow the troops to start it was required of Canada that the rights and privileges of the existing population should be respected, and the English Government were to be the judges in case an agreement was not arrived at. The force was to consist of British Regulars and Canadian Militia, the whole to be put under the command of Colonel (now Lord) Wolseley; and he at once set about making preparations for the expedition.

In the midst of the preparations I returned to Toronto, and

was anxious to have an opportunity of joining the force, but I found that the Dominion Government had excluded from its ranks all those who had been in any way mixed up with the troubles during the previous winter, which was to me a great disappointment. The expedition was to be one of peace, for the purpose solely of re-establishing law and order.

Sir Garnet Wolseley selected the route for his expedition by way of the chain of lakes and rivers which had been so frequently used during early explorations, as well as by the traders of the North-West Company. Colonel Crofton, on one occasion, took his troops to the Red River by this route, and Lork Selkirk, in his struggles with the North-West Company, had also brought troops over it. The history of this expedition is an exceedingly interesting one.

The expedition was admirably managed throughout, not a single life being lost. Colonel Wolseley arrived at Fort Garry on the 24th day of August, 1870, and Riel only gave up the reins of power a few moments before his arrival, preferring not to remain to render an account of his short but iniquitous reign.

The rule of the Hudson's Bay Company, in the absence of any other constituted civil authority, was at once reinstated by Sir Garnet Wolseley, in the person of Mr. Donald A. Smith, the Chief Commissioner, who played so important a part throughout the troubles. He in turn, a few days after, handed the country over to the Honourable Adams Archibald, who had been appointed Lieutenant-Governor in the place of Wm. McDougall, and who arrived on the 2nd of September. The Queen's proclamation was read, and all the legal requirements were complied with to make the old Hudson's Bay Territory part and parcel of the Dominion, and a new era commenced in the development of the region. Colonel Wolseley, without delay, despatched his regular soldiers on their return journey to Quebec, leaving the two battalions of Canadian Militia, under Colonels Jarvis and Cassault, to preserve law and order, and protect the settlement.

On Sir Garnet Wolseley's arrival, Riel quietly slipped across the river, where he was sheltered by his friends. A warrant for his arrest was procured by private individuals, and he with-drew from the country and took up his residence at St. Joe, an American village on the boundary line. The feeling was very strong against him; but, on the other hand, his own people applauded the success of his winter's work, and the settlement was still in constant danger from the excited population.

Lieutenant-Governor Archibald and his successor, Lieuten-ant-Governor Morris, had a most difficult task to perform during their terms of office. They were isolated from Ottawa, the means of communication with which were still slow. They had an excited population to deal with, that took totally differ-ent views of the events which led to the acquisition of the North-West Territory by Canada. By their prudence, firmness and moderation, however, they avoided very serious difficulties, which might have befallen the country. Individuals are not apt at all times to weigh their words or consider their actions in places of trust, or to feel their responsibility in the adminis-trative affairs of the nation. It is this that frequently leads to difficulties, which often get beyond the control of the civil authorities.

The most delicate subject the Government had to deal with during this period was the question of a general amnesty. When Archbishop Taché arrived in March he took upon himself the responsibility of promising a full and complete amnesty on behalf of the Governor-General; and he and Father Ritchot pressed with the utmost vigour, by correspondence and by interviews, the fulfilment of this promise. Archbishop Taché claimed that the condition of the country warranted his making this promise of an amnesty, and having once made it, he would be considered to have deceived the people did he not make every effort to keep his word.

The position the Government assumed was that as the coun-try had not been a part of Canada at the time of the troubles, the amnesty question was one for the Imperial authorities alone to deal with.

In the autumn of 1870, the Fenians took advantage of the

excited state of the country to make a raid, at the instigation of O'Donoghue and others, who were intriguing against its peace. "General" O'Neill managed to find his way to the borders with an armed force, invaded the territory, and took possession of the Hudson's Bay post at Pembina. O'Neill, however, was promptly followed by the American troops and compelled to return. Finding that the American authorities were firm in their desire to preserve international amity, he abandoned the enterprise. In the meantime the settlement was thrown into great excitement and alarm, and Governor Archibald issued a proclamation asking for volunteers to serve against the Fenians. Shortly after the issue of this proclamation he received a letter from Riel, Lépine, and Parenteau, telling him that they had organized several companies of half-breeds for service against the Fenians, and containing assurances of loyalty. The Governor went over to St. Boniface to inspect these volunteers, and publicly thanked them for their services, shaking hands with them as they marched by, Riel and Lépine being present. In his communication to Sir John Macdonald on the subject, the Governor says in reference to this act:

> If the Dominion has at this moment a province to defend and not one to conquer, they owe it to the policy of forbearance. If I had driven the French half-breeds into the hands of the enemy, O'Donoghue would have been joined by all the population between the Assiniboine and the frontier; Fort Garry would have passed into the hands of an armed mob, and the English settlers to the north of the Assiniboine would have suffered horrors which makes me shudder to contemplate.

The Government felt, however, that Riel was playing a double game. He continued to be a menace to the peace of the settlement, and realizing the difficulties of protecting the country, should its peace be broken, Sir John Macdonald arranged with Archbishop Taché to get Riel to leave the territory. To effect this the Government sent Archbishop Taché one thousand dollars to pay Riel's expenses, but this sum was not considered sufficient, and on Governor Archibald's guaranteeing to repay the amount, Mr. Donald A. Smith, then Chief Commissioner of the Hudson's Bay Company, advanced three thousand more to Archbishop Taché, which was some time after repaid by the Dominion Government.

In September, 1872, Riel was nominated to the House of Commons for the constituency of Provencher, but he declined the nomination in favour of Sir George Cartier. In 1873, in consequence of Sir George Cartier's death, Riel was elected by acclamation for the same constituency, and in the election of 1874, he was again returned. Some time in March of that year, Riel signed the roll in the clerk's room of the House of Commons at Ottawa, without any one being aware that he was in the capital. The question was brought up in Parliament, and by a vote of 124 to 68, Riel was expelled from the House, but was again returned by his constituents. In October, 1874, Lépine was tried for the murder of Scott, convicted and sentenced to death, while a warrant of outlawry was issued against Riel by the Court of Queen's Bench of Manitoba. Lord Dufferin sent a despatch to Earl Carnarvon, Secretary of State for the Colonies, reviewing at length the circumstances which were urged as entitling Riel and Lépine to clemency, placing especial stress upon Lieutenant-Governor Archibald's acceptance of their services on the occasion of the threatened Fenian invasion, and the public expression of confidence and thanks tendered them by the representative of the Crown in Manitoba. In reference to the application for a commutation of Lépine's sentence, he said: "This commutation, when the proper time arrives, I propose to order on my own responsibility, under the powers accorded me by my instruments." In January, 1875, Earl Carnarvon stated that in Lépine's case, neither amnesty nor entire pardon was possible, but that his sentence should be commuted; that Riel should have similar punishment, and that both should be politically disqualified. The next day Lépine's sentence was commuted to two years' imprisonment, and he was deprived of his political rights. On the 12th of February an amnesty was granted to Riel and Lépine, on condition of five years' banishment and forfeiture of political rights. Lépine, however, having already served a portion of his sentence, preferred to complete his term in lieu of banishment.

Another duty that fell to the lot of Lieutenant-Governors Archibald and Morris was the extinction of the Indian title by treaty. Governor Archibald, with the assistance of Indian Commissioners, negotiated the Stone Fort and Manitoba Post treaties, or treaties numbers one and two. The Honourable Mr. Morris negotiated treaties numbers three, four, five and six respectively, called the North-West Angle treaty, the Qu'Appelle treaty, the Winnipeg treaty, the treaties at Forts Carlton and Pitt. The Blackfoot treaty, number seven, was negotiated by Lieutenant-Governor Laird, when Lieutenant-Governor of the North-West Territory.

In 1875 a circumstance occurred which might have resulted in difficulty for the country, had it not been for the prompt action of Lieutenant-Governor Morris. He received information that Gabriel Dumont had organized a provisional government in the Batoche district, where a new settlement had the previous year been started. It was ostensibly established for the purpose of governing the half-breeds, on the principle that used to prevail in their hunting expeditions. This act Governor Morris realized would excite the Indians. General Selby Smyth, with two officers, had been visiting him in Winnipeg, on his way across the continent to British Columbia, and had already left for Fort Pelly to visit the Mounted Police stationed there, when this information was received. He had been gone two days; but Mr. Morris despatched Captain Cotton after him to advise him of the circumstance, and requesting him to take a detachment of Mounted Police and visit the disaffected region. At the same time Mr. Morris availed himself of the services of Mr. McDougall, who was then in Winnipeg, and who had the misfortune afterwards of being frozen to death, having lost his way in a blizzard, far away from any settlement. He entrusted Mr. McDougall with a despatch to the Indians, signed and sealed with his official authority as Governor of the North-West Territory, and despatched him with all haste to the western tribes, counselling them to be quiet, and promising to visit them the following year, which he faithfully did. General Smyth took a detachment of fifty Mounted Police from Fort Pelly and visited Batoche, and had an interview with Gabriel Dumont, who agreed to abandon his enterprise. Having done this, the Mounted Police were sent back, and General Selby Smyth continued on his way across the continent. This, among many other similar events in the history of the North-West Territory during the previous fifteen years, shows the disturbing element that existed among the half-breeds and Indians, and the facile material Riel found ready to work upon to enable him to carry out his schemes.

Riel, being banished from the country, took up his residence for a time at St. Joe, and in 1878 went to Sun River, Montana. There he taught in an industrial school, where he remained until waited on by the delegates from the Saskatchewan. In Montana he seems to have illegally mixed himself up in the politics of the country, according to the newspaper accounts which occasionally came to hand. There, at any rate, the delegates found him, and, as we shall see, induced him to return to the territories and again bring trouble upon the country.

The country now settled down to peaceful pursuits, and a gradual stream of immigration came in, penetrating everywhere, in advance of surveys, as fancy dictated. The Province of Manitoba organized its governmental machinery, and laid the foundation of the laws of the country under the inspiration of the native population, which was, however, gradually absorbed in the new elements that so rapidly came into the territory. It is worthy of remark here, and to the credit of the excellent educational institutions established under the Hudson's Bay Company rule, that a native of the country, the Honourable Mr. Norquay, for many years occupied the highest position in its political life.

With the population scattered far and wide over the country, the Government found it necessary to organize a Mounted Police force to institute legal machinery in the scattered districts, and to throw over the whole country its protecting arm. The force was at first composed of three hundred men; afterwards it was increased to five hundred; and then again was increased to one thousand strong.

Having now attempted to supply a narrative of the first rebellion, I shall endeavour to give an account of the second one, which, unfortunately, was far more disastrous in its effects upon the lives and property of the people. Happily, in the new outbreak, the Government was enabled to assert the power and dignity of the country; and in this it was in no small degree aided by the means of communication afforded by the construction of the Canadian Pacific Railway.

Part Two

The North-west Rebellion, 1885

VI

RIEL'S SECOND REBELLION

Fifteen years had elapsed since the rebellion of 1869-70 and the transfer of the country to Canada. In this interval great progress had been made. Two main lines of railway were constructed, one from the south through the Western States, and one from the old provinces of Canada, through Canadian territory north of the Great Lakes. The population of the newly acquired territory had at the same time largely increased and spread over the face of the country, in numerous small bands of settlers, forming the nucleus of what must soon be populous districts. The half-breeds, having in numerous instances sold out their claims to newcomers, migrated westward in large bands, taking with them their families, their stock and worldly possessions, and carrying all in the rude Red River cart. In those days it was no uncommon thing to see a train of sixty or seventy of these primitive conveyances, freighted with these nomadic people, proceeding westward along the trail to select other localities on the banks of the great rivers, where they could settle down for a while by themselves, untrammelled by the laws and habits of civilization and apart from the incoming population. And now, throughout those distant regions, may be found small settlements of three or four hundred souls, mostly composed of those who formerly resided on the Red River in the neighbourhood of Winnipeg. In this newly acquired territory, in which the half-breed sought a new home, four, six, or even eight hundred miles' travel by cart is little thought of. The horses pasture on the luxuriant vegetation of the prairies, and the people, while thus travelling, live on the game that everywhere abounds. Thus isolated, though accompanied on all occasions by their faithful priests, who as a rule are alike their temporal and spiritual advisers, these people preserve their primitive habits and customs, and retain sufficient of their savage nature to relish the excitement of the chase and not infrequently that of battle.

The half-breeds comprising these communities select the banks of the larger rivers and apportion off for themselves farms with but a few chains of frontage on the river, making up their area by running them two miles deep, out on to the prairie. This is done that their houses may be built close to one another, and that they may have the benefit of the river water for their cattle, and thus save themselves the labour of digging wells. Besides this, the quantities of fish to be got in these rivers are a great help towards the family's subsistence.

Between the north and south branches of the Saskatchewan River, and adjacent to the English community of Prince Albert, which comprises some six thousand souls, is situated the mission of St. Laurent, containing a population of twelve or fifteen hundred people. Both these settlements have made great progress during the last few years. Their means of communication with the outer world is however necessarily imperfect, and the cost of freighting is heavy, as they are distant about two hundred and fifty miles north of the main line of the Canadian Pacific Railway. But, like the settlements planted by Lord Selkirk on the banks of the Red and Assiniboine Rivers in the early part of the present century, they have struggled, grown, and prospered; yet, owing to their great distance and isolation from the civilized world, their voice has been faintly heard, and their complaints indifferently listened to.

The Canadian Government during these years was busy surveying the country, endeavouring to keep pace with the rapidly advancing settlements, and connecting the territory by base and meridian lines from east to west and from north to south. In consequence of the previous growth of the settlements in and around Prince Albert, surveying parties had been early sent forward to locate townships and divide them into lots. The prevailing system of surveys is by townships six miles square, subdivided into sections one mile square, separated by road allowances one chain and a half wide. When the surveyors came into the settlement of St. Laurent, they were at once met with the difficulty of the locations made by the half-breeds, which we have before described. Having no instructions, they continued their surveys upon the recognized principle, leaving, however, any lands occupied by squatters intact. The surveyors in due course made their returns to Ottawa, and a land agent was appointed. For some time, however, the land office was not opened for business, and the settlers were unable to make entries for their lands or to obtain their patents.

A good deal of confusion arose during the early settlement of this district, owing to the numbers who sought to obtain the most eligible locations having no guide to go by, or survey to direct them. They clung on, however, to the locations they had first taken up, irrespective of the closeness of neighbours. The settlement of these claims, and the policy of permitting the half-breeds to maintain their own surveys, was no doubt the cause of the great and apparently unnecessary delay in satisfying the settlers, who were anxious to know what land their titles covered. In addition, these half-breeds contended that they should be allotted the scrip for two hundred and forty acres of land, the same as their brethren in the Province of Manitoba, a policy that had always been contemplated by the country but was held in abeyance. Many of them had already received scrip in that province, but without question they nevertheless hoped to get it again. This had been petitioned for frequently, but apparently no attention had been paid to them.

The reason given by the Government, in the debate upon the alleged grievances, was that Archbishop Taché and other friends of the half-breeds represented that until the half-breeds had become more acquainted with the civilization that was surrounding them, and better able to hold their own, it would be wiser not to accede to their demands. Archbishop Taché wanted reserves made for the half-breeds, to be held in trust for them for three generations. Lieutenant-Governor Laird and the North-West Council recommended that ten years should elapse before the half-breeds should have the power to part with their privileges. These were all sensible recommendations, but the people themselves wanted to secure the few dollars the issue of scrip would give them. Their friends, moreover, felt that if patents were granted them and their scrip distributed, a repetition of the exodus that had taken place from the settlements around Winnipeg would ensue, and that these settlements, which were now contented and happy, would be broken up and the people would migrate further west into the Peace River and other isolated districts. It is a benefit to the country to have pioneers like these forming outposts for the advancing tide of immigration; and looking at it from that standpoint, it was a mistake postponing the issue of their scrip. But the Government inclined to take a paternal view of their circumstances, and yielding no doubt to the suggestions of their friends, delayed the appointment of the Commission to award the scrip to those entitled to it.

The Commission, however, was appointed in January, 1885, previous to the outbreak of disturbance; and before the campaign was over it had completed its task, allotting the scrip to those who were entitled to receive it. Speculators accompanied the Commission to the various settlements and purchased from the half-breeds the valuable rights and privileges which were thus granted. It is perhaps well to give here the result of their labours and enquiries, to show that their friends were right in postponing as long as they could the realization of these valuable privileges.

The Commission appointed to inquire into the half-breed claims and to make the award to those entitled to the scrip granted altogether about nineteen hundred to heads of families and their children. So just and liberal were the awards that, included in this nineteen hundred were a number of half-breeds who had been drawing treaty all the time but resigned it and took scrip, and about three hundred who had died of small-pox some years previously, during an epidemic that had

visited the district near Edmonton. The latter had become entitled to the scrip by virtue of their residence in the territory in
1870, the date of the transfer, and their scrip was awarded to
their heirs. It is also worthy of note that in the parish of St.
Laurent, where Riel made his headquarters, and which was
the scene of the rebellion, only sixty souls were entitled to the
scrip. The remainder belonged to families who had emigrated
from the Province of Manitoba and had already received the
benefit of the half-breed grant. Eighty-seven were entitled to
it in the Prince Albert district. The scrip they received, in the
case of heads of families, granted the right to locate one
hundred and sixty acres of land, or one hundred and sixty
dollars in scrip, good to purchase Dominion lands at the current
price. In the case of minors, it conveyed the right to locate two
hundred and forty acres of land, or two hundred and forty
dollars in scrip. Of those who obtained their scrip, nearly ninety
per cent elected to take the money value in preference to the
land, which they parted with in many cases for about thirty-
five cents on the dollar. A half-breed with any Indian blood
can take treaty as an Indian, and can resign it at his pleasure
for scrip.

Withholding the patents and the scrip, and the system of
surveys, were the chief causes which excited the people and
enabled Riel to stir up an armed rebellion in the country for
his own glory and personal advantage. Although, according
to Père André's evidence, a telegram came on the 4th of March
to say that the Government had acceded to the issue of scrip
and patents and river surveys, no word had come in regard
to Riel's compensation, and so he went on with the rebellion.

This is how the half-breeds reasoned. Riel, in the year 1869,
had been successful in his stand against the Honourable Wm.
McDougall and the Hudson's Bay Company, where for six
months he had served out the stores of the Company to pay
his people for their services to him and to feed them, and had
also obtained for them scrip for two hundred and forty acres
of land, each, and the recognition of their existing privileges
and titles. Hence, they thought, he could not fail to accomplish

similar great results for these new settlements, many of which were made up of those who migrated from the neighbourhood of Winnipeg, and had realized the temporary advantages and other gains of the previous rebellion.

Riel had spent most of his time, after his banishment, in the United States, where he became an American citizen, and in 1884 was teaching a small school of half-breeds in a settlement in the territory of Montana. The people of this settlement were imbued with the same sentiments and feelings, and inherited much of the same blood, as the half-breeds in Canada. While there, Riel had on two or three occasions got himself into trouble with the American authorities by interfering illegally in the politics of the country, showing that the spirit of agitation was still strong in him, and that he was there striving to use the influence of the half-breeds for his own ambitious ends.

The thoughts of the half-breeds of the Saskatchewan valley naturally turned to Riel in their desire to secure their rights and privileges, which so far had received little attention from the Government. In the summer of 1884, four men, Gabriel Dumont, Michel Dumas, Moise Ouellette, and James Isbister, went to Montana, sought an interview with Riel, and persuaded him to come up to the Saskatchewan to assist them in their cause. Riel did not require much persuasion; in fact, it is stated that he brought about this mission himself. As his answer to this delegation is of interest, I give it below:

To Messrs. James Isbister, Gabriel Dumont, Moise Ouellette, and Michel Dumas: –

St. Peter's Mission, June 4th, 1884.
Gentlemen, – You have travelled more than seven hundred miles, from the Saskatchewan country across the international line, to make me a visit. The communities in the midst of which you live have sent you as their delegates to ask my advice on various difficulties which have rendered the British North-West unhappy under the administration of the Ottawa Government. Moreover, you invite me to go and stay amongst you, your hope being that I, for one, could help to better in some respects your condition, and cordial and pressing is your invitation. You want

me and my family to accompany you; I am at liberty to excuse myself and say no; yet you are waiting for me, so that I have only to get ready, and your letters of delegation assure me that a friendly welcome awaits me in the midst of those who sent you.

Gentlemen, your personal visit does me honour, and causes me great pleasure, but on account of its representative character, your coming to me has the appearance of a remarkable circumstance, which I record as one of the gratifications of my life – an event which my family will remember; and I pray to God that my assistance will prove so successful to you as to render this event a blessing among the many blessings of this my fortieth year. To be frank is the shortest. I doubt whether my advice given to you on this soil, concerning affairs in Canadian territories, could cross the border and retain any influence. But there is another view of the matter. I am entitled, according to the 31st and 32nd clauses of the Manitoba treaty, to land, of which the Canadian Government have directly or indirectly deprived me, and my claim to which is valid, notwithstanding the fact that I have become an American citizen. Considering then, that my interests are identical with yours, I accept your very kind invitation, and will go and spend some months amongst you, in the hope that by petitioning the Government we will obtain the redress of our grievances.

Montana has a population, of which the native half-breed element constitutes a considerable portion, and if we include those white men, who through being connected by marriage, or in other ways, have a personal interest in their welfare, I believe it is safe to assert that this element is a pretty strong one. I am just getting acquainted with them, and I am one of those who would like to unite and direct its vote for the furtherance of their best interests. Moreover, I have made friends and acquaintances amongst whom I like to live. I go with you, but I will come back in September.

I have the honour to be, Gentlemen delegates,
Your humble servant,
Louis Riel.

Riel accompanied the delegates on their return to the Saskatchewan, and took with him his wife and family. His crimes of 1869-70 had been condoned, though he was permanently deprived of his political rights. His term of banishment, however, had now expired, and he was once more entitled to return a free man.*

A number of the Prince Albert settlers, who had grievances similar to the half-breeds, were inclined to make common cause with them, and welcome Riel to their midst; but upon discovering the extreme measures he intended taking, they afterwards refused to have anything to do with him. He held meetings in the various parishes, and explained his policy, and commenced a constitutional agitation for the redress of the grievances of the people who had sent for him.

It is a wonder that Riel would again venture to head a violent and treasonable agitation of the half-breeds. He had narrowly escaped the consequences of his acts of 1869-70, through the sympathetic interference of Archbishop Taché. He had put the Canadian Government and the Imperial authorities to a large expense in sending troops into the country, and he had taken the life of a fellow countryman without rhyme or reason, which had stirred the hearts of the Canadian people to the depths. On the other hand, however, there was a chance of personal profit, and he no doubt came with the intention of pushing his agitation to extremes until that profit should come. Sir John Macdonald declared in Parliament that Riel had made an offer to the Government to leave the country for five thousand dollars, which offer was more moderate than the amount stated by Riel himself, in his speech to the jury during his trial in Regina. In this speech he claimed that there was a balance of thirty-five thousand dollars due him since the time he was

---

*That the French half-breeds, at the outset, were anxious to have Riel come among them, and lead an agitation in the district, is clear from the following letter of Father André, which has recently been published. Says this priest:

My dear Mr. Riel, – The opinion here is so pronounced in your favour and longs for you so ardently that it would be a great disappointment to the people of Prince Albert if you did not come. So you see you absolutely must come. You are the most popular man of the country, and with the exception of four or five persons all the world impatiently expects you. I have only this to say – Come. Come quickly. With kind remembrances,

I am,
A. André.

at the head of the provisional government in 1870.

As in 1869, Riel prepared a "bill of rights," which contained extensive provisions for the half-breeds and the Indians. In 1869 the half-breed grant was computed by apportioning one-seventh of the lands of the Province of Manitoba to their use and that of their children. Riel wished a similar principle to be carried out with regard to the North-West Territories. I do not think this principle of one-seventh was ever formulated before the Government, but I believe this was the inducement he held out to the half-breeds and the Indians; and to further every interest on his behalf he made promises of liberal grants of land, etc. The "bill of rights," which was adopted at the meetings held in the various settlements, contained liberal provisions for the half-breeds and their children, as well as for the Indians.

Riel continued his agitation through the winter and held meetings in the English settlements, which were attended by many sympathizers, who thought some good might come of the agitation, although open rebellion was never hinted at or contemplated by the sympathizers. But the latter were playing with fire in having anything to do with Riel, for he had personal ends to serve, and was using these settlers merely as his tools.

In order to get some sort of authority for the proceedings he now determined to take, he formed a provisional government upon the same basis as that formed by him in the year 1869. The ostensible reason he gave for the formation of this government was that the "bill of rights" which they had prepared, and which had been so long neglected, would have to be demanded. It is a wonder that he did not see danger in his proceedings, or in his assuming this leadership; for having been deprived of his political rights, he could not claim, as a new settler, the same status or the same justification as those could claim whom he was leading. It was urged as an injustice, that the white settlers had the privilege of entering second homesteads, after having performed settlement duties on the first, while the half-breeds who had come west were not entitled to, or could not receive, their scrip a second time.

This was a specious argument. The difference lies in this: that in one case the Government gives a free grant of land, and in return obtains a settler whose industry will add to the wealth and prosperity of the country; in the other case, the Government gives a transferable right to two hundred and forty acres of land, which is reserved to meet that obligation. This right passes into the hands of a speculator at a low price, and the land lies fallow for years to come, to the detriment of the country, to the detriment of the neighbourhood, and to the detriment of every one except the holder. But more than that, the half-breed who chooses to go to the land-office and say: "I want to take up a homestead under the conditions of the Land Act," is perfectly free to do so, whether or not he has obtained the patent for his land in the old Red River settlement of 1869, and his half-breed scrip in addition. And after he has performed the settlement duties of that homestead, he is still at liberty, under the land regulations, to take up another homestead, the same as his fellow citizen from Ontario, Quebec, or anywhere else. Nothing could be more liberal; nothing should so little justify the armed rebellion which these men instituted.

VII

DUCK LAKE

On the formation of Riel's second provisional government, in March, 1885, it immediately became necessary to levy contributions to sustain its dignity. From levying they got to seizing, and from seizing stores they got to seizing prisoners. Of the possession of prisoners, Riel, in days gone by, well knew the value.

The first overt act was committed when Riel requested the French half-breeds to bring their arms with them to a meeting to be held on the 3rd of March; and from that day matters grew worse. On the 18th of March the stores of Walters and Baker, and Kerr Bros. at St. Laurent, were raided; and Indian agent Lash, Astley, a surveyor, Tompkins, the telegraph repairer, and other Government employés were taken prisoners.

Major Crozier, head of the Mounted Police detachment stationed at Fort Carlton, received this news on the 19th, and at once sent over to Prince Albert to Captain Moore and others asking for reinforcements. A meeting was held, and it was determined to send a force of forty men, who on the 20th marched to Fort Carlton, forty miles distant, arriving there about 10 o'clock the same night.

Major Crozier had already received a letter from Riel through Mr. Mitchell, the owner of stores at Duck Lake, demanding surrender. Crozier at once sent Thomas McKay with Mitchell to the half-breeds to endeavour to get them to disperse. McKay, who is an intelligent English half-breed, started for Batoche with Mitchell during the night of the 20th, and arrived at

Walters and Baker's store, which is on the opposite side of the river to Batoche. They were there met by a guard and were escorted across the river to the council-chamber, which Riel had set up in the church. McKay's sworn account of this interview is important as showing the determination of Riel to shed blood. Mr. Mitchell introduced McKay to Riel, and having ascertained that he came with Mitchell, who was the bearer of correspondence, he was accorded the same protection as was guaranteed to Mitchell.

Upon being introduced, McKay said, "There seems to be great excitement here, Mr. Riel." He said, "No, there is no excitement at all; it is simply that the people are trying to redress their grievances, as they had asked repeatedly for their rights." McKay then told him that it was a very dangerous thing to resort to arms. Riel said that he had been waiting fifteen long years, and it was time now, after they had waited patiently, that their rights should be granted, as the poor half-breeds had been imposed upon. McKay disputed his wisdom and advised him to adopt different measures. Riel accused McKay of having neglected the half-breeds. The latter told him that this was simply a matter of opinion, that he had certainly taken an interest in them, and that his stake in the country was the same as theirs, and that time and again he had so advised them, and had not neglected them. He also said that Riel had neglected them a long time if he took as deep an interest as he professed to. Riel became very excited, and got up and said: "You don't know what we are after. It is blood, blood; we want blood; it is a war of extermination. Everybody that is against us is to be driven out of the country. There were two curses in the country – the Government and the Hudson's Bay Company."

Riel now told McKay that he was a traitor to his Government; that he was a speculator and a scoundrel, a robber and a thief. He finally said it was blood, and the first blood they wanted was his. There were some little dishes on the table, and he got hold of a spoon and said, "You have no blood, you are a traitor to your people, your blood is frozen, and all the little blood you have will be there in five minutes," putting the spoon up to his face, and pointing to it. McKay said, "If you think you are benefiting your cause by taking my blood, you are quite welcome to it." Riel called his people and the committee, and wanted to put McKay on trial for his life; and Garnot got up and went to the table with a sheet of paper, and Gabriel Dumont took a chair on a syrup keg, and Riel called up the witnesses against McKay. He said McKay was a liar, and he told them that McKay had said all the people in that section of the country had risen against them. He said that it was not so; that it was only the people in the town. Champagne got up and spoke in McKay's favour. McKay told them that Riel was threatening to take his life, and said, "If you think by taking my life you will benefit your cause, you are welcome to do so." Champagne said no, they did not wish anything of the kind; they wanted to redress their grievances in a constitutional way. Riel then rose and said he had a committee meeting of importance going on upstairs, and he went off. McKay spoke to them for quite a while, and Riel occasionally came down and put his head in, and said McKay was speaking too loud, that he was annoying their committee meeting. When he had said what he had to say, McKay asked for something to eat, as he was pretty hungry. After he had eaten, McKay lay down on some blankets in the corner till Mitchell was ready. Mitchell was upstairs, and when he came down, they prepared to leave for Fort Carlton. Riel presently came in and apologized to McKay for what he had said, adding that he did not mean to harm him personally, but that it was McKay's cause he was speaking against, and he wished to show that he entertained great respect for him. He said he was very sorry not to have McKay with him, that it was not too late to join him yet. He also said that it was Major Crozier's last opportunity of averting bloodshed, and that unless he surrendered Fort Carlton, an attack would be made at twelve o'clock.

It had been arranged with Mr. Mitchell at the committee meeting upstairs that Riel should send two delegates to meet Major Crozier half way; and an hour after the arrival of McKay at Fort Carlton, he turned round and accompanied Captain Moore to meet Riel's delegates. At the appointed place McKay's party were met by Charles Nolin and Maxime Lépine, who had been sent as delegates to demand the surrender of Fort Carlton, with all its stores and property, undertaking if it were quietly given up that the Police should be allowed to go unharmed. As Major Crozier's instructions to the delegates were that the people should disband and give up the leaders at once, or suffer the penalty of their criminal acts, the meeting resulted in nothing; and Lépine did not present the document intended for Major Crozier. It was afterwards found among Riel's papers in Batoche subsequent to its capture.

Things remained as they were for a day or two, everyone awaiting anxiously the arrival of Colonel Irvine. This officer had been despatched with a force of a hundred men in great haste from Regina, upon the receipt of the first news of the outbreak. He arrived at Prince Albert on the 24th of March; but in the meantime, Major Crozier had determined to send a guard with some sleighs to take the forage and provisions that were in Mitchell's store at Duck Lake to a place of safety. So, on the morning of the 26th about four o'clock, he sent a small detachment off with a dozen sleighs to remove the stores, under Sergeant Stewart. They advanced, with four men in front acting as advance guard, and when within a mile and a half of Duck Lake, the guard were seen returning at full gallop with a number of half-breeds after them. The sleighs were halted and turned round, and McKay, who was with them, awaited their coming. They were a party of between thirty and forty, headed by Gabriel Dumont. He was very excited, jumped off his horse, and loaded his rifle, cocked it and went up to McKay and threatened to blow his brains out. McKay told him that two could play at that game, and that he had better be quiet.

Dumont talked wildly, and wanted McKay's party to surrender. He said it was McKay's fault that his people were not assisting them, and that McKay was to blame for all the trouble. McKay refused to surrender, and said that they had the best right to the property. Some men got into the sleighs and attempted to snatch the lines, but the teamsters held on to them. Gabriel Dumont fired his rifle over their heads, and they then stepped out of the road and allowed the sleighs to return to Carlton, without, however, having secured the forage and provisions. Sergeant Stewart had sent a message back to Major Crozier to say that he had met with resistance and wanted support, and about three miles from the fort they met Major Crozier coming with his whole force to assert the law. He sent back young Retallack with a despatch to Colonel Irvine to tell him that he had started out to support some teams that had gone over for provisions, and that help would be needed. McKay and his party turned round and accompanied him. Crozier's force, numbering in all about one hundred, now advanced along the trail towards Duck Lake. About four miles from there the advance guard reported that there were some Indians in a house belonging to Beardy, whose tribe had joined the insurgents, and whose reserve they were then crossing. They advanced past this house to where McKay had been stopped in the morning.

On nearing Duck Lake the advance guard was seen galloping back, pursued by a large body of the rebels, and one of the guard, Ernest Todd, reported to Major Crozier that the half-breeds were advancing in numbers, and that he had been fired upon, receiving a bullet in his saddle. Major Crozier at once called Joe McKay, and said, "I will hold a parley with them before attempting to advance;" but, while holding this parley, he saw an attempt on the part of the enemy to surround his men, and at once gave the order to fire. At the same time, one of the Indians who was parleying with Major Crozier tried to wrest the rifle from Joe McKay, and in the scuffle that ensued the Indian was shot. The nine-pounder was loaded, ready for action, but Major Crozier was in the line of fire, and it could not be used upon the enemy until he moved, and the gunners could not make him hear. Before he got out of the way, the great body of the rebels had disappeared over the hill out of danger. Major Crozier turned round angrily and said, "Why don't you fire that gun?" He was told that he was in the line of fire, and the answer was, "Well, I am only one man, you should have fired anyway." To this circumstance a number of the rebels owed their lives.

The fight that ensued was nearly a complete massacre, and only by the coolness of Major Crozier and his force was this avoided. Captain Morton took his men to the right flank, near a rail fence, where, only seventy-five yards distant, and not seen at first for a bluff, they were terribly exposed to the fire from the neighbouring house. The Police were formed up near the sleighs. The skirmish lasted for thirty or forty minutes, and was most disastrous. Nine Prince Albert volunteers and three policemen were killed and about twenty-five wounded. There was no possibility of an advance through the deep snow, and the enemy kept well out of sight, though the gallant men managed to kill six of them, and in this fight Gabriel Dumont got a severe scalp wound. The mistake Major Crozier made was in attempting to hold a parley. Riel took advantage of this to send his men round, under cover of the gullies, and made an attempt to surround the Police and capture the whole party.

Major Crozier ordered his men to retire. The horses were hitched up under fire, and the withdrawal took place in the most orderly manner. Captain Moore, while he was stepping into one of the sleighs, had the misfortune to receive a bullet, which shattered his leg, and the injury was so great that the limb had to be amputated. The little force reached Carlton about four o'clock, and half an hour afterwards Colonel Irvine marched in with his men. Colonel Irvine, now being in command, determined to evacuate the fort and to retire to Prince Albert. This was done on the morning of the 28th. A portion of Fort Carlton caught fire by accident and was burned; and on the 3rd of April, Riel and his men marched up and took possession of the ruins of the fort, where they remained for a time in the unconsumed buildings.

Major Crozier was quite unprepared for such an encounter, and, no doubt, did not contemplate that, in the execution of his duty, he would meet with such murderous opposition.

Otherwise, he would have hesitated to expose his men without greater military precaution, as Colonel Irvine was expected shortly with an increased force. Though brave lives were lost in the endeavour to uphold the laws of their country, and to protect the isolated settlements from the insurgents, they were not sacrificed in vain. This engagement was the signal to the Government to take decisive steps to prevent the recurrence of such a rising, which now seemed inevitable, and to show the power of Canada to maintain her laws, to punish offenders, and to control her Indian population scattered throughout the immense territory.

The danger that presented itself was not so much the half-breed rising under Riel, which was confined to a certain locality, but the fear that in the excitement of war and at the instigation of Riel, the whole Indian population of the country might rise, and the various bands and reserves scattered over it would commit depredations, and bring death and desolation to the peaceful homes of the settlers. I may here say that such was not the case, owing to the excellent system under which Canada always managed her Indian population. Although there may be faults arising from individual instances of bad management, yet the general system, and the good faith and honesty which prevail in the management of Indian affairs, have been productive of the very best results, and on this occasion prevented widespread disaster reaching the far distant homes of the enterprising and defenceless settlers. The Indians have shown themselves capable of appreciating all that had already been done for them, and sensible of the advantages yet in store.

With the exception of a few evil spirits, who committed some atrocities, the general demeanour of the Indians showed the white settlers that on future occasions there need not be that alarm which fills the mind in having these savage tribes as neighbours. Of course, from their nomadic habits and savage nature, for many years to come they will require controlling; but, out of thirty thousand Indians, spread over the country, there are probably fewer individual instances of crime among them than there is in the same number of white people. It does not do for us to judge them by our own standard; they are a conquered race, they are narrowed down from their wonted privilege of roaming free over the whole country to occupying reserves set apart for them, which, though liberal in area, are, nevertheless, a restraint upon their freedom.

It was at once felt by both Government and people that if the half-breed rising in the North-West was allowed to assume important dimensions and become an Indian rising, great disaster would befall the commercial interests of the country, and throw its prospects back for many years by retarding immigration, which is so essential to its development. It was true statesmanship, therefore, on the part of the Government, to realize this fact in time, and to throw promptly into the North-West a force strong enough to ensure the speedy re-establishment of law and order, and to show the outer world the determination of Canada to protect the lives and property of her most distant citizens.

The Government's call for troops brought out a national feeling that will prove to all political parties that when the interests of Canada or her national existence are at stake, the people are a unit. Every province enthusiastically desired to join in the expedition, and the Canadian spirit that was aroused dominated every sectional and provincial feeling. This attitude of the nation has done much to raise the character of our people in the eyes of the world.

It would seem unaccountable that Major Crozier, an officer of twelve years' experience in the country, should have been led into a trap which proved so disastrous. But Major Crozier was resting under the insult offered by Riel, who sent to demand his surrender, and as an officer of the country with an armed force at his back, he deemed it his duty, for the honour of his men, to go out to support the teams and the little detachment which had been stopped. It must also be remembered that the whole of this vast region, eight hundred miles long by four hundred broad, filled with a half-breed and Indian population, had hitherto been well and peacefully governed by a small force of five hundred Mounted Police, which, in themselves, combined military and civil elements. By this force the law had been well administered and well upheld. By their coolness and courage, on occasions without number, they had entered the camps of the excited Indians, and, with an escort of two or three, been accustomed to take their prisoner. Their ability to do so has frequently excited the admiration of American officers to the south of the boundary, who were engaged in the same duties, where, for the capture of a murderer or a horse thief, or in putting down whiskey sellers, a force would have to be put in motion and often lives lost in the attempt.

On our side of the line these duties were accomplished by the determined action of two or three policemen; and Major Crozier doubtless thought that the same determined action on his part would nip in the bud a serious outbreak, which would prove disastrous to the country. On this occasion, however, a new element had sprung up in the person of Riel, who had not yet interfered on this side of the line. He was prepared to resort to force to accomplish his purpose, or die in the attempt. Besides this, Riel worked upon the superstitious beliefs of his people; he worked upon their feelings, and overawed them by the fears he excited for their safety, the while holding out large promises of reward to stimulate their courage and devotion.

After the battle of Duck Lake, the half-breeds returned in an excited state to their headquarters, where they held the prisoners, and in the wild excitement of their savage nature some of them wished to wreak their vengeance upon their harmless captives; but they were valuable as a hostage to use in the future, when Riel must have felt that he would have to give an account of his actions. He at once set to work to enlarge his plans for the defeat of the whole country and to hold at defiance the authority of Canada. Immediately he sent his runners to the different tribes of Indians, hundreds of miles away, with letters indited by himself, instructing them to rise, to seize the forts, and to secure all the provisions and ammunition. These runners came to my own neighbourhood in the

Shell River district, to the Indians and half-breeds in the thickly settled Qu'Appelle district, to Poundmaker in the Battleford district, and Big Bear in the Fort Pitt district, and wherever Riel knew of a tribe of Indians or a settlement of half-breeds. He cunningly took advantage of an eclipse of the sun, which was to occur during March, and told the Indians that upon a certain day the sun was to darken, and that was to be a sign that they should rise, and also be a sign of his power. It is here worthy of remark that "John Smith's" tribe at the Company's crossing, near Prince Albert, Mis-ta-wa-sis (Big Child), near Carlton, Chic-a-sta-fa-sin (Star Blanket), on the road to Green Lake, Moosomin, near Battleford, besides many other tribes whose reserves were near the scene of the outbreak, left their reserves to avoid being compelled to join in the rising. Riel, moreover, instituted a policy for his own aggrandizement by attempting to overthrow the religion of his church; he declaimed against the interference of the church in the temporal affairs of the people, limiting it strictly to its spiritual power; he formulated a new religion, constituting himself the head and prophet; he baptized Jackson, the secretary of his provisional government, into this new religion, and gave a feast in the village of Batoche in honour of it, inviting all his people. Those who came he held as soldiers, and did not allow them to return to their homes. This all occurred during the latter part of March. He then cut the wires in the neighbourhood of Batoche, which severed telegraph communication between Prince Albert and the East. The telegraph communication crosses the Saskatchewan at Clarke's Crossing on its way to Battleford, and there branches off in a northerly direction to Prince Albert. It has been a matter of astonishment that he never attempted or permitted the cutting of the wires elsewhere, which was an easy thing to accomplish all through the country, and would have hampered the movements of the forces sent to overthrow him. His object in this was supposed to be to allow the fullest information to go to the world of the events that were now likely to occur in rapid succession, in the hope that the Fenian element in the United States would come to his assistance, or that the half-breeds, to the south of the boundary, would send him aid. Possibly also, he expected that the Indians on the boundary line of the United States would harass the Canadian troops. Such were the desperate measures of Riel, into which he had drawn his people, and he assured them of the co-operation of these forces to assist them in their cause.

Colonel Irvine's plans were now altered, and instead of taking his whole force to punish the rebels, he deemed it more prudent to act on the defensive, and take steps for the protection of the settlers, whose property and lives were considered to be in great danger. The half-breeds who committed the dastardly act at Duck Lake now felt that they carried their lives in their hands, and under the command of Riel were determined to go on to further victories, and rouse the half-breed and Indian population throughout the whole district. This, no doubt, led Colonel Irvine to abandon Fort Carlton and concentrate his forces in Prince Albert, for the protection of that populous district, and in the altered state of affairs to await the action of the Dominion Government.

VIII

The Canadian Militia

Before giving my readers the details of the prompt measures which the Canadian Government took to meet the grave emergency which had arisen, I desire to give some idea of the military forces that Canada has at her disposal, and to draw attention to the fact that the Canadian people had now to deal with the most serious military operations they had yet been called upon unaided to undertake.

The North-West is to Canada very much what the colonies of England have for centuries been to her. England has always rushed to their defence and helped them to maintain their laws inviolate. Formerly Canada was a station for British troops, which were always available for her protection and use; but in the year 1870 a new policy had been dictated by Mr. Gladstone's Government, of withdrawing from Canada the troops that had for so many years been maintained there, and throwing upon Canada the responsibility of maintaining her own defences, retaining only a sufficient force at Halifax for the protection of a coaling station for the British fleet. The withdrawal was so complete that the stores were sold, the guns handed over to Canada, and even the sentry boxes in the citadel of Quebec removed to England. It was a sad day for Canada when the forces that added so much to her prestige, whose expenditure was so beneficial, and whose leisure added so much to the amusement and social life of the country, were withdrawn. But it was a step in the direction of making the colonies self-supporting and self-reliant, a policy which was intended to extend to England's entire colonial empire, but which led to such adverse criticism that it was checked.

The military force of Canada, in its present organization, was instituted in the year 1855, and consists of two divisions – the active militia and the sedentary militia. Canada, from the Atlantic to the Pacific, is divided into military districts, and in these the active militia is composed of a number of battalions of cavalry, artillery and infantry, officered after the fashion of the British service, during good behaviour, and recruited by men who undertake to serve for three years. The sedentary militia consists of all those, under the age of sixty, who are not enrolled in the active militia, and are capable of bearing arms with the ordinary exemptions. At the head of each military district is a permanent staff officer, a deputy adjutant-general, assisted by a brigade-major and a district paymaster. The whole is commanded by a major-general, with the assistance of an adjutant-general and permanent staff. The general is selected from among the distinguished officers of the British army, and his term of service lasts for five years. The civil head of the military organization is a minister of militia assisted by a deputy-minister and the staff of his department.

Canada has at her disposal a drilled force of about two thousand regulars, an active militia force of about forty thousand, and a reserve of all the available muscle in the country, which numbers about seven hundred thousand. The growth of this military force has been very gradual, additions and modifications continually being carried out as time and experience dictated. The General at present in command of the forces in Canada is General Sir Fred Middleton, formerly of the 29th Regiment, and late commandant of the Royal Military College at Sandhurst; where for several years he governed that training school for officers in the British Army.

General Middleton* was appointed to his present position

---

*Major-General Middleton is the third son of Major-General Charles Middleton, who saw a great deal of service in India. He was educated at the Royal Military College, Sandhurst, from which he obtained his commission, without purchase, 30th December, 1842. He served as an ensign in the 58th regiment in New South Wales, Norfolk Island and New Zealand, and was present at most of the fighting in the operations in the latter country against the Maoris, in 1845-46. He was mentioned twice in in the year 1884, and came out to perform the routine duties which are generally the work that falls to the lot of this office, consisting of inspecting the forces and endeavouring to improve their drill and efficiency. Little did he think, when he was appointed, that it would fall to his lot to command the first active expedition ever organized solely from the citizen soldiery which he commands, the responsibility of which was to fall upon the shoulders of Canadian statesmen and Canadian officers and men. Without the guiding experience of past expeditions, without any knowledge of how to deal with an armed rebellion, thousands of miles from the central authority, and without the steady military training in the field of any of her officers or men, Canada had to undertake the task of arming, equipping, transporting and commanding the military expedition which was now deemed necessary.

Before the Duck Lake fight had taken place, the seizure of prisoners and stores by Riel was sufficient warning to the

---

despatches, and was promoted to a lieutenancy in the 96th regiment, August, 1848, and served in that regiment in India until October, 1854, during which time he passed the required examination in surveying, and was promoted Captain, July, 1852. He served as a volunteer in the suppression of the Santhal rebellion, in 1855, in command of a troop of the Nawab of Moorshedabad's cavalry, and received the thanks of the Indian Government. He exchanged into the 29th regiment, June, 1855, and served with it in Burma. He served during the Indian mutiny, 1857-58, in General Frank's column, on the march to the relief of Lucknow, and was present as A.D.C. at all the engagements and affairs which took place on that march; also as A.D.C. to General Sir E. Lugard, K.C.B., at the seige and capture of Lucknow in the pursuit of Roor Singh and the subsequent engagements. He was five times mentioned in despatches, and recommended for the Victoria Cross for two acts of bravery, but being on personal staff, was not considered eligible by Lord Clyde. He received the brevet of Major, served as Brigade-Major to the field forces in Oude employed in attacking the forts of the rebel chief. He served with the 29th regiment in England from 1859 to 1861; A.D.C. to General Franklyn in Gibraltar; Brigadier-Major and temporary Police Magistrate in that fortress, and A.D.C. to General Sir Henry Bates, at Malta, until November, 1862. He passed through Hythe School of Musketry and the Staff College, obtaining a first-class certificate at the former. He rejoined the 29th regiment in Canada in August, 1868, and held various important appointments in the service until the removal of the Imperial troops from Canada. In July, 1870, he became superintending officer of garrison instruction to the forces, and inaugurated that system. He was Commandant of the Royal Military College from September, 1874, until his appointment to the command of the Militia of Canada in July, 1884. He was promoted Lieutenant-Colonel in March, 1869, and Colonel in July, 1875. He has the New Zealand medal, the Indian Mutiny medal and clasp, and the Cross of the Commander of the Bath. He was married to Miss Doucet, of Ottawa, while serving in Canada.

Government that more than ordinary exertions would be necessary. Therefore, on the 24th of March, 1885, the Government hurriedly despatched General Middleton to Winnipeg, after only a hasty and imperfect consultation, to be prepared for any emergency that might arise.

The General arrived in Winnipeg on the 27th of March. In the meantime, the news of the fight at Duck Lake had been transmitted over the wires, and its sad sacrifice of life brought forcibly before General Middleton and the Government the necessity for a strong force to successfully cope with armed resistance in the territory. Calling at once for troops on his arrival at Winnipeg, the General found that the only available forces there were the 90th Battalion, which had just been organized under Colonel Kennedy; a troop of cavalry under Captain Knight, and a field battery of artillery under Major Jarvis. The 90th had been called out on the 23rd, and promptly answering to a full roll-call at their headquarters, had armed and equipped themselves for service, and were soon ready for the field. The left wing of the 90th was sent forward on the 25th, under Major Boswell, to Troy, a station on the main line of the Canadian Pacific Railway, which was to be used as the base of operations for the column under the immediate command of the General himself. In the emergency many retired military officers in Winnipeg came forward and offered their services.

The other troops called out and promptly answering the call were, the Governor-General's Body Guard, under Colonel Denison; the 10th Royal Grenadiers, under Colonel Grassett; the Queen's Own Rifles, under Colonel Millar, and "C" School of Infantry, under Major Smith, all of Toronto. These regiments were brigaded under Colonel Otter, Commandant of the Infantry School. Colonel Williams was authorized to raise a provisional battalion, which came to be familiarly known as "The Midlanders," being composed of two companies from the 46th Battalion and one each from the 15th, 40th, 45th, 47th, 49th and 57th Battalions, all situated in the Midland district.

Colonel O'Brien was authorized to raise a battalion called

the "Simcoe Rangers," composed of four companies of the 35th Simcoe, and four companies of the 12th York Rangers. The 65th Mount Royal Rifles, of Montreal, under Colonel Ouimet, were also called out for active service. Colonel Scott, of Winnipeg, was commissioned to raise a regiment, known as the 91st Battalion, which was drawn from Winnipeg and the surrounding towns. Lieutenant-Colonel Osborne Smith, C.M.G., was also commissioned to raise a battalion in Winnipeg, called the 92nd, or Winnipeg Light Infantry.

In addition to these forces, a detachment of fifty sharpshooters was selected from the Governor-General's Foot Guards, under Captain Todd, of Ottawa. On the 31st of March the 7th Fusiliers, of London, under the command of Lieutenant-Colonel Williams, and the 9th Battalion, Quebec, under Colonel Amyot, were also called out. A provisional battalion was formed from detachments of the 66th, the Halifax Garrison Artillery, and the 63rd, under the command of Lieutenant-Colonel Bremner. The Quebec School of Cavalry, under Colonel Turnbull, and "A" and "B" Batteries, of Quebec and Kingston, were also called out and ordered to the front. Later on, the Montreal Garrison Artillery, under Colonel Oswald, were ordered to proceed to garrison Regina.

Captain Dennis was commissioned to raise an Intelligence Mounted Corps, composed of surveyors; and local companies were gazetted at Birtle, under the command of Captain Wood, at Regina, under Captain Scott, at Battleford, under Captain Nash, at Emerson, under Captain Whitman, at Yorkton, under Major Watson, at Qu'Appelle, under Captain Jackson, besides a local company at Calgary. The Rocky Mountain Rangers, under Captain Stewart, and the Moose Mountain Scouts, under Captain White, were also put in commission.

The whole of the Eastern corps, numbering about four thousand men, were called from their homes and vocations to take part in an expedition three thousand miles away, before the winter had yet closed; and within a few days from the 27th of March, the date on which the Government had received news of the Duck Lake fight, most of these troops had actually embarked upon the Canadian Pacific Railway for transport to Winnipeg.

The Canadian Pacific Railway was not quite completed to the north of Lake Superior, there being several gaps where the rails were not laid. These gaps, some seventy miles in length, had to be crossed by the troops. The difficulty of these marches was very great, for the snow was still upon the ground, and the country frozen up; but by the energy of the Canadian Pacific Railway authorities, who admirably performed their part in transporting the troops to the North-West, these difficulties were got over without any mishap. The teams which were engaged upon the construction of the line were used to assist the troops in passing over the gaps, and they were of material assistance in this service, though the exposure of the men was very great. An unfortunate accident happened to Lieutenant Morrow, of the Grenadiers, in crossing the gaps: a rifle went off accidentally and gave him a severe wound, which necessitated his return.

I happened to be visiting Winnipeg at the date of General Middleton's arrival, and having served with him on former occasions, I waited on him, and offered to raise a force of mounted men that would prove serviceable in the proposed expedition. The men, I urged, resided on their homesteads in the interior, not very far from the scene of the action. He asked at what cost this could be done, and I told him at the same rate as the Mounted Police, viz., seventy-five cents per day, with clothing and equipment. The General transmitted my proposal to Ottawa, and in two days I received authority from the Minister of Militia to raise and equip my force.

My home is in the Shell River district, about three hundred miles west of Winnipeg, and nearly seventy miles north of the Canadian Pacific Railway. I received my authority on the 31st of March; and before leaving Winnipeg, I ordered from the Hudson's Bay Company my equipment of rifles, blankets, tents and saddlery. I came out by train to Moosomin, and drove north to Birtle, where I left a notice with Mr. Pentland, land agent there, asking for thirty men and horses to be ready for inspection in two days. I then drove north to Russell, and there put up a similar notice. By the 6th of April, I returned to Moosomin with sixty men and horses, besides officers, order-lies, cooks, etc. – in all eighty-two men, including six teams for transport of provisions, equipment and forage. I had travelled in the six days two hundred and twenty miles by rail and one hundred and forty miles by road. I purchased all my horses in the district, at an average of one hundred and sixty-five dollars a piece, giving orders on the Hudson's Bay Company posts, at Fort Ellice and Russell, which were duly honoured.

I formed up at Moosomin, gave my men their mounts and equipment, and took the train for Qu'Appelle, one hundred and twenty miles farther west, there to march to join General Middleton's column, which was about one hundred miles on its way to Clarke's Crossing. When I arrived at Qu'Appelle, I divided my men into two troops, and appointed to be captain of the Russell troop Meopham Gardiner, from Brighton, England, who came with me to Manitoba in 1880, and had been my neighbour ever since. Mr. Pigott, son of General Pigott, who with his family had settled in the country three or four years previously, I made lieutenant. Captain Johnston, of Seaforth, Ontario, now of the village of Birtle, I appointed captain of the Birtle troop; with Mr. Gough, a nephew of Lord Gough, lieutenant. Mr. Cox, a surveyor, from Buckingam-shire, England, I appointed quartermaster, and Dr. Rolston, late surgeon of the Royal Navy, surgeon. All my officers and men had been living on their homesteads, and now sacrificed the prospects of their season's crop to serve in the campaign.

General Middleton remained but twelve hours in Winnipeg. On the evening of the 27th of March, before leaving, he ordered the right wing of the 90th Battalion, under the command of Major McKeand, to take the train for Fort Qu'Appelle, and gave instructions to the artillery to follow in the morning. The General accompanied these troops (numbering in all about three hundred and fifty men) to Qu'Appelle station, and from there marched to Fort Qu'Appelle, eighteen miles further north, on the trail to Clarke's Crossing, where he organized his force.

Fort Qu'Appelle is one of the old established posts of the Hudson's Bay Company, and is prettily situated in a broad valley, with the Qu'Appelle lakes lying on each side of the fort. It is now the site of an enterprising town. These lakes form part of the Qu'Appelle River, so called from the echo that the valley produces.

It was at Fort Qu'Appelle that General Middleton commenced the real preparations for the campaign; and one of its first necessities was the want of mounted men. Knowing that it would be some days before my troop could join him, he empowered Captain French, an Irish officer who had been in the Mounted Police, to raise a mounted force in the vicinity of Fort Qu'Appelle. This troop, with the 90th Rifles, under Major McKeand, and the Winnipeg Field Battery, under Major Jarvis, constituted the General's force at that time. Soon afterwards it was reinforced by Colonel Montizambert, in command of "A" Battery, and a few days later by a detachment of "C" School of Infantry, under Major Smith. With these forces the General determined to push on with all expedition to the scene of the rebellion; and he now developed the plan of the campaign.

As he explained it to me, General Middleton's original plan of campaign was to march his column from Fort Qu'Appelle to Clarke's Crossing. The second column, under Otter, was to march from Swift Current to meet him at the Crossing; and from that point the two columns were to move down the river on both sides to attack Batoche. There he proposed to join the two columns, and march to relieve Prince Albert, then to relieve Battleford, and after punishing Poundmaker to proceed with a portion of his force to Fort Pitt. At this latter post he had ordered General Strange with his column to await his arrival, when it was his intention to attack Big Bear and release his prisoners. This plan was necessarily altered in consequence of the alarming reports received from Police Inspector Morris, at Battleford, of the danger the women and children were in. Learning of this, he now directed Colonel Otter to proceed straight to Battleford, and hold Poundmaker in check until he came up, while he marched with his own column to attack Riel in Batoche. These three columns were organized with great rapidity from the forces sent from the Eastern Provinces, and those raised in the Province of Manitoba and the North-West Territory.

The troops from Quebec had a journey by rail of two thousand five hundred miles, and the troops from Nova Scotia and New Brunswick had three thousand miles to get over before they arrived at the various points from which they were to march to occupy and protect the isolated and defenceless northern country.

Colonel Otter's column was composed of the Queen's Own Rifles, "B" Battery, under Major Short, a company of the Governor-General's Foot Guards from Ottawa, fifty Mounted Police, under Colonel Herchmer, and part of "C" School.

Before sketching the plan of the campaign, it is necessary to give a description of the country General Middleton was about to enter.

IX

GENERAL MIDDLETON'S ADVANCE

About two hundred and fifty miles north of the line of the Canadian Pacific Railway is the north branch of the Saskatchewan River. This noble stream takes its rise in the Rocky Mountains. About forty miles east of Prince Albert, the south branch of the same river empties into the north branch, flowing from the south-west, where it is crossed by the Canadian Pacific Railway, at Medicine Hat. It flows past the headquarters of Riel, at Batoche, Clarke's Crossing and Saskatoon, the latter a pretty village that was afterwards used as an hospital. Both of these rivers are navigable at high water. On the north branch are posts of the Hudson's Bay Company, which, upwards of a century ago, were established for trading purposes by the rival fur companies. These posts have settlements around them, commencing with Prince Albert on the east. Forty miles farther west stands Fort Carlton; and one hundred miles west of that lies Battleford, at the junction of the Battle River and the Saskatchewan. One hundred miles farther west, on the North Saskatchewan, is situated Fort Pitt; one hundred and fifty miles from the latter is Victoria and one hundred miles still farther west lies Edmonton, all on the same river. Numerous tribes of Indians hold their reserves in the neighbourhood of these posts, which are occupied by small bodies of Mounted Police. It was to these tribes of Indians that Riel sent his most pressing letters to secure their co-operation, instructing them to rise, defeat the troops, and seize all the ammunition and provisions. He hoped that by being so far north, and the territory being difficult of access, troops could not reach him, and he would dictate his own terms.

In attempting to give a description of the operations, which were brought to so successful a completion within three months of the rebel outbreak, occupying long and arduous marches and fighting several battles, I will first follow the fortunes of the column under the immediate command of General Middleton.

The period of the year in which these columns had to undertake their marches was an inclement one. The snow was about leaving the prairie, when wet and slush prevail, when the frost comes out of the ground leaving stiff, muddy roads and sloughs filled with water, and when the winds blow cold and damp; the difficulties of marching and the exposure of soldiers unaccustomed to hardship making a very trying and arduous task. Yet all was undertaken and overcome with little grumbling but with great cheerfulness and enthusiasm.

I arrived with my men at Fort Qu'Appelle on the 8th of April, having already met with one serious mishap. Mr. Maclurcan, whom I appointed lieutenant, was unfortunate enough, in handling a vicious horse in the stable, to get kicked and trampled upon so seriously that his life was despaired of. Throughout the campaign he was confined to the hospital at Winnipeg, where he slowly recovered.

I arrived at Qu'Appelle on the same day with the Grenadiers, under Colonel Grassett. By the instructions of General Middleton the Grenadiers were ordered to the front, with teams to hasten their march and save the men. The call for transport at this time was enormous. It shows the marvellous progress of the country within the previous few years that to transport these three columns fifteen hundred teams were available – the number at one time on the pay-roll of the Hudson's Bay Company – for the transport-corps, in addition to the teams necessary to carry on the agricultural operations of the country.

General Middleton, on his arrival at Fort Qu'Appelle, at once called for two hundred teams to convey the equipment, forage and supplies for his column. This naturally created a "boom" for the farmers; and under the energetic efforts of Archibald McDonald, of the Hudson's Bay Company, the teams were all procured in two days' time, at ten dollars per day and "found." A transport corps was organized by the General, under Mr. Bedson, Warden of the Manitoba Penitentiary, who took the direction-in-chief of the transport, assisted by Mr. Secretan. Major Bell, manager of the Bell Farm in the Qu'Appelle Valley, remained at the base of operations, to see that all went right and to continue to engage transport for the rapidly increasing necessities of the campaign.

Comment has been made upon the cost of this transport, but to those acquainted with the rapidity of the movement General Middleton deemed essential to the success of his expedition, and the scattered district from which the teams had to be collected, there is little occasion for criticism. It has also to be borne in mind that farmers were loth to leave their operations at a time when their whole summer's gains depended upon the early seeding of their land. The price, ten dollars per day, was therefore not excessive for the work that was demanded of them, and the exposure to which their horses would necessarily be subjected. Nor was the cost to the Government of the supplies and forage of the expedition much more than the early settlers who penetrated far into the interior were themselves called upon to pay. For two years I paid six dollars per bag for flour before our own crops came in. I paid one dollar and fifty cents per bushel for oats, and occasionally two dollars per bushel for potatoes, and everything else in proportion. I mention this as an evidence of the difficulties that have to be overcome by the settler or by the soldier who penetrates a country unknown and unpopulated.

I was ordered by telegraph to use all possible speed, and I marched on the morning of the 9th, at the rate of thirty miles a day, to join the main column, covering the whole distance in seven days. To show the energy people are capable of in this country, I may say that in sixteen days from the date of receiving instructions in Winnipeg, namely, between the 31st of March and and the 16th of April, I was enabled to place a mounted force in the field, after visiting the farming districts, raising the men, purchasing the whole equipment, and making a march by land of three hundred and sixty miles. The trail over which we had to march was muddy and wet, without bridges and without improvements, and thirty miles of it was across the salt plain, unusually difficult in wet weather.

As an extreme example of the exposure, I might mention one incident that befell me on the second day's march. The freshets were high, and the previous night the thermometer had gone down to 15 degrees below zero and frozen streams over solid, but in the very centre, where the stream was rapid, the ice was thin. I was in front and leading my horse, feeling my way, when down I went up to my waist and my horse nearly on top of me. I scrambled out, and in a minute my clothes were frozen as hard as boards. It was five o'clock in the morning, and the thermometer, as I have said, 15 degrees below zero. My clothes were so stiff that I had to be lifted on to my horse, and I rode in that condition for six miles, after making a detour to avoid this bad place, to a house where we were going to halt for breakfast, and where I was able to get a change of clothing and dry myself out. There is no exaggeration about the incident. During this halt, Dr. Rolston, our surgeon, tumbled down the cellar of the house, and narrowly escaped finishing his military career, and the same day poor Maclurcan was trampled by a vicious horse. Need I say, that I was afraid my casualties were heaping up too fast?

My corps overtook General Middleton's column the day before the Grenadiers, with the horses in fairly good condition and the men in high spirits. The morning after, we reached Clarke's Crossing, the ferry on the South Saskatchewan River forty miles south of Batoche, upon the same river. General Middleton's march had been so rapid, and his force had increased so much, that he had got a little ahead of his transport. Although provisions were ample, forage was short, and there was no grass for the horses. At Clarke's Crossing, however, we were able to purchase sixty tons of hay, at fifty dollars a ton – a "bonanza" for the farmers of the district.

When within a day and a half's march of Clarke's Crossing, and before we had reached it, General Middleton felt anxious about its safety. He fixed upon this point as a depôt for his supplies, and as the headquarters for his reinforcements, which were to come from Swift Current by boat, or from Fort Qu'Appelle by the trail we had followed. As the place was also on the main trail to Battleford, and on the telegraph line to the west, it became a strong objective point to reach and hold as a second base of operations. The General's anxiety was so great that, without waiting for his infantry, he took all the mounted men and one gun, and in one day made a rapid march of thirty-five miles, and reached the Crossing in the midst of a North-West blizzard.

On Saturday morning, the day after his arrival at the Crossing, the General ordered my corps out on a reconnaissance towards Batoche, under Lord Melgund, Captain French accompanying him as guide. After proceeding about seven miles, the first excitement of the campaign commenced. Two of my troopers, Fisher and Henderson, sighted some rebel scouts who were running for "dear life." They chased them for about four miles, the rest of the corps in pursuit; but the rebels kept under the bank of the river, which was covered thickly with underbrush and trees, and when we thought we had them, after attempting to surround them, we found we hadn't them. They had slipped like eels from under our noses, when we had to take up the pursuit once more. Captain Gardiner and half a dozen others, however, brought the three Indians to bay in an opening, while they were crossing a deep gully. There they stood, back to back, their rifles pointed, with their fingers upon the triggers of their rifles; and we were at a loss how to capture them. One of my men, named Dunkin, volunteered to go down and speak to them. I told him to leave his rifle behind, that they might not suspect treachery. He went down to the bottom of the gully, which was about seventy feet deep, but the language he knew was not their language. Two more of my men, Neil and Lyons, followed, who knew other Indian dialects, and spoke to them, gave them some tobacco, and assured them that no harm would be done if they surrendered. But they steadfastly refused, and Lord Melgund ordered me to send down ten men to take them prisoners. Before I had time to do so, however, Captain French, who was on the opposite side of the gully, went down, smoked their pipe, shook hands with them, and brought them up. I took their rifles from them, and sent trooper King to bring a transport waggon to convey them to camp, in the meantime marching them along under a guard of six men. On our way out along the trail we picked up a piece of a newspaper, which Lord Melgund found fastened in a split stick, with pictures on it, resembling guns, evidently intended to convey intelligence to other scouts.

We marched with our first quarry about twelve miles to camp, which we reached amidst much excitement. After a thorough cross-questioning by the General, through an interpreter attached to my corps, as to what they knew and what their movements were, they were handed over to me. I placed them in a small tent, put up especially for their use, as they fought shy of the whole camp, fearing the soldiers. The officers purchased at "boom" prices all their trinkets, knives, pouches, necklaces, armlets, etc., and I doubt whether prisoners of war were ever treated better. Captain Haig, of the Royal Engineers, came to my tent and made sketches of them for the London *Graphic*. Two of them were the sons of White Cap, the chief of the Sioux, whose reserve is near Saskatoon, and the third was a brother-in-law of the same chief. They said they had been down to the reserve from Batoche, to hunt for their ponies, and when captured were on their way back to join Riel. They described the entrenchments Riel had constructed, and told us the number of armed half-breeds and Indians he had with him. Riel, we learned, had been to Saskatoon, to White Cap's reserve, to get the Sioux chief to join him, at the same time seizing his cattle and horses. The settlers about Saskatoon, who were on friendly terms and in constant intercourse with the chief and his band, asked White Cap not to go. White Cap replied that if they would help him to regain his cattle and ponies, he would not go, but otherwise he could not resist the half-breeds. The white settlers did not feel inclined to mix themselves up in the disturbances, and White Cap went his way. But under the circumstances the settlers considered White Cap blameless.

General Laurie, a half-pay officer of the British service living in Halifax, who had accompanied General Middleton as far as Humboldt, returned to hasten the boats from Saskatchewan Landing, near Swift Current, as the General felt it was a risk to rely upon the muddy trail for reinforcements and supplies. The great rivers of the North-West take their source in, and are fed from, the Rocky Mountains, and do not depend upon the rains and drainage of the country. The water, therefore, does not rise to a sufficient height for deep laden vessels until the snowy peaks of the Rocky Mountains pour forth their torrents. In consequence, an annoying delay occurred in the river transport. Notwithstanding these drawbacks the General determined to lose no time, but to push on with the force he had with him, trusting that the supports would soon get over the minor difficulties that presented themselves.

The General's present plan of attacking Riel in his stronghold was to divide his force and march upon Batoche on both sides of the river. The information he had received underrated the strength of the enemy, and their determination to fight was doubted; so this disposal of the forces was more for the purpose of preventing the escape of the rebels. Subsequently learning that entrenchments had been prepared by Riel on both sides of the river at Batoche, the General concluded to advance as first agreed upon, and be prepared to attack the place from both sides. It took three days to transport across the river the Grenadiers, twenty of my corps, under command of the late Captain Brown (then a sergeant), all of Captain French's men, the Winnipeg Field Battery, and a portion of "A" Battery, under the command of Colonel Montizambert, with Lord Melgund as chief of staff. The only means of crossing was a scow, of a rather ricketty description, worked by means of pullies and a wire rope, and propelled by the current. This was a tedious affair. All the teams and forage necessary were transported to the other side with difficulty, as the banks of the river at the landing, and for some yards on each side, were composed of apparently bottomless mud.

General Middleton had with him his own telegraph operator with his instruments, whom he kept busy communicating his orders to the distant parts of the territory; regulating the movements of Colonel Otter's and General Strange's columns; and conducting the whole campaign, covering six or eight hundred miles of country. He had on his shoulders, besides the conduct of the campaign, the anxiety of the transport, upon which so much depended, and the safety of the various settlements throughout the country. Not a little of his troubles at this time arose from the pressing applications from all parts for protection, many of which were conceived in a speculative spirit, for the benefit that might be derived from the presence of the troops. In consequence, he had to sift the motives for these appeals, so as not to be misled or imposed upon. From the number of stories and unfounded rumours now current, he became sceptical as to the truth of any reports brought to him, causing him frequently to exclaim, "That is another of your nor'west'rs!" I can here testify to the prudence, caution and penetration of General Middleton in all his actions.

On the morning of the 23rd of April, seven days after our arrival at Clarke's Crossing, everything was ready for an advance. Signalling parties had been practising during this time, from both sides of the river, to telegraph information between the two columns as they marched parallel to one another. In addition to the day-signalling, Major Jarvis and Captain Peters organized a corps of signalmen for night-work, by means of the ordinary bugle sounds, upon the phonetic principle. Lord Melgund, in an enterprising spirit, had the day before made a reconnaissance for ten miles north, on the left bank of the river, and discovered scouts watching our movements. He gave chase, and exchanged shots with them; but the scouts disappeared, and the party returned to the camp.

On Thursday morning, the 23rd of April, both columns marched simultaneously from Clarke's Crossing. My corps, now reduced to forty armed men, constituted the advance guard of the right column, the remainder going with the left. The order of march was a line of sixteen scouts, covering half a mile of front, fifty yards apart from one another. I marched with the remainder of my men on the trail, about two hundred and fifty yards in rear of the advance scouts. About three hundred yards in rear of us came the advance guard of the 90th, consisting of a file followed by the usual formation; and some three hundred yards in rear of them came the column, followed by the transport, with about two hundred teams. I told off two men to march on the flank of the General wherever he might move. Generally, however, he marched in front of me, at the head of my men, with his two A.D.C.s and Captain Haig, of the Royal Engineers. The scow, with the wire rope and a party on board, floated down the stream to accompany the columns, and to be ready for use should the necessity arise for either column to cross the river.

Our noon halt was similar in every day's routine: the column formed up in companies, piled their arms, fatigue-parties rushed off for wood and water, and in a trice fires were lit, and the boiling of tea and unpacking of hardtack and canned beef were proceeded with. After an hour and a half's rest, and the solace of the brier-root, the fall-in sounded once more. During the halt we remained in advance with videttes out, acting as sentries, to give the alarm if such should be necessary. The A.D.C. conveyed the word to continue our march to the evening camping-ground. There was the same routine every day.

An interesting sight to the uninitiated is the formation of a zareba or corral for the protection of the transport. It is formed by the teams following one another, under the direction of the transport officer, round and round in a circle, the leading team turning inwards and each team in succession forming up alongside, until an impenetrable wall of waggons presents itself to the enemy. The camp is pitched in front, with the mounted men on the right, the artillery next, the infantry next, with the headquarter staff in rear. The column bivouacked for the night eighteen miles from Clarke's Crossing, and twenty-two miles from Batoche. The General intended to make a second day's march to Gabriel Dumont's Crossing, within six miles of Batoche. He ordered me to continue my march and make a reconnaissance in front. I advanced in the same order for about three miles and a half without observing anything unusual, until I came to a house where I found a lot of forage, consisting of barley and oats, with half a dozen Red River carts in front of the door. I returned to camp about six o'clock in the evening, picketed the horses and pitched the tents, and reported to the General the result of my reconnaissance.

Strong pickets were mounted under the command of Lieut. Hugh J. Macdonald (son of Sir John Macdonald) and Lieutenant Laurie; and at half-past nine o'clock, being field officer of the day, I waited upon General Middleton, who invariably visited the sentries and pickets himself every night before retiring. He took unusual pains on this occasion, instructing the sentries, officers and non-commissioned officers in charge regarding their duties, and was fully two hours going the rounds, not returning to camp till half-past eleven o'clock. In the meantime, as forage was short, Colonel Houghton, the deputy adjutant-general, thought it advisable to secure the forage I had reported seeing on my reconnaissance, more especially as we were told by a farmer, near whose house we were camped, that the carts belonged to the enemy, and were evidently there for the purpose of removing the forage. I told off twenty of my men, under Captain Gardiner, with Quartermaster Cox, and with twenty of the 90th under Captain Clarke, Colonel Houghton went to secure the needed supplies. Though the night was dark, and the enemy were watching their proceedings from a short distance off, the forage was secured, and the party returned to the camp unmolested. We heard afterwards that it was Gabriel Dumont's intention to attack the camp that night, and Colonel Houghton's enterprise no doubt assisted in causing them to change their plans. At any rate, they must have observed that we were well on the alert, although up to this time we had no idea that they were so close, or that they intended making a stand on the morrow. I visited my rounds once more at half-past one, after the return of Colonel Houghton's expedition, and found the sentries keenly alive and watchful. Our quartermaster secured half the forage as his share of the night's spoils.

X

Fish Creek

Next day, reveillé sounded before daylight, and the camp was all astir, breakfasting and striking tents, and loading up for our march. We little thought that before sunset many of our comrades would find a soldier's grave, sacrificing their lives to uphold the integrity of their country. We started the day's march in our usual order, with sixteen scouts out skirmishing to the front, under the command of Captain Johnston. I took the precaution of making five of my men, who were dismounted on account of used-up horses, march in rear of my troop. We moved off at half-past six o'clock, with General Middleton, Captain Wise and Captain Doucet, A.D.C.s, and Mr. McDowall, of Prince Albert, in front. Mr. Chambers, the war correspondent of the Montreal *Star*, an enterprising civilian, marched alongside Captain Gardiner and myself, then came our twenty mounted and five dismounted men immediately behind us. The column followed in the usual formation, the head of the advance guard being about four hundred yards in our rear. We advanced about four miles.

The first unusual thing we came across was a house with all the windows smashed, where destruction was clearly intended. It was the property of a Mr. McIntosh, whose brother's place we had just left. Grain was lying about here and there, as if placed to feed horses, in which operation the enemy had but a short time before been evidently disturbed. We spent a few minutes examining the premises, which was fortunate for the General and for us, as it gave the scouts in front an opportunity of getting a little further in advance, thus giving the General so much more warning of the presence and intended action of the enemy.

We had hardly left this house to proceed on our way, when Captain Johnston, commanding the advanced scouts, reported to me that he had struck thirteen camp-fires still warm, and a heavy trail leading away from them. I reported the circumstance to the General, who told me to obtain further information. I then ordered Captain Johnston to take the leading section, follow up the trail, and report to me. We meantime marched on.

They had not been gone many minutes when I heard, bang! bang! and immediately after, a volley was fired at us, which, however, struck the trees in front. I gave the command "Left wheel, gallop!" and we charged down upon thirty or forty mounted men who were standing in the shelter of a bluff. When we came upon them they at once turned their horses and bolted for a ravine, or gully, about a hundred and fifty yards distant, dismounting as they galloped. I instantly gave the word to my men, "Halt! Dismount! Extend in skirmishing order, and lie down!" Simultaneously, the enemy, who were in the ravine and out of sight, opened a murderous fire upon us. I said, "Fire away, boys, and lie close; never mind if you don't see anything, fire;" my object being to keep the enemy down in the gully and hold them in check till the supports came up. The rebels would pop up from the ravine, take a snap shot, and disappear in an instant. The General at once sent back Captain Wise, A.D.C., to hurry up the main body, in which duty his horse was shot. We here sustained the whole of the enemy's fire, which was very hot, and unfortunately fatal. Captain Gardiner, who was beside me, was the first to say, "Major! I am hit." Almost immediately, Langford called out that he was hit. Bruce was the next victim. Then poor D'Arcy Baker called out, "Oh Major! I'm hit!" as he received his death wound by a bullet crashing into his breast. Then Gardiner called out, "I am hit again!" Langford, too, was wounded a second time. I told the wounded to drag themselves to the rear the best way they could and get out of further danger; and ordered the remainder to hold on and fire away.

The anxiety of the moment, hearing the groans of my comrades and the continuous and disastrous fire of the enemy, was very great. But to have allowed the half-breeds to come up from the ravine upon the approaching supports, I felt, would have been so fatal, that I kept my men firing away, and I looked anxiously back for the arrival of the infantry, which, when we attacked the rebels, was half a mile in our rear.

The scouts who were extended in skirmishing order, and who had been in advance of the column, now began to gallop in. They attacked the enemy from other points, which tended somewhat to draw their fire from us. But so far, having sustained little damage, the enemy were becoming bolder, and one brave came out in full view at the top of the bank, and danced a war-dance for the purpose of stimulating his comrades. He was, however, promptly disposed of by a bullet from Sergeant Stewart's rifle, which effectually prevented any further foolish exposures, for the half-breeds now kept themselves well under shelter of the ravine.

Feeling certain that in a few minutes all the horses would be slaughtered, I had ordered them to be let loose to save them, and they went galloping back to the rapidly approaching column. The first detachment came up in about fifteen minutes, during which we managed to keep the enemy in check and under cover of the gully. Captain Clark's company of the 90th was the first to come up, and he himself was one of the earliest victims, among the riflemen, of the rebel bullets. "C" School of Infantry, under Major Smith, arrived about the same time, and next came the artillery, which was speedily brought into action, Captain Drury opening fire upon the enemy over our heads. The remainder of the troops marched up in rapid succession, the enemy the while keeping up a hot fire from the ravine, only exposing themselves for an instant as they took a snap shot.

The ravine at this point forms an angle, the left arm of which descends almost perpendicularly to the bottom. Both bank and bottom were densely covered with bush, and this formed an excellent protection for the rebels along the course of the ravine, and up and down the stream. The flat is about a hundred yards broad, through which the stream, about ten feet in width, meanders. The abrupt banks are five or six feet high, and were covered with long grass and occasional willow bushes, forming a second protection for the rebels, as they stood up to their waists in water in the bed of the stream. Stretched along this ravine, occupying a tract a quarter of a mile in length, the enemy lay, some two hundred and fifty strong. At the beginning of the engagement they had their horses, to the number of about a hundred, tied up to the trees in the bottom of the ravine, showing that they evidently did not expect defeat, and that they intended to entrap General Middleton's column as it crossed by the trail. But the formation of our column, by the line of scouts that had always preceded our advance, precluded the possibility of a surprise. So, instead of the enemy drawing us into a trap, they got themselves into that position, little thinking that the General's movements would bring him and the force so early to the spot, or that our advance would be so well protected. Fifty-five of the enemy's horses were shot before the day was over, causing as much sorrow to the half-breeds as the loss of their comrades. The horses they had when they fired at us first were allowed to run loose when the rebels jumped off their backs, and some of my men, while under fire, captured fourteen of them, and tied them up in a bluff to await the close of the battle.

The companies of the 90th, under Colonel McKeand, arrived in quick succession, General Middleton directing them. Two companies of this battalion, under the command of Major Boswell, were ordered to advance to the left where an attempt was being made to out-flank us. With a few of the men left we joined Major Buchan, who was in command of three other companies of the 90th, and Major Smith, in command of "C" School of Infantry. Our object was to defeat a flanking move-ment of the enemy on our right.

The same tactics displayed by the half-breeds with Major Crozier at the Duck Lake fight were being pursued here, and

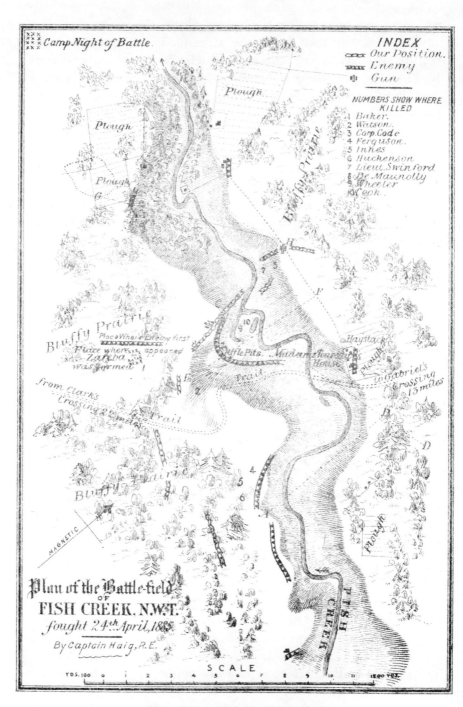

Plan of the battlefield of Fish Creek

an attempt was made to enclose us on three sides. But the steadiness of the troops, who advanced without flinching, and with a well-directed, independent fire, checked this attempt, and confined the enemy to their snap-firing, as they popped up above the crest of the embankment for an instant. This snap-firing, however, was well-directed as well as murderous upon all the troops engaged, one poor fellow after another falling, some killed outright, and some to be consigned to the tediousness of the hospital. The General could be seen moving from one flank to the other, directing, urging and commanding with the utmost coolness, and eliciting the admiration of some and the dismay of others lest a stray bullet should deprive the force of the Commander upon whom so much now depended.

The enemy were soon made to feel that an attack upon so large a front, showing such determination and obstinacy, was greater than they had calculated upon, although up to this time I doubt if they had sustained much loss. The position cannot be better described than by reciting an incident which Captain Gardiner relates: As he was dragging himself to the rear, after having received his second wound, one of the 90th then coming up called out to him, "Say, Chummy, are you hit?"

"Yes."

"Where are they, anyway? I can't see them! This is new to me; I was never at this kind of thing before."

The artillery opened fire upon a house on the opposite side of the ravine, where some of the rebels were to be seen moving about, and were made to scatter in all directions. Meanwhile a few of my men, with some of the 90th and several dismounted artillerymen, had crept up to the angle before referred to, where the bank was precipitous, and here they commanded a view of the ravine looking east, while under cover of a slight rise at the crest. Having safely gained this vantage-ground, Lieutenant Ogilvie brought his gun to bear and raked the whole flat with good effect. The heaviest casualties of the artillery occurred here, as the rebels tried to silence their fire. But the gunners nobly did their duty; one man after another, as his comrade was picked off, being ready to take his place. Lieutenant Ogilvie sighted his gun and fired in rapid succession, and soon let the enemy know that it was no longer a safe place for them, although he was not able to sufficiently depress his piece to reach the rebels who were immediately under the steep embankment. Gunner Armsworth was killed at the gun, and out of eighty-six men belonging to this battery fourteen fell, dead or wounded, nobly doing their duty while taking an important part in the battle which up to this time had been so hotly contested. The artillery action cleared the ravine in front of us, though not before Ferguson, Ennis and Hutchinson, of the 90th, and Watson of "C" School, had been killed, and many others wounded.

We gradually crept up to the ravine on the right, Private Dunn, of the 90th, being the first to gallantly cross the open on my calling for a volunteer to see if our immediate front was clear. With some of the 90th, under Lieut. Hugh J. Macdonald, a portion of "C" School, and a few of my men, we advanced across the ravine and entered the bush on the opposite side; while Major Buchan and Major Smith, with the remainder of the force on this flank, extended further up the ravine to the right.

About this time we saw forty or fifty men, some of whom were mounted, retiring up the ravine, about half a mile away. We afterwards learned that they were under the command of Gabriel Dumont, who graphically described his position at this time in his official report of the battle he made to Riel, which was found among the rebel chief's papers on his hasty retreat after the capture of Batoche. He therein states that seeing there was necessity for reinforcements, he deemed it his duty to return to Batoche to obtain them, and left the scene of the battle about ten o'clock on the morning of the fight. Some of the 90th opened fire on Dumont's party with their Martini-Henry rifles, and Captain Drury directed his gun on a house to which they retired, about fifteen hundred yards off, and set it on fire with the second shot. The General now ordered us to withdraw across the gully, and, with Major Buchan, who had been ordered to retire from the right, we now joined the centre attack.

While what we have described had been occurring on the right, Colonel Houghton, with Major Boswell, and "B" and "C" Companies of the 90th, had attacked the left flank, causing the retreat of a portion of the enemy down the ravine to escape in that direction. The casualties on our left were as great as in other parts of the field, for the men had crossed the ravine, under the immediate command of the General, and cleared the front on that flank, afterwards returning and taking up a position on the brow of the hill, below which the rebels made the first stand.

About this time the fire of the enemy considerably slackened, and their comrades at this point discovered that they had been deserted by the main body to the right and left of them. But the firing was resumed with great vigour when they found that it now became necessary for them to sell their lives as dearly as possible.

An attempt was here made to clear the bush at the bottom of the angle of the ravine, which was humourously described as "the hornet's nest." With this object, Captain Ruttan, with his company of the 90th, and Captain Peters, with the dismounted artillery, descended to the bed of the creek. The former crossed it, and pushed into the bush, while the latter advanced up the right bank. But the enemy retired through the bush, keeping out of sight and picking off the advancing troops, so that they had to take up a position, under cover, in the bed of the creek, where they were joined shortly after by Colonel Houghton and Captain Wise, with reinforcements. At the same time, eight of my men under Quartermaster Cox, with a few of the artillery and 90th, co-operated by attempting to advance over the brow; but all were obliged to retire with several casualties. At the bottom of the ravine, Lieutenant Swinford received his death wound, and Wheeler of the 90th, and Cook of the artillery, were killed. Captain Wise, A.D.C., was wounded at this time, and many other casualties also occurred. A gun was brought up to cover the retirement of this advanced line, which, though it failed, was a gallant attempt to clear out "the hornet's nest."

The General shortly afterwards sent Captain Drury with a gun (supported by his own men, and by "C" School, under Major Smith), across the ravine to the left, to shell the apparently impregnable position. Though the range was too close to effect much with a shell, Captain Drury for a time silenced the enemy's fire. Nor could the infantry accomplish much, as the rebels, while the gun was operated, lay at the bottom of their rifle-pits, secure from harm. It was simply impossible to see anything of them to fire at. One gunner was wounded here, and my horse was shot from under me, while I was standing beside the gun.

While this was going on, the column under Colonel Montizambert and Lord Melgund, some two miles distant on the left bank of the river, heard the heavy firing and the rage of battle proceeding, and their chagrin at not being with us was very great. But they vigorously set to work to make preparations to cross; and, happily, General Middleton's foresight, in bringing the ferry with the wire rope from Clarke's Crossing, gave them the means of doing so. But, before a crossing could be effected, oars had to be hewn out of the poplar timber, as the wire rope could not be speedily stretched; and the scow was rowed over the current, a tedious operation. Many of the men, in their eagerness to cross, were anxious to swim over, not knowing what was happening and fearing the danger our small column might be exposed to. One can well imagine their feelings as they were forced to listen to the fire of artillery and the rattle of musketry for several hours before they could ascertain the cause or the result. However, by the combined exertions of the officers in command of the various corps forming the left column, a crossing was effected, and early in the afternoon, a portion of the Grenadiers, under Colonel Grassett, and the Winnipeg Field Battery, with Colonel Montizambert and Lord Melgund, immediately marched up to the scene of action. By this time the battle may be said, however, to have been over, for the enemy had all retreated, excepting the small detachment hidden in the narrow angle of the ravine. Protected by their rifle-pits and the woods, like rats in a hole, there they were, completely surrounded and preparing to sell their lives as dearly as possible. The Grenadiers now relieved some of the companies of the 90th, and took up the position so gallantly held by the Winnipeg Rifles.

The question now was: "Will the surrounded rebels be cleaned out by a charge upon their position?" and an appeal was made to the General to decide the question. With characteristic humanity, the General, however, replied: "No, it will cost more lives, and I have lost too many already; their capture will not affect the work of the day." The men who had borne the brunt of the battle were ready to undertake the task; but the General was obdurate. Knowing the determined character of the men we had to deal with, and the difficulties of approaching them through bush and brush to find their whereabouts, there is no doubt that had the charge been made many more valuable lives would have been sacrificed to gain a slight advantage. The General's good sense in refusing to make the charge was therefore to be commended.

No greater bravery, heroism, devotion to duty, or discipline could be expected from any troops, than was manifested at this unequal fight at Fish Creek. There was no wavering, no thought of a retreat, but rather a dogged determination to hold their ground, under the galling fire of an unseen enemy. The critics who sympathize with the rebels have tried to represent that with the superior arms and the superior numbers of General Middleton's force, no other result was to be expected over the foe. But without wishing to disparage the bravery of the enemy, it is well to remember that on this occasion the actual fighting force which took part in the battle did not exceed three hundred. The rear-guard, the orderlies, and the non-combatants of the force, with few exceptions, were ordered to remain in rear to protect the transport. Gabriel Dumont, over his own signature, on the other hand, acknowledges to having had two hundred and eighty men on the rebel side, which I feel sure, from what I saw and heard, was below the number. Besides this force, the enemy had the advantage of knowing the country, and had selected a naturally strong position, rendered still more strong by their ingeniously constructed rifle-pits. Moreover, every man of them had been accustomed from boyhood to the use of fire-arms, by which numbers of them live. Out of our three hundred men engaged, one officer and nine men were killed, and four officers and thirty-eight men were wounded, besides minor casualties which were never reported.

Out of my total strength, which was forty armed men, mounted and dismounted, D'Arcy Baker received a death-hurt, and seven others were severely wounded. About the same percentage of the other forces engaged fell during the day, besides Captain Wise and Lieutenant Doucet, the General's two A.D.C.s, both of whom were severely wounded, and the General himself came off with a bullet hole through his fur cap.

Major Buchan, of the 90th, was the first to arrive after the fight commenced, and writing shortly after to a friend, thus describes the opening of the battle:

> Volley after volley broke the stillness of the clear morning. Vaulting into my saddle – for I had been walking quietly along with my horse's bridle over my arm – and passing the various sections of the advanced guard, who were already extending for attack, I galloped to the front. When I got around the curve on the trail and came to the edge of the bluffs, where a plain opened, a terrible sight was before me. Riderless horses were scattered about, half a dozen or so of them struggling in death's agonies. Some wounded scouts endeavoured to crawl to the rear, while the remainder were lying flat and briskly returning the fire of the enemy, who were unseen, save by the puffs of smoke which came from the further side of the plain, but whose presence was made very manifest by the whizzing "zip" and "ping" of the bullets as they flew over our heads. My appearance was the signal for a volley at myself, which made me realize, as I did all through the day, that mounted officers were the enemy's special targets. The men extended in good shape as they came up, and immediately

opened fire from an advantageous position on the edge of the scrub, and gradually crept forward towards the enemy, while the wounded scouts crawled back behind the first bluff in front of which were our fellows. Not five minutes afterwards, Captain Clark of "F" Company was struck as he was kneeling in the scrub directing the fire of his sharpshooters. Presently the guns of "A" Battery came up, and Captain Peters opened fire, dropping his shells with splendid effect. The roar of the cannon and the scream of the bursting shells gave encouragement to those engaged on our side and evidently dismayed the enemy.

Towards four o'clock in the afternoon, the General ordered the firing to cease, and the small body of the enemy still remaining were only too well satisfied to abandon the conflict. Comparative quietness now reigned, and an opportunity was given the doctors to attend to the wounded, among whom they had already been busy. Dr. Orton, M.P., brigade-surgeon; Dr. Rolston, of my troop; Dr. Grant, of the artillery; Dr. White-ford, of the 90th, were all doing their best to relieve the distressed and suffering men. They were moderately well-prepared with instruments and bandages, although, not being accustomed to war or expecting such calls upon their resources, they were somewhat deficient. A corral, about six hundred yards from the ravine, had been formed of the transport by Mr. Bedson, assisted by Mr. Secretan, and in the centre of this an hospital was improvised. The casualty list was anxiously conned, and was found to amount to eight killed, and forty-four wounded.

The war correspondents, Mr. Chambers, of the Montreal *Star*; Mr. Ham, of the Toronto *Mail* and the Winnipeg *Times*; Mr. Davis, R.M.C., of the Toronto *Globe* and the Winnipeg *Free Press*; Mr. Johnstone, of the St. Paul *Pioneer Press*, and Mr. Flynn, of the Winnipeg *Sun*, were now busily engaged completing their hastily written reports, conveying information of the fight to the people of Canada, whose anxiety was great to know the fate of their friends among the troops, and whose hearts were to be torn by the sad news.

The General ordered me to supply two couriers for the

conveyance of despatches to the telegraph station at Clarke's Crossing, twenty-four miles distant. The honour of bearing these despatches fell to Sergeant Dalton and Corporal Marriott, and the correspondents took advantage to send by them their accounts of the engagement. I sent a telegram to my wife, to acquaint our friends of the result of the day – being off the line of communication – so that no unfounded rumours might distress them. Before the following night it was received, the message having travelled twenty-four miles from Fish Creek at our end, and sixty miles by road to Russell at the other end, which, it will be admitted, is remarkable despatch.

The General had now to determine what his next best course should be. But his first anxiety was for the wounded. He instructed Lord Melgund and Captain Haig to select a suitable camping-ground in the neighbourhood, which would at the same time protect the crossing of the remainder of the troops from the left bank of the river, and be safe from surprise. They found an open space, about half a mile to the left of the battle-ground, near the Saskatchewan, and close to the gully of Fish Creek, which there empties into the river.

The wounded were conveyed thither in the ambulance, the transport next, and then the troops were gradually withdrawn from the scene of the conflict. Thus ended the most severe battle that the Canadian soldiery of the present day have had to fight.

Had we had supports, the day might have been carried with less loss of life by a charge on the enemy's position at the commencement of the fighting; but the men lacked the experience they gained after the battle of Batoche. Apart from this fact, however, it would have been too risky with so small a force at disposal to have charged down into the ravine, without reinforcements to fall back upon.

The Grenadiers were the last to leave the field towards dusk. When they had got about three hundred yards from the battlefield, a party of about fifty horsemen came out of the woods on the opposite side of the ravine and gave their war-whoop. These were evidently the reinforcements Gabriel Dumont had sent down from Batoche, for they did not show themselves while the troops were on the field. The word was given, "right-about-turn," and the troops were returning to the battle-field, when the enemy once more disappeared in the bush. As the General determined to pursue the attack no further, the order was once more given to march into camp.

We all went into camp, and put out strong pickets and sentries, which, after the fatigue of the day, was no light task for tired officers and men to perform. But it was done with cheerful alacrity and steadiness. Our night duty consisted in furnishing a mounted patrol, which every two hours circled the camp outside the pickets.

This was the most risky duty the mounted men had to perform. We kept from a quarter of a mile to half a mile outside the pickets, and had to run the gauntlet of every sentry and answer to their challenges. The sentries performed their duties with a great degree of faithfulness. Lord Melgund, going the rounds one very dark night, was met by, "Who goes there?" "Rounds." "What rounds?" "Grand rounds." "Stand, Grand rounds, and put up your hands," and the sentry came down to the charge. Lord Melgund called out, "Come to the port, sir." The sentry's reply was, "No, you don't," until he became convinced that he was not being taken in by a deceitful enemy. On another occasion the patrol came and woke me up about one o'clock in the morning, and told me that one of the sentries had drawn a bead on them, and that the sentries' orders were to shoot on sight. I had to get up and go to see that the orders were corrected. This was after we had joined General Strange's men, in our chase after Big Bear, and when the sentries who were on piquet the first night that we joined forces had not been accustomed to the mounted patrol. This duty General Middleton always required to be performed, and hearing my patrol moving through the dark, they took them for Indians, and very nearly fired upon them.

One sad but necessary duty had on the following day to be performed – the burial of the poor fellows who had been sent to their last home by the fatal bullets of the enemy. Wrapped up in their blankets, the bodies were placed on stretchers, and mournfully the troops followed them to their last resting-place, the General reading the burial service in an impressive and solemn manner. Their graves were covered up, and a sketch made of the position in which they lay, for the benefit of their friends. The General, before dismissing the troops to their separate parades, addressed them in these brief but affecting words: "Men! your comrades did their duty and have nothing to regret." Before leaving the camp a hundred waggon loads of stone were hauled, and a huge cairn, surmounted by a wooden cross, was erected over the spot where lay in honour the country's dead.

Two nights after the battle of Fish Creek, we were alarmed by the report of a rifle and the summons, "Guard, turn out!" The whole camp was astir at once, and, in the most orderly and self-possessed manner, fell in on their parade-grounds within three minutes from the first alarm. The General, who was on horseback in a moment, rode off to visit the pickets and ascertain the cause of alarm. Three mounted men were reported as having been seen approaching the near picket and not answering to the challenge; the sentry fired, but nothing more was heard of them. After half an hour's anxious wondering the troops were turned in.

At dawn I was awakened by a stranger, a transport officer, who related his adventures of the past night. It appears that he was in charge of thirty-five transport waggons loaded with supplies from Humboldt, and just in time discovered that he was on the wrong trail and marching straight into the enemy's camp. At six o'clock the previous night he had left the teams formed up for defence, to try to find our whereabouts, and struck the camp about one o'clock in the morning. This was the cause of the alarm. Not knowing whether we were friends or foes, he refused to answer to the challenge, and on hearing the whiz of the bullets, dismounted and lay down on the prairie till daybreak. He now wanted an escort to go off and convoy his teams into camp, which the General ordered me to furnish, and we arrived back in safety with the waggons, about six o'clock in the evening.

Poor D'Arcy Baker, who was lying severely wounded in one of the hospital tents, on hearing the shots fired at this night alarm, raised himself up, called for his horse and rifle, staggered to the door of the tent, and fell dead from the exhaustion of his efforts. He was buried the following morning beside his comrades in arms. The following lines on the gallant trooper's death, from the pen of Mr. Murdock, of Birtle, indicate the sympathy of our friends:

"My rifle and my horse," the soldier said,
As forth with vigorous step he quickly came;
On his young brow the morning sunlight play'd,
And life was centred in his active frame.

By winding streams far o'er the plain we go,
Where dark ravines and woody bluffs appear,
Where'er a swarthy, treacherous Indian foe
May hide, to burst upon our flashing rear.

'Tis ours to guard the friends who come behind,
'Tis ours to find and search the dangerous shade;
Perchance our lives we lose, but never mind,
When duty calls let no man be afraid.

The sulphurous smoke is drifting to the sky,
And horse and rider on the plain are spread;
The ambushed foe, in sullen terror fly,
The bold and brave are now amongst the dead.

With shattered heart, the stricken soldier lies,
The fatal wound has almost ceased to bleed;
The dying warrior vainly seeks to rise,
And begs once more, his rifle and his steed.

Forever more the youthful limbs are still,
The young, the gallant, and impulsive brave
Now rests beside the far-off western hill,
And wild flowers blossom by his lonely grave.

The General now resolved to place his left column again on

the other side of the river. It took two days to complete the crossing, and when that was accomplished there was nothing to relieve the routine of camp-life which now set in. The infantry took advantage of the time to drill their men and to instruct them in the various military duties which they were daily called upon to perform. Our time was more actively employed in furnishing escorts to hay trains and transports, and in sending couriers with the Grenadier's despatches, which were frequent and on long distances, as we were twenty miles from the telegraph station. Gunner Wood, our excellent telegraph operator, soon laid a field-line, however, into the camp from across the river, where the wires ran on the way to Prince Albert.

The General went over on Sunday morning to visit the scene of the battle; and the fight of Friday was had over again in vivid descriptions of individual experiences. The houses were all deserted, and left evidences of a hurried flight having taken place. We found the dead bodies of three Indians, which, with the eight killed and the eleven wounded that Gabriel Dumont, in his official report to Riel, stated were his casualties, made up the total loss of the rebels. The shelter of the ravine had reduced their casualties very much below ours, who had to fight in the open and exposed prairie.

There was, of course, a little sadness in camp on account of the death of so many comrades, and this was deepened by the receipt of the news of the death of Lieutenant-Colonel Kennedy, of the 90th Battalion of Winnipeg Rifles, who at the time of the outbreak of the rebellion was in Egypt in connection with the brigade of Canadian boatmen, formed for the transport service. As soon as the news of the insurrection reached him he started to join his own regiment, which he had raised only the previous year, and made all haste to return to Canada. It had been arranged that he was to be received by the Queen at Windsor, on his way through England, but stricken with smallpox almost at the moment of his arrival, he lingered only a few days, to die far from his own home. The news of his death was a deep shock to all ranks in his battalion, who had eagerly looked forward to his soon joining them.

The General now awaited the arrival of the steamboat, which had left Saskatchewan Landing, near Swift Current, but was much delayed by low water. He was anxious to send the wounded away by it to the village of Saskatoon, some forty miles up the river on the other side of Clarke's Crossing, whose inhabitants had written to say that they would be pleased to give their houses for their accommodation, and that their wives and daughters would nurse the wounded. But the boat was so long in coming that the General was obliged after all to send them by road. Through the ingenious invention of the chief transport officer, rude ambulances were made out of the transport waggons, by stretching across them the hides of the cattle we had killed; and on the 2nd of May I was ordered to escort them to Clarke's Crossing, where they were to be met by representatives from the settlement at Saskatoon. The wounded were accompanied by Drs. Orton and Rolston, and the day after their arrival at Saskatoon, Dr. Roddick, with his staff and excellent hospital outfit, arrived and took them in charge, where, by all accounts, the arrangements for their comfort were perfect. The kindness and hospitality of the settlers of Saskatoon were at once supplemented by experienced nurses under the excellent superintendence of Nurse Miller, of the Winnipeg General Hospital.

I might here state that all the arrangements for conducting the campaign were excellent. The troops were never once without the most liberal rations, and all of good quality. The transport, though costly, did its work well; and with the exception of the two days at Clarke's Crossing, never failed to bring up the most liberal supplies of forage and rations.

I might here also remark upon the excellence of our mail arrangements. Soldiers' letters went free, and two or three mails a week arrived, bringing greatest solace to the soldier far from home. The newspapers were eagerly scanned for information, especially when the first news came back to us of the battle of Fish Creek. Mr. Nursey, who is a bombardier when he is soldiering, and Provincial Auditor when he is not, was our obliging post-master. The only thing that put him out was when every man in camp came to ask him each evening when the mail was going out or had it come in. He was assisted by one of the Honourable Mr. Norquay's sons, two of whom were with the column, one in the fighting ranks, the other in the post-office. The thanks of the whole force are due to the Postmaster General for the liberal postal arrangements he made for the troops.

On the 4th of May the General had a brigade parade, with the view of practising his troops, which lasted for several hours. On the 5th we made a reconnaissance towards Batoche, under the personal command of the General, accompanied by Lord Melgund. The reconnoitring force consisted of my own and Captain French's men. We marched in the usual formation, with sixteen mounted skirmishers well to the front. We found all the houses completely deserted, everything being left as it was, excepting blankets, which the half-breeds had taken with them for their nightly camp covering. On the trail we observed numerous heavy tracks of horses, as if a large body had lately passed over it. The country was thickly covered with bluffs or clumps of trees, affording excellent coverage for an enemy. After we had proceeded about nine miles, some of my men signalled signs of the enemy, and almost immediately Sergeant Fisher came up and reported having seen a dozen or more men galloping off at full speed. The General now rode on to the front, and, with an escort, went down to the houses from which the enemy had escaped, leaving the main force on the trail. He found in the house they had so hurriedly left the dinner cooking on the stove and their bannocks in the oven. After further search nothing unusual was discovered. They proved to be an outlying picket of the enemy stationed there to give warning of our approach. We resumed our march for a couple of miles until we arrived at Gabriel Dumont's Crossing, the homestead of Riel's lieutenant-general. We found a store here containing a few articles, chiefly blacking, braces, strings of beads, and such like, but nothing of value, except a billiard table. Dumont's house, which was built of logs, was neat and commodious, with ample outbuildings, and the store referred to attached. From this store everything of value had been removed. The General gave orders that he would allow nothing to be touched, and turned all of the men out of the buildings, not, however, before some mementoes of the campaign had been secured.

After having lunched off our hardtack, which we had with us, and fed our horses, each with a nose-bag of oats, we returned by the river bank, about a mile and a half to the west of the main trail, passing by all the houses overlooking the river. They were all open, and the interiors showed evident signs of comfort and prosperity. In almost every other house was seen a fiddle on the walls, to help in whiling away the long winter evenings in a Red River jig. But beyond a few chickens, which we caught for the wounded, nothing was touched; and we left the doors closed to await the return of the occupants.

During this reconnaissance a courier followed us to say that the long-looked-for steamboat had arrived from Saskatchewan Landing, having on board Colonel Williams, with two companies of the Midland Battalion. On board also was the gatling gun, in the charge of Captain Howard, a representative of the manufactory where these guns are made. The troops disembarked to form part of the column. The gatling was attached to "A" Battery and put under the command of Lieutenant Rivers.

On the 5th of May General Middleton completed his arrangements for a further advance on Batoche. At the time he was, I believe, urged to advance directly on Prince Albert, in order to effect a junction with Colonel Irvine and his corps of Mounted Police, leaving Batoche for future attack; but no doubt feeling that this would be a sign of weakness, the General determined to march on to Batoche, and to attack Riel in his stronghold without further delay, sending a message to Colonel Irvine to co-operate with him from the north.

In order to give the Indians an opportunity of abandoning their alliance with Riel, the General, on the 4th of May, wrote out a proclamation in French, and sent half a dozen copies to be distributed in Batoche. He selected one of the three Indian scouts we still held as prisoners to take them. This proclamation was to the effect that if the Indians and friendly half-breeds would return to their reserves they would be protected. Riel took this messenger prisoner and suppressed the proclamation before he had distributed any of the copies.

About this time, I lent two of my best horses to couriers McConnell and Linklater, to carry despatches, both of whom were, however, captured by the enemy. McConnell became a prisoner, but Linklater escaped with the loss of his horse.

General Middleton's two A.D.C.s, Captain Wise and Lieutenant Doucet, having been wounded, Lieutenant Frère, Adjutant of the School of Infantry at St. John's, Quebec, now joined to take their places. Another visitor also turned up in the person of Mr. Henty, correspondent of the London *Standard*, having been sent out by that enterprising paper to report the campaign. He arrived on the 9th of May, the first day of Batoche.

XI

THE ADVANCE ON BATOCHE

The General had the steamboat barricaded for protection for the conveyance of supplies down the river, and also to co-operate with his troops on the river at Batoche. On board he placed Major Smith with "C" School of Infantry in command; and on the morning of the 7th of May, the column marched from Fish Creek, the scene of the late battle, leaving our dead comrades in their lonely resting-place. My men led the advance, followed by the column, now reinforced by Colonel Williams with his two companies and the gatling gun, an addition which made up for our Fish Creek casualties. On the first day we advanced as far as Gabriel Dumont's Crossing, arrving there at noon. We camped at Dumont's for the night, my men being sent out as videttes about half a mile to the front of the camp. The picket we had surprised two days previously we saw in position, about three miles from their old station, and they fired a few shots at some stragglers, who had wandered away from camp, without, however, doing any damage.

After dinner I was ordered to turn out for a reconnaissance towards Batoche, the General himself commanding. We circled out on to the open prairie to get clear of the bush, which is dense only within two or three miles of the river bank. After proceeding some distance, we ascertained that the prairie was open to the north, and that the column could thus avoid dangerous ravines and heavy timber, which obstructed our march along the main trail through the settlement. Under the guidance of Mr. Reid, a surveyor, who was acting as paymaster to the Midland Battalion, the General marked out his line of march for the following day, and we returned to camp.

The next day was an anxious one; we were encamped within six miles of the stronghold of Riel, who was aware of our presence, and there was ample cover to make a night attack, with little warning. But our pickets were strong and well placed, and were kept vigilant by being visited by the General himself as usual, who was followed later on by the field officer of the day. General Middleton never failed to assure himself every night that the pickets were well placed and doing their duty.

On the following morning we marched eastward at six o'clock, to reach open prairie, and then turned north to the trail that leads directly into Batoche. On the edge of the bush, some six miles from Batoche, the General halted, and ordered camp to be pitched on a rising ground, protected by a lake on the bush side, and the open prairie on the other. Without halting, the General took my men on and made a reconnaissance to within a mile and a half of the rebel headquarters, to ascertain for himself the lay of the country, to see that our front was clear, and to select a spot nearer Batoche for the following night's camp. We passed through the reserve of One Arrow, whose tribe had joined the insurgents, leaving his reserve deserted. Beyond a scout or two, who were seen watching our movements, nothing unusual occurred.

In the evening the General assembled the officers commanding corps and explained the duties each was expected to perform on the morrow, when an attack on the enemy's stronghold was to be made. Previous to leaving Gabriel's Crossing, the General had given instructions to Major Smith and Mr. Bedson, on board the steamboat, to drop down the river and join us at eight o'clock on the following morning, opposite Batoche, to co-operate in the contemplated attack.

On the morning of the 9th of May, the camp was astir before daybreak, making preparations for the important day's work before us. We were ready to march punctually at six o'clock, and as we were assembling for parade, a box of cigars, which had come by that morning's mail, was handed to me as a present from Messrs. Davis & Sons, of Montreal, who for the comfort of the troops generously sent up ten thousand cigars to our column. By this thoughtful act I was enabled to serve out a cigar to each man, and we marched off amidst great good humour and lots of chaff.

The General left the camp intact, to await the result of the day, leaving a small guard to protect it. Our order of march was as usual. My men covered the front with a line of sixteen skirmishers, supported as before, followed by "A" Battery of artillery and the gatling, the Grenadiers, the 90th and the Midland, with the Winnipeg Field Battery and Captain French's Scouts. My skirmishers had to go through dense bush, swamps and gullies, on each side of the trail, but the reconnaissance of the previous day had given them confidence, and they kept their position and touch remarkably well.

When within about a mile of the river, we heard sounds of a hot contest in the direction of the stream, volley after volley and shot after shot being fired in rapid succession, and the steamboat blowing her whistle "for all she was worth." We knew at once that this part of the programme had miscarried. The General ordered a shot to be fired by the artillery to advise them of our approach, and if possible to draw the attention of the enemy from them in case they were in danger. We then advanced rapidly to the scene of the action.

On our approach to the village, which lay on the high ground before descending to the valley, we found the houses barricaded. It took some little time to form up the column from the line of march preparatory to going into action. Two guns were brought up and opened fire on the barricaded houses, from which men were seen issuing. I dismounted some of my men and advanced in skirmishing order, as we saw men moving about at the edge of the bush which encircles the prairie ridge at the top of the valley. Right before us, about four hundred yards off, lay two large buildings near the trail, and out of one of them, after Captain Howard had fired two rounds of the gatling at it, came two or three people who waved a white handkerchief; this being reported to the General, he advanced with us to ascertain the cause. He found that this house was occupied by a number of priests, some Sisters of Mercy, and several families, who were in a great state of anxiety and fear, and who luckily had not been touched by the gatling, which only hit the corner of the house. The General assured them of his protection, and shook each kindly by the hand. We now again advanced.

My line of scouts went on beyond the church and seminary, as we found them to be, and into the brush that lay about two hundred yards the other side of the church, and there we received the fire of the enemy from the concealed rifle-pits. The General's orders to me were, that the moment I felt the enemy I was to retire my men and form them up to await further orders, which I now did, in the neighbourhood of the church.

The Grenadiers now came up, and two companies extended in skirmishing order to advance upon the position. The artillery were advanced and opened fire upon the other side of the river. Two more guns were pushed still farther forward until they commanded the village and the ferry, and there commenced shelling the position to protect the advance of our skirmishers and draw the enemy's fire from the steamboat. By the time these positions were taken up, the fire in the neighbourhood of the steamboat had ceased, and she was not to be seen near the ferry, so we hoped she had made her escape in safety.

The Grenadiers advanced into the bush, were received by a hot fire from the concealed rifle-pits, and were ordered to lie down. The guns, which were shelling the village, were ordered to change their position. The General and all his staff, besides a number of officers, were watching the effect of the shelling, and just as the guns were being limbered up preparatory to changing their position, a body of the enemy, who had crept through the bushes which lay a short distance in our front, poured in a volley and wounded two or three men and killed a horse. The gatling, which was being worked for the second time and was just getting into action, with Captain Howard at the crank, turned its fire on the concealed foe, and for the moment silenced them. Captain Howard on this occa-

sion showed his gun off to the best advantage, and very pluckily worked it with great coolness, although the fire from the
enemy was very hot for a time. This is the incident that was
magnified into the "gatling saving the guns." The illustrated
papers drew vivid pictures of our artillery, surrounded by a
horde of savages, and Captain Howard's gatling pouring forth
its bullets for our salvation, and "mowing 'em down." These
absurd illustrations and absurder comments unfairly reflected
upon our artillery and their officers; but Captain Howard did
nothing more than what was repeatedly done by our gunners,
and were it not that he was an officer belonging to the American service partaking of our hospitality and serving with us,
I do not suppose his name would have been mentioned. I say
this in justice to our own men, and not in any way to discredit
Captain Howard, who behaved himself throughout the
campaign with the greatest coolness and courage, and worthily
upheld the character of the great people who were our neighbours. On this occasion we were all anxious to compliment him
on the service his gun had performed, the first time it had
been in action, and this considerate act of ours was unfortunately made the pretext for which at one time seemed a dere-
liction of duty on the part of our own gunners and their
supports.

We had now received a decided check. Immediately in our
front lay a thick bush, beyond which we could not penetrate.
We had been driven by the heavy fire of the enemy from the
position which the guns occupied overlooking the village, which
was within easy range of the rifle-pits that were covered by the
bush.

I here attempt a short description of the ground that we
were fighting on. The trail by which we had approached
Batoche from the east made a turn and came up parallel to
the bank of the river for half a mile, and only a few yards from
the edge of the valley to the church. A short distance beyond
the church the trail disappeared in the bush, down the slope
of the valley leading to Batoche. The bank of the river is very
steep, sloping abruptly down to the water about one hundred

and fifty feet below, the valley between these two high banks being about a mile wide. On one side, opposite the village, where a few houses with a store stood, a portion of Riel's men were camped, protected by a semi-circle of rifle-pits and entrenchments, whose points touched the banks of the river to the north and south. The river bank on our side was covered with heavy timber, and afforded good cover to the enemy, further protected by a semi-circle of rifle-pits which enclosed the slope towards the village, and the ferry. Near the church a short gully formed an indentation leading down to the river, clothed with brush towards the bottom, where the enemy were in force. On the prairie level was an open space, about half a mile square, surrounded by clumps of trees and flanked by the river. This position we occupied, making the neighbour-hood of the church our headquarters. The enemy were on two sides of us; in front of us, in their rifle-pits, and on our left, covered by the protection of the river bank and the shelter afforded by the bush in the gully. On the south side of this short gully, farthest from Batoche, and next our position, was a graveyard with a fence around it, resting on the edge of the bank and overlooking the magnificent valley below.

General Middleton now lined the edge of the river bank, with the 90th occupying the graveyard and the slope of the hill to the river. The Grenadiers occupied the front, opposed to the rifle-pits of the enemy. Some of my men, with Captain French's, flanked the crests of the short gully, joined by the dismounted artillery. At this point, Gunner Phillips was killed, and two of Captain French's men were wounded. The mouth of the gully evidently contained the enemy in force. Colonel Williams was ordered to charge down this gully with his two companies, which he gallantly did, clearing the front in this direction; and Captain Peters, accompanied by Dr. Codd, took advantage of this movement to go with three or four of his men to recover Phillips' body, which was lying under fire. The position was unknown to the troops, and the danger from the unseen rifle-pits was so great to our inexperienced men that no further advantage was gained; but a continuous fire from both sides was maintained in a determined manner, the enemy not venturing out of their rifle-pits and our troops not venturing into them. We were somewhat annoyed at this time by a galling fire from the opposite side of the river, two or three long-range rifles reaching us, sending occasional bullets into our midst. But the artillery opened fire and silenced it; and so the day wore on. The casualties were not heavy.

The question that was discussed with a great deal of interest and anxiety during the afternoon was what did the General intend doing. On the previous evening during our reconnaissance the General had selected a spot upon which to camp after the morrow's engagement at Batoche; but he had altered this arrangement, and the orders which had been issued to strike camp at four o'clock in the morning had been countermanded, and the camp was left standing to await the events of the day. The question privately discussed was whether the General intended retiring to the camp, or would he bring the camp up to the position?

The news of Colonel Otter's engagement with Poundmaker reached the General before he left Fish Creek, and the wires between Battleford and Clarke's Crossing being down, no further information from that quarter had been obtained, which added to the anxiety of the moment.

The General gave no intimation of his policy until about half-past three, when he gave me orders to take my men and go with Mr. Secretan, the assistant transport officer, strike camp, and escort it up. As soon as the General had given this order, his face brightened up; and the load of anxiety that had rested upon him, in determining his policy, seemed to pass off when he had made up his mind as to the course he should follow. He was now relying on the valour and determination of his troops, and casting upon them the fate of the day. He was not to be disappointed in the result. There was a certain element of risk in thus moving up his whole equipment close to the enemy's lines, but the General determined upon a bold policy.

We cheerfully returned to the last night's camp at a brisk

pace, and the tents were struck and loaded up. Lord Melgund returned with us on his way to Humboldt to convey the despatches of the General, and continued his way to Ottawa, to confer with the Government upon the present situation, and if necessary to bring up reinforcements. We were sorry to lose him, for a more kind, gallant officer no troops ever served under. I fancy, he felt the affair was likely to be of longer duration that was at first supposed, owing to the stubborn resistance of the enemy, or else he would not have left us at all.

We returned with the transport and camping outfit by half-past seven in the evening, very much to the relief of everyone, who had a long, fatiguing and harassing day, and unproductive of any material results. The houses had been burnt down in our neighbourhood as a precautionary measure, and a place selected, and lines for an entrenched camp marked out.

A corral was soon formed about a quarter of a mile distant from the church, in a ploughed field, and about two hundred yards distant from the bank of the river. Inside this small space the whole of the troops were placed, using the waggons as a barricade in case of attack. The skirmishers were now withdrawn, and as they retreated, they were followed by the enemy with a hot fire, which was kept up till they reached the corral, some bullets taking effect upon the horses, and several men being wounded inside the corral. As dusk had now come on, the firing ceased, and the troops were allowed to get supper in quiet and prepare for the night.

The General now ordered up reinforcements. Colonel O'Brien's battalion, York and Simcoe Rangers, were ordered to reinforce Colonel Denison at Humboldt; the 7th Fusiliers, under Colonel Williams, of London, to go to Clarke's Crossing, and the remainder of Colonel Williams's battalion, the Midland, were ordered to the front. Colonel Scott's battalion, the 91st, was also instructed to garrison Fort Qu'Appelle, and Colonel Turnbull's School of Cavalry was ordered to remain at Touchwood Hills, and the Winnipeg troop of cavalry under Captain

Knight, to remain at Fort Qu'Appelle, thus bringing the reinforcements closer to the main column.

The night which we had now to spend will ever be a memo-
rable one to the little force encamped before Batoche. In the
corral, formed by about two hundred and fifty waggons, were
enclosed some six hundred horses and about eight hundred
men, besides teamsters. As soon as the men had their supper,
strong pickets were placed outside the corral, in front of the
waggons. The Midland, under Colonel Williams, with one
company of the 90th, under Captain Forrest, took up a position on the edge of the bank overlooking the valley to prevent
a surprise from the enemy at that point; and during the whole
night our men kept up a dropping fire into the bush, which
clothed the bank of the river. This was done to prevent the
enemy in any numbers sneaking up under cover to surprise
the little force; and to keep the men awake, two-thirds of the
force kept vigilant watch on all sides, as sentries, pickets and
skirmishers; for it was felt by the General that if there was any
enterprise in the enemy we would be exposed to a night attack,
which, in our crowded position, would have been very harassing, if not serious.

Before dawn next day the teamsters were all aroused, and
the troops astir, in case that hour should be selected for an
attack. The greatest danger would have been the stampeding
of the horses, as it would have embarrassed our movements,
so the teamsters were ordered to stand by them. But dawn
came and early morning passed without any disturbance, and
the men got their breakfast in peace; thus a bright Sunday
morning opened upon a scene of war and anxiety.

About seven in the morning we saw through our field-glasses
a party of men digging near the graveyard. It was a funeral
party of the enemy, burying their dead of the day before, and
we refrained from interfering, or making any attack, until all
was over.

At eight o'clock the General ordered out the Grenadiers and
directed Colonel Van Straubenzie to advance them to their

position of the day before. My men were also ordered out, as a line of skirmishers, in front of the right flank of the corral, to protect the camp from surprise in that direction. The Midlanders again occupied the position on the left flank. The enemy took up a more advanced position in front of their rifle-pits and in the rear of the church, so we lost some of our ground of the previous day; but as the General was occupying the ground only to ascertain further the lay of the country, no attack was ordered. The men put in some practice by firing at the enemy in front and across the river, and by throwing up temporary entrenchments to protect themselves, taking lessons from the enemy's mode of warfare. Captain French with his men, and one of my troops, was sent on a reconnaissance to ascertain the position of an open plain, reported to the north. He made a circuit of some distance, returned in the evening, and reported having found it. The Winnipeg Field Battery turned out in the afternoon and opened fire from the right of the line across towards the graveyard, and Lieutenant Bolster, of the 90th, with a small detachment, made some blind rifle-pits to occupy and protect the line of skirmishers as they made their usual retirement in the evening.

The Reverend Mr. Gordon, who had joined the force as chaplain of the 90th, and who had been sent up by the parishioners of Knox Church, Winnipeg, of which he was pastor, held service in the evening. During his sermon the retirement took place, which was accompanied by heavy firing to cover and protect the retreating troops. This made his remarks so much the more impressive, as he had to raise his voice above the din of the firing. To show how completely we had lost track of the days, the arrangements about divine service were being put in orders and Mr. Gordon was consulted, when he had to tell the Brigade-Major that Sunday was over.

On Monday morning the General ordered out my men and Captain French's with the gatling to make a reconnaissance on the plain to the north of Batoche. We marched out about ten o'clock under the command of the General himself. Just as we were going out, one of the priests was being carried to the hospital tent; he had been severely wounded by one of the enemy's bullets, which had entered the window from the rear of the seminary. We made a short cut across, just skirting the prairie where it dips into the thick bush towards the valley; and after a march of about a mile we came to a fine level plateau, of about fifteen hundred acres in extent, and nearly half a mile wide. We discovered that the edge of this plain, next the valley of the river, was lined with men, who were sheltered, as we afterwards found, by the customary rifle-pits which formed part of the semi-circle of entrenchments with which Batoche was surrounded. After dismounting, we threw out our skirmishers, under shelter, in order to draw the fire of the enemy and to ascertain their strength. The gatling opened fire upon some houses half a mile distant, where some men were seen, which had the effect of bringing out from a house about forty or fifty men who were there assembled, and who scattered in all directions under the rapid firing of the gun. After gaining all the information we could at this point, without exposing the men more than was necessary, the General continued his reconnaissance down the plain. Two scouts were observed in the distance watching our movements, and a view halloo! was given, and a chase and chevy ensued, led by the General himself, on his horse, "Old Sam," as he called him.

After an exciting gallop for a couple of miles, we pulled up, but the enemy had escaped us. On our return, we found that the General, who had been left by himself, had made a capture on his own account of a half-breed who had been lurking in the bush. He was unarmed, represented that he had come out for cattle and was not a fighter. He observed, as we marched him off, that the men would have to go hungry to-day for dinner. Before leaving this point we burned down some log houses that might afford shelter for the enemy, in case further operations were needed here, and we returned to camp in good humour after our morning's excitement, driving before us a herd of cattle, some heads of which had been intended to supply the rebels with their dinner. We also drove off, during these days, all the ponies we could find, and herded them in the neighbourhood of our camp, to prevent the enemy obtaining them for offensive purposes or for flight.

We returned to camp, where the day's work had been similar to the previous one, Colonel Van Straubenzie with his Infantry Brigade occupying the positions in front of the enemy, and keeping up the same excellent practice, making experienced soldiers of his men. The Winnipeg Field Battery turned out in the afternoon and from the neighbourhood of the graveyard, which position had been regained during the day, had a little practice, shelling the opposite side of the river, where we observed that the shells created great consternation among the rebels, making them scatter and get well beyond range, and silenced the long-range rifles which were a constant source of annoyance. The retirement was effected in the evening in the same manner, with the same heavy, independent firing from both sides. It was on this evening that poor Dick Hardesty, the son of the well-known and respected Hudson's Bay officer, who acted as secretary to Mr. Donald A. Smith in 1869, was brought in on an ambulance to breathe his last in a few short hours. His death and a few wounded made up the casualties of the day. Among the latter was Captain Manley, of the Grenadiers, who was wounded while covering the retirement of the 90th. During this movement, the General was engaged shaving himself in the centre of the corral (a daily duty he never neglected). His pocket-glass was resting on the wheel of a waggon, and a bullet struck the waggon-box behind the glass. The General, with the utmost composure, took no notice of it, but went on with his shaving, though the incident was sufficiently exciting to make most men give themselves a gash or dispense with the ceremony on that occasion.

XII

BATOCHE CAPTURED

The General having now ascertained the exact situation and lay of Batoche, determined on the following day to make an attack and carry the position. Both officers and men had gained valuable experience from their three days' fighting, and were, doubtless, getting impatient over the tedium of their daily skirmishes. But nothing of the General's intention was known until the following day; and I may say here that I never met a man who was so thoroughly able to keep his own council, no one knowing until orders were issued what his projects were. His plan was to make an attack, with all the mounted men, upon the enemy from the plain to the north, so as to draw them from the front of the camp, and to allow the Infantry Brigade to advance beyond the shelter trenches which they occupied, and then to return rapidly and with the whole force capture the position. Captain Haig, R.E., of the General's staff, told me as we marched out in the morning that Batoche was to be taken that day. I was ordered to furnish two mounted men for the Infantry Brigade to act as gallopers, and I detailed Logan and Flynn, who remained behind with the infantry. On Sunday we were joined by Captain Dennis, in command of fifty mounted men composing the Intelligence Corps, most of whom were surveyors and their assistants. The arrival of this corps was opportune, for they were a useful, hardy, intelligent lot of men, and were of material assistance in the campaign and a valuable addition to the mounted force.

Captain Dennis's corps, my own corps, and Captain French's, in all numbering about one hundred and thirty mounted men, one gun of "A" Battery, under Captain Drury, and the gatling, under Lieutenant Rivers, accompanied by Captain Howard, marched off under General Middleton to the position we occupied the day before. Before setting out, the General gave orders to Colonel Van Straubenzie to advance his brigade to the old position, and as much farther as he could, after he heard that we had engaged the enemy. We debouched on the plain at the same point as on the previous day; the Intelligence Corps dismounted and extended in skirmishing order to support the gun about to open upon the enemy, the gatling took up a position a little farther down the plain, the main body of the mounted men keeping out of sight behind a knoll. The General went out on horseback in advance of the skirmishers to view the position through his glass before placing the gun, thus offering an excellent mark to the enemy as he sat there still and immovable as a target. The enemy were tempted to try a shot at him at four hundred yards, though they were careful of their ammunition. Ping! Ping! the bullets whizzed past him, when he deemed it prudent to retire, and in a temper to make it hot for them.

The gun being placed in position opened fire, and was viciously answered by volleys from the enemy about three hundred and fifty yards distant. Lieutenant Kippen, of the Intelligence Corps, who was skirmishing with his men in support of the gun, here received a death wound, and presently breathed his last. Dr. Rolston, assisted by his dresser, Mr. Kinlock, attended him instantly where he lay, in the line of skirmishers. Captain Drury dropped several shells into the enemy's entrenchments, and the skirmishers kept up an independent fire at the rebels as occasional opportunity offered. The General took the gatling farther down the plain to another position, a couple of hundred yards off, supported by some of my men, and brought it again into action. A few shots had been fired, when a man, riding quickly, appeared waving a white flag. The General called "cease firing," and rode out to meet him. He proved to be a Mr. Astley, one of Riel's captives. Astley, it seems, was confined in a cellar with a number of other prisoners at Batoche, when Riel came to the trap-door, called him up, and sent him with a letter addressed to the General, which he now presented, saying that if we murdered the women and children by our shell fire, he would massacre the prisoners. The General wrote an answer to say that he did not wish to harm them, and that if Riel would place the women and children together in one spot, and let him know where they were, he would take care that no shot should be fired in that direction, adding that he trusted to his (Riel's) honour that no men would be placed with them.

After a quarter of an hour's conversation with Astley as to where the prisoners were, the position of the ground, etc., he was sent back. Before leaving, however, Astley asked the General upon what terms he would accept Riel's surrender; as he (Astley) was anxious for the safety of the prisoners, and expected to bring about Riel's surrender. The General told him that he would be glad to see Riel in camp and would protect his life until handed over to the Government; but that his surrender must be unconditional; and with that Astley returned. As he was leaving, another messenger, named Jackson, came out from the same direction, on the same errand. He was the brother of Riel's secretary, and said he had been a prisoner in the hands of Riel. Having, however, got clear of the place, he refused to go back with an answer to his message, although the General urged him to do so, lest it should affect the safety of the rest of the prisoners.

The General now gave us orders to form up preparatory to returning to camp, keeping us for a while just out of sight of the enemy, occasionally showing a mounted man or two to puzzle the rebels as to our movements, which always drew a volley from them. About half-past eleven we returned to camp, and the General was annoyed to find that the advance ordered had not been made. Shortly after the General left the camp in the morning, Colonel Van Straubenzie had ordered out the Grenadier and Midland Battalions, who took up a position in front of their respective lines, in quarter-column, waiting to hear the attack which he expected would be made on the position to the north. Owing, however, to a strong wind blowing from the camp, he only heard a little firing, and not knowing exactly what to do, determined upon waiting the return of the General. Colonel Van Straubenzie took this opportunity to address a few words to each corps, telling them that a resolute attempt was now to be made to capture the position. Immediately on his return to camp the General dismounted from his horse, sent him to be fed, and went down on foot towards the high ground overlooking the river, to examine the position. From there he walked over in the direction of the church, where he was received by a hot fire from the enemy, and took shelter, for the first time in the campaign, in one of our newly constructed shelter-trenches. Colonel Van Straubenzie, Colonel Williams and I stood watching him from the outside of the corral, greatly apprehensive that he would be hit. What his object was in going out, I could not imagine, unless it was to see if Riel made any attempt to withdraw his men, or if he had sent any message to the priests in regard to the women and children, or was only using the negotiations he had opened as a ruse to gain time, for Poundmaker and his braves were daily expected. In half an hour he returned to camp to lunch.

In the meantime the Grenadiers and Midlanders had had their dinner, and, according to orders, again turned out. Colonel Van Straubenzie now gave instructions to the commanders of the corps to advance to the old ground and as much farther as they could, telling them what was expected of them, and himself accompanying them. Colonel Grassett advanced his regiment straight to the front, and Colonel Williams advanced his men to the graveyard, and threw his line down the bank of the river till his left touched the water's edge and his right was near the graveyard. At this point the river takes a bend, and in advancing, it became necessary to change the front by throwing forward the left, so Colonel Van Straubenzie ordered Colonel Williams and Colonel Grassett to throw the left flank forward, which was well executed under a brisk fire from the front as well as from the opposite side of the river. This movement was performed at the double, the men responding with

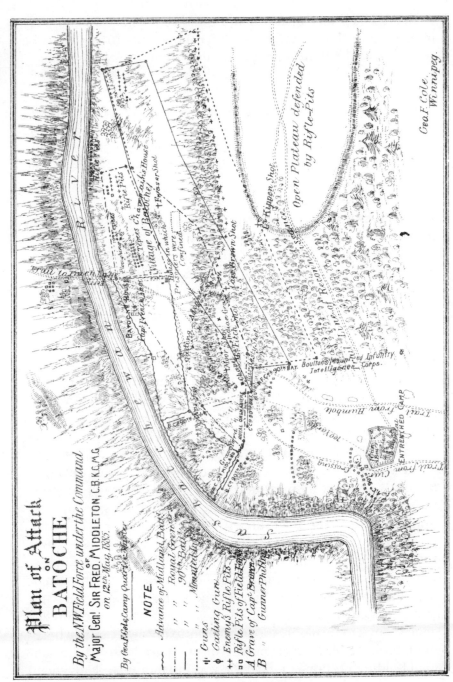

Plan of the attack on Batoche

a cheer, which was taken up along the whole line, warning us in the camp that operations had commenced in earnest. A company of the 90th, under Captain Ruttan, was ordered out to support Colonel Williams, and another company, under Captain Wilkes, to support the Grenadiers. Colonel Van Strau-benzie now sent word asking for the guns, which the General ordered out, at the same time mounting his horse and going to the scene of action, taking up his position at the church, surrounded by his staff. My horses having been fed I told the men to saddle and fall in to wait for orders, and rode out myself to join the General. I knew that there was likely to be some warm work, and determined to be on the spot to take instructions.

The excitement now increased, and order after order issued in rapid succession from the General. One gun of the "A" Battery and both guns of the Winnipeg Field Battery had been ordered out, and I galloped back into camp with the General's commands to hasten the movement. I met them all coming thundering along at full gallop, with the little gatling in their midst, followed by the ammunition waggons, under Lieuten-ant Desbrowe, who was indefatigable in supplying the troops with ammunition. Other mounted officers galloped to and fro carrying orders, and making a stirring scene. "E" and "F" Companies of the 90th, under Colonel McKeand, and Major Buchan, followed the artillery, to prolong the line to the right.

All this time the infantry were steadily advancing through the bush, supporting one another by hearty cheers. The guns took an advanced position and opened fire, one shelling the opposite side of the river, and two more shelling the enemy's position in the valley, and clearing the houses, which were filled with men, to make way for the advance of the infantry. I now received orders from the General to bring the mounted men out and prolong the line to the right of Major Buchan, so I galloped back into camp and gave orders to the Intelli-gence Corps to turn out, and went over to my own camp, where the men were all ready standing on the parade-ground, each man holding his horse. I gave the word to mount and advance, and within a few minutes of receiving the order we had galloped up to the skirmishing line and dismounted. Leaving the horses in the charge of three or four men, the former standing perfectly quiet in the midst of the din, we formed up on the right of the 90th with a hearty hurrah! In this movement we were quickly followed by the Intelligence Corps, which had marched up on foot. Cheer after cheer rose from one end of the line to the other, as the men saw that they were being supported by their comrades.

The whole line, stretching upwards of a mile from the river bank, now advanced steadily but rapidly through the bush to the open space which lay between us and the village. Before getting through the bush we came to a gully, at the bottom of which lay a number of the enemy. I shouted to the men not to hesitate, but to rush down, as it was dangerous to stand in the exposed position they had gained. At this moment poor Ted Brown, who had only lately been promoted to his captaincy, and was a universal favourite, became a mark for the enemy and was instantly killed, having time only to say, as his head dropped upon his arm, "I am hit, boys!" This exasperated our men, who, with the 90th on the left, rushed furiously down the gully and drove the enemy before them. As they ran from us, five of them dropped under the fire of the now excited men, and pit after pit was cleared in front of our skirmishing line, as we took them on the flank.

From the hillside, as we advanced straight to our front, we could see the line of skirmishers advancing on the left, in the form of a semi-circle. We could also see the rapid rush of the Midlanders on the left and the Grenadiers in the centre, mixed with the 90th, all rapidly advancing and concentrating on the clump of houses which formed the village. My own men, with the remainder of the 90th and the Intelligence Corps, advanced straight to the front to protect the flank of our comrades who were now capturing the village. We were further reinforced by Captain Coutlee, with a gun from the Winnipeg Field Battery, supported by the gatling. The latter had been ordered round to open fire upon the village from the right flank, to assist the Grenadiers and Midlanders.

It was now evident that the day was ours, and that the winding up had only to take place, although the enemy still kept up a stubborn fire. From our new position we could see the soldiers, who had now reached the village, sheltering themselves from behind the houses, the enemy having retreated to the bed of the river, protected by a bank of some twenty feet, from which they poured a hot fire upon the victorious soldiers. The men, little heeding the fire they had become so accustomed to after three days' fighting, went from house to house to take possession, the first one visited being that in which the prisoners were confined in a cellar.

A piece of timber jammed between the ceiling and the trap-door of the cellar was used to prevent their escape, and all these unfortunate men were confined for some time in this dark, foul place, and had been prisoners in Riel's hands ever since the 18th of March. They came out, looking pale and wan, but greatly relieved to be once more at liberty. During the time the charge was made upon the houses, Major Jarvis, with the remaining gun of the Winnipeg Field Battery, opened fire from the left upon a clump of trees up the gully, where the enemy was in position, and after a few well-directed rounds he succeeded in silencing them. After the village was captured the advance was continued by Captain Harston and a company of Grenadiers, who gained Champagne's house, near by the river bank; and Captain Young, the Brigade-Major, with some men took possession of the Council Chamber, where all the rebel documents were found intact.

The two companies of the 90th continued their advance, now under Major Buchan, as Colonel McKeand had sprained his ankle and was obliged to retire, though not before knowing that the day was practically won. My men and the surveyors also continued their forward movement on the right of the 90th, clearing the front for a mile beyond the village, where the enemy kept up a most determined fire. In this advance one more of the enemy fell under the good marksmanship of Sergeant Burton. After we had passed the village, Hope Hay, another of my men was badly wounded in the arm; and Fraser of the 90th was the last man killed in Major Buchan's advance late in the afternoon. About five o'clock we halted to await further orders from the General, and I came down the hill to the village to ascertain what were the results of the day.

The first thing I heard, and from everyone's lips, was that poor French was killed. With some of his men he had advanced with the Grenadiers and Midlanders, and after taking possession of the houses in the village, made a rush for Batoche's, which was about a hundred yards nearer the bank of the river and standing by itself. With characteristic gallantry Captain French entered the house with others, rushed up-stairs and went at once to a window to open fire on the enemy below. The latter, observing the movement from the shelter of the bank only a short distance off, and waiting their opportunity, concentrated their fire on the windows. An old French half-breed, named Ross, was standing at the corner of a house nearly opposite Batoche's house, and fired the fatal shot, then made a run for cover, but paid the penalty for shooting French just before reaching it. Captain French was a gallant, kind-hearted Irishman, and a friend of everyone. Just at the moment of victory, death met him in triumph, his last words being, "Remember, boys, who led you here!" I now heard for the first time of the death of Lieutenant Fitch, of the Grenadiers, who, with Captain Brown, Captain French, Lieutenant Kippen, and Fraser of the 90th, made up the day's casualties. Happily, owing to the impetuosity of the advance, which forced the rapid retreat of the enemy, the killed were confined to these few, who, in their country's cause, nobly met a soldier's death.

Under the shelter of the bank of the river, concealed by a bluff, we found numbers of women and children huddled together, frightened and anxious. Their household property lay in a confused mass in the middle of the village. The captives were kindly treated by the General, as well as by the officers and men, who sincerely pitied them in their unfortunate position, and who did all they could to relieve their anxiety, as well as to assist them in collecting their effects.

I should have mentioned another circumstance that occurred as I was standing beside the General before receiving the order to bring my men, and that was the approach once more of Astley, who had brought the flag of truce in the morning from the enemy's lines. He gallantly galloped through the line of fire pouring in from front and rear, and received several bullet marks in his clothes in his anxiety to bring about the safe release of the prisoners. He was the bearer of another despatch from Riel, thanking the General for his prompt and courteous reply, and informing him that he would put the women and children in some place of safety and send word, Astley all the time hurrying him up, as the firing was getting warmer and the time short. Riel sealed the letter up as he heard the ominous cheers of our men; and the fire increasing, he hurriedly wrote on the envelope, hoping to stay proceedings thereby, "I don't like war, if you do not cease firing, the question will remain the same as regards the prisoners." This despatch Astley handed to the General, but further negotiations were now out of the question. Astley returned to Riel once more, in order to give him the opportunity of surrendering, not knowing what the fate of the day might yet be. Riel by this time was anxious to surrender, and if he could have got safely into the General's hands he would have done so, but it was too late. In discussing the advisability of his surrendering with Astley, Riel was anxious to have his safety assured; "but," he said, "there are three things that will save me: one is politics; another that I have assumed the office of priest, and that will save me; and the papers which are all here will implicate the council more than me." From this latter circumstance it may be assumed that the papers were left behind purposely. Riel's actions at this time were so selfish that he completely lost the sympathy of his own people.

I would here hold before the eyes of those who sympathize with Riel, his course during this eventful day, to show how little he deserves sympathy, and how he was working, not for the good of his people, not for the cause for which they were fighting, but for his own self-glorification, and, above all, for his own safety. For this he sent Astley out in the morning to open up negotiations, though, ostensibly, his motive was the protection of his women and children. But this was far from being the real motive. Astley returned with the humane assurances of the General, and, at the same time, with the promise of personal protection for Riel until handed over to the civil authorities. Astley returned with this message, and Riel, anxious to carry on the negotiations in a politic way, and to obtain some terms, wrote four different letters, as Astley informed me, and tore them up, one after the other, not being satisfied with the part he wished to play. He thus allowed four precious hours to elapse after the General had answered him, and only completed his letter on hearing the vigorous fire of his assailants.

General Middleton would have been glad to have saved the lives of his gallant officers and men, who fell in that charge; he would have been glad to have saved the lives of the nineteen half-breeds and Indians who lay prone in death after the battle was over, and for whose death Riel, in refusing the General's offer, was responsible. But instead of thinking of them, Riel was thinking only of himself. In his anxious desire to couch his letters in such language as might ensure his own safety, he wasted the moments which were given him by the General to put an end to the warfare. In wasting these precious hours, what consideration did Riel show for the lives and property of his people, and what advantage or honour did he gain for them in the wicked extremity to which he drove them? In taking advantage of their excitable nature, and their ignorance and superstition, was he not making profit only for himself, and causing them to ignore the counsel and solicitude of their priests? If he had been allowed to escape unharmed, what security had the country from a like danger from other adventurers at some future period, in settlements as isolated in the more western districts; and what security had his people against having their homes and property destroyed, and their lives lost in fruitless opposition to the power of the country? It is to these questions those who condemn the hanging of Riel should give heed before allowing their sympathy to go out to a man who showed so little consideration for his people's welfare. Not for Riel, but for his unfortunate dupes, who are now undergoing the penalty of the crimes for which he is responsible, should there be sympathy, and only for them should Executive leniency have been invoked.

The teamsters now brought down the picks and shovels for the troops to throw up entrenchments for their protection, for they were to hold the position during the night. This, however, proved quite unnecessary, as the enemy were thoroughly beaten and threw up their cause without another shot being fired. The delight of the troops over their day's work was unbounded, and congratulations and compliments passed round and great enthusiasm prevailed. After the men had captured every position and driven the enemy completely off, they took up their quarters in the village for the night, during which time the looting complained of took place.

The troops for four days had lain before Batoche, being killed, wounded and harassed by the residents of this village, where the schemes had been hatched and which had been used throughout as the rebels' headquarters, and it is hardly to be expected that the soldiers, who had thus suffered, were at once to enter upon the burdensome duties of guard and picket, to protect this property, especially as most of it had been stolen at the commencement of the outbreak, and appropriated by Riel to keep up the sinews of war. I can say this as an eye-witness, that notwithstanding the provocation, notwithstanding the murderous fire they had been subjected to, after the battle was over there was not a particle of ill-feeling for these misguided people. There was rather a feeling of sympathy for their misfortunes, in having left their comfortable prosperous homes, to take up arms and bring upon themselves these troubles, at the instigation of a few ambitious leaders. The General did all he could for their relief; he gave them provisions, and assured them of his protection. By nightfall, such was the collapse of the rebellion that friend and foe alike were perfectly safe in the neighbourhood.

The half-breeds had any number of ponies, and the soldiers

were soon seen galloping about on their backs, and every man who wished had a shagannappi for his own use and amusement for the time being. They, however, proved too great an encumbrance to them to care for on the line of march, and so were left behind.

Before dusk General Middleton took a survey of the position, visiting and inspecting the entrenchments, and as he rode round with his A.D.C., Lieutenant Frère, he was received with enthusiastic cheers from the men, in their admiration of his coolness and gallantry, and in acknowledgement of the successful manner in which he had led them to victory.

His plans were undoubtedly well laid; his attack on the position to the north, and the complete silence in the direction of the camp, put the enemy off their guard and drew their strength in the other direction. When we seized the rifle-pits, one after another, in our front, we found that the timber defences, with which they were surmounted, had been changed from the south side to the north side of the pits. This showed that the sudden movement of the troops in the afternoon had caught the enemy unawares, made the victory so much the more complete, and unquestionably prevented a greater loss of life. My men picked up forty or fifty pairs of blankets in these pits, besides camping utensils and food, showing that the pits had been occupied for some time, and that men had slept in them.

At dusk the General ordered me to take my men back to the corral to remain on guard. During the day it had been under the command of Colonel Houghton, with Major Boswell and one company of the 90th, and half of "A" Battery. To guard the corral, while Batoche was being taken, was an unpleasant but necessary task that fell upon this portion of the expeditionary force.

The effect of the fall of Batoche was decisive for the country. The Indians had been greatly excited by the false news concerning the battle of Fish Creek, which Riel had reported to them as a victory. At Fort Qu'Appelle, the numerous tribes assumed a threatening aspect, and it took the combined exertions of Colonel McDonald, an experienced Indian agent, and Mr. McDonald, chief factor of the Hudson's Bay Company, united with Colonel O'Brien's good judgment, to keep them quiet and avoid a conflict between the Indians and the troops who were stationed there under the command of Colonel O'Brien. But the capture of Batoche nipped all this in the bud; and having now disposed of Riel, the General had only to gather in the insurgent Indian tribes farther west to bring the campaign to a close.

About nine o'clock that evening the troops which had taken part in the charge were, by the General's orders, formed up in the square inside the corral, and were addressed by him. He paid them a high compliment for their gallantry, and said he was the proudest man in Canada, to be at their head. He was answered by hearty cheers from the men. The troops did their duty well, the officers gallantly led their men, and all ranks have a proud feeling and satisfaction that a grateful country acknowledges the service rendered.

The charge, if it could be called such, was gallantly made; it was in reality an advance by a long line of skirmishers through thick bush, and it was impossible that orders could be received or given to any but those under immediate command. A great deal had to be left to the individual intelligence of the force. The ardour with which the troops charged was such that had the enemy been five times the number, they could not have withstood the troops. In fact, it could not be properly called a charge, but a steady advance of four hundred and fifty men in skirmishing order, vying with each other in rapidity of movement, clearing everything before them as they steadily advanced on the enemy's position, and brought to a close by undaunted pluck and determination. The capitulation of Batoche ended the half-breed rebellion and enabled the General now to turn his attention to quiet the excited Indians, who were threatening trouble all over the country while the fate of the battle was still undecided.

About six o'clock in the evening the whistle of a steamboat was heard, and shortly afterwards the *Northcote* steamed up to the ferry with all on board safe. It appears that, on the morning of the 9th instant, those in charge of the boat had miscalculated their distance, and had dropped down upon the ferry before they were aware, and were at once attacked by the whole strength of Riel from both sides of the river. But the steamer was well barricaded, and "C" Company, under Major Smith, so steadily and rapidly returned the fire from their portholes, that no loss was sustained beyond the three men wounded, although she was in a most dangerous position. The hottest fire had been directed at the pilot-house, which was also well barricaded; but the captain of the vessel remarked that this kind of thing was not in his articles of agreement, and steadily refused to guide the boat, taking shelter from the enemy's bullets on the floor of his pilot-house. The vessel was allowed to drift for a short distance at will, but fortunately keeping clear of the many shoals in the river. She was followed for some miles by a few excited half-breeds, but finally escaped to the Hudson's Bay Crossing; where Mr. Bedson communicated with Colonel Irvine, and obtained from him a small detachment of Mounted Police, under Mr. White-Frazer, and returned just in time to be present on the day of the victory.

At five o'clock in the afternoon the General called upon me for a courier to carry his despatches, which honour was entrusted to Mr. VanKoughnet, who galloped off to convey the good news to the people of Canada, who for four days had been torn with anxiety as to the result of the engagement. VanKoughnet returned during the night with messages of congratulation from the Minister of Militia. A congratulatory telegram was received from Lord Wolseley on the following night, all of which were put in orders.

The day after the battle the General had his wounded, numbering in all thirty-five men, placed on board the steamboat to be taken to Saskatoon, and made preparations for a forward march. I had to perform the painful duty of burying poor Captain Brown. We selected a quiet spot, half way down the bank of the river in front of our corral, on top of a slight rise overlooking the valley and surrounded by trees. A prettier spot could hardly be chosen for a soldier's last resting-place, and within view of the scene of the battle where he fell. The Reverend Mr. Gordon performed the burial service, and as we marched out of camp the band of the 90th Battalion played the Dead March. His comrades followed his remains to the spot selected, where a grave was dug and the coffin lowered into it amid the most sincere grief of all.

A second time I had to appoint a commander to the Russell troop. I now appointed Captain Campbell, a son of an old Hudson's Bay officer living at Straithclair. He was installed amid the cheers of the men, reminding us forcibly of the truth of the old motto: "Le Roi est mort, vive le Roi!"

On Thursday morning the General ordered us to strike camp, which we were thankful to do, having spent four days crowded together in the centre of a ploughed field, without tents or the ordinary comforts that may be obtained in a well-appointed camp. We quitted the scene with regret only for our fallen comrades; and left it to the imagination of the owner of the field to endeavour to make out the peculiar formation of the entrenchments we vacated. Each corps, according to its fancy, had thrown up earthworks for the protection of the face where it lay; each teamster had, according to his fancy, secured himself as he thought from harm by digging a pit under his waggon, where he lay for four days, preferring to risk inflammatory rheumatism for life rather than expose himself to the rebel bullets.

The General now set out for Prince Albert, intending to cross the river at Gardapuy's Crossing, about ten miles north of Batoche. In doing so we passed through a portion of the half-breed settlement we had not yet visited. We found the people coming in great numbers, carrying white flags, to surrender themselves as peaceable citizens. One and all were treated kindly by the General and by the troops.

On our way we heard that Riel and Dumont had fled to the Birch Hills, not many miles distant from this point. After reaching the Crossing the following day, the General ordered me to take the mounted men, with the gatling, and scour the country in search of the rebel leader. Before leaving Batoche the General sent a letter to Riel, at the solicitation of Astley, telling him that if he would surrender he would give him protection until being handed over to the civil authorities. We marched back on the trail by which we had come the day previous, towards Batoche, and there we met a guide who undertook to lead us to Riel. We now branched off into the country towards Birch Hills, where we got ample information of Riel having been seen a short time previously. I divided my men into parties and they scoured the country. They came across a place where a camp of women and children had for some time taken shelter. Some of my troopers caught sight of a mounted man, to whom they gave chase, but he was on too fleet a horse for them. We afterwards heard that this was Gabriel Dumont, who had been in company with Riel.

In the afternoon a message came from the General to say that Riel was captured. Hourie, Deal and Armstrong, three scouts who knew the country and the people, accompanied me about a half a mile in advance of the column, and on the main trail Riel had surrendered to them with the General's letter in his hand. Dreading the approach of the troops, he asked them to take him out of our way lest he should be ill-treated. They made a detour across the country, which happened to be in the same direction that we had taken, and when about five miles from the trail they passed through some of my scouts, who did not know Riel, and Hourie in his anxiety to take him into camp himself, gave no intimation of his capture, sending word that he had lost his horse and was going back to camp for another. He took Riel into camp and delivered him up to the General, before it was known that he was captured. The General had a tent pitched near his own, and put Riel in it, in charge of Captain Young, of the Winnipeg Field Battery, who kept guard over him until he handed him over to the police authorities at Regina. We returned to camp that night, and gave up further pursuit of the rebel leaders. Gabriel Dumont, with his companion Dumas, evidently left the country at once, for a week after a telegram brought the news that they had been arrested south of the boundary, in United States territory. In this short time they covered the distance, some three hundred and fifty miles, fear lending wings to their flight. They were released by the American authorities, no application having been made for their detention, and there they have remained ever since.

Riel decamped so suddenly before the rapid and determined onslaught of the troops at Batoche that he left behind him all his papers and documents, with the official record of his provisional government, containing all the evidence necessary to enable the Ottawa authorities to prosecute those implicated with him in the rebellion. Two days after, he surrendered himself to the General, preferring to take his chances upon a judicial trial to wandering about among his people and the Indians, who now apparently were hostile to him, on account of the troubles he had brought upon them. The General sent Riel by steamboat to Regina, in the charge of a guard commanded by Captain Young, there to be handed over to the civil authorities. In the meantime the half-breeds had surrendered a large quantity of arms of all sorts, from the repeating-rifle to the single barrel shot-gun.

The day after the capture of Riel, I was sent to Batoche with a list of the names of men the General wished me to make prisoners. I took them and brought them into camp, whence they were sent to Regina, to stand their trial for complicity in the rebellion.

The crossing of the river at Gardapuy's took two days, and on the 16th we set off for Prince Albert. Before leaving, the General sent two waggon loads of provisions to the priests at Batoche, with instructions to relieve any distress that might arise among the people. At noon on the 17th, we arrived at Prince Albert, having marched eighteen miles that morning over very dusty roads, the men being much weather-beaten and fatigued. We were met by Colonel Irvine and his police force, and were warmly welcomed by the citizens of the place, who for two months had been locked up without telegraphic or mail communication, and who had been in a constant state

of excitement and anxiety over the stirring events which so
materially affected their safety. They were, however, well-
protected by the Mounted Police force, some two hundred
strong, and by a local corps, lately organized, under Colonel
Sproat.

The troops made a march of eighteen miles, with only half
an hour's rest, the day of reaching Prince Albert, arriving there
by twelve o'clock noon, literally black with the dust of the march.
At Prince Albert they had a day and a half of rest before
proceeding. I will now follow the fortunes of Colonel Otter's
and General Strange's columns.

XIII

COLONEL OTTER'S COLUMN

For the present, we shall leave the movements of General Middleton's column to relate what had been occurring in the other parts of the territory.

Colonel Otter had instructions to take command of his column at Swift Current, a station on the Canadian Pacific Railway, about thirty miles from Saskatchewan Crossing, where the ferry provides a crossing over that river *en route* to Battleford. Colonel Otter had orders to march speedily to the relief of Battleford, whose residents and neighbouring settlements were threatened by Poundmaker and the various bands of Indians who had joined him.

His column consisted of the Queen's Own Rifles, two hundred and seventy strong, whom he had commanded previous to his appointment to the Toronto School of Infantry. The Queen's Own, during the Fenian raid of 1866, had seen service near Fort Erie, a Canadian town opposite the city of Buffalo, where a number of the corps fell in an engagement with some Fenians who had invaded our territory at that point. In addition to the Queen's Own, he had a company of fifty from the Governor-General's Foot Guards, Ottawa, under the command of Captain Todd; "B" Battery, from Quebec, one hundred and ten strong, with two nine-pounders, under command of Major Short; a portion of his own Infantry School, called "C" School, forty-six strong, under command of Lieutenant Wadmore, the other half of which was with General Middleton, under Major Smith; fifty Mounted Police under Colonel Herchmer, and a gatling gun.

Previous to the arrival of Colonel Otter's column in Battleford, Poundmaker's Indians had committed a number of
murders in the vicinity. Bernard Tremont was the first victim.
He was a Belgian, engaged in stock raising, and while at work
in his yard was shot by four Indians. Ickta, one of the tribe of
the Stonys, confessed to the murder to General Middleton.
James Payne, farm instructor on the Stony Reserve, was
murdered in his own house while the Indians were claiming
rations. This murder was also confessed to the General. Poor
Payne had an Indian wife who, apparently, deserted him in
his time of need. Mr. Smart, a trader, while on patrol at Battleford, was shot dead on the night of the 22nd of April, by some
Indians who were hidden in a coulée, three or four miles from
the town. He was an enterprising citizen from Battleford, and
his loss was much felt.

Battleford is a rising town on the Upper Saskatchewan, about
two hundred miles north of Swift Current. It is very prettily
situated, at the junction of Battle River with the Saskatchewan,
on a high level plateau overlooking these two deep valleys to
the north and to the south of the town, and high enough to
command a good view of the surrounding country. One of
the first impressions of a stranger on reaching Battleford is
what a beautiful place it is to live in. It was originally a Hudson's
Bay post, and has gradually grown to be a place of some importance in the northern portion of the territory. Before the
construction of the Canadian Pacific Railway it was selected to
be the capital of the North-West Territories, and there the
Honourable Mr. Laird, the then Governor, resided. Mr. Laird
was most popular in his time, and exercised a beneficial influence in the country. At Battleford also a considerable force of
Mounted Police was maintained, and the North-West Council
annually met to conduct the local affairs of the territories.
There are some fine settlements in the neighbourhood, which
help to maintain the town, and intermingled with these settlements are a number of Indian Reserves, chief among which
are Poundmaker's and the Stonys, an offshoot of the Sioux.
The trade of these Indians, for the fur that they bring in, is

also valuable to the town. As in the case of Batoche, there is, some eighteen miles from Battleford, on the Saskatchewan River, a half-breed settlement, founded by some of those who had left their locations on the Red River to seek other districts in which to settle.

Upon the news of the Duck Lake fight, which was apparently the pre-arranged signal of those who intended to commit depredations and commence hostilities, warnings reached the settlers in the neighbourhood of Battleford that danger was imminent. I might here say that the Duck Lake fight was so precipitated that the Indians and half-breeds were taken unawares, and were themselves unprepared for the outbreak. Undoubtedly, had they the choosing of the time, they would have postponed hostilities for another month; because the snow was still on the ground, there was no feed for horses or ponies, and it was at a time when the natives find it difficult to move about or obtain provisions from the hunt. For that reason, the act of Major Crozier, in his attempt to secure the provisions and stores at Duck Lake, was a fortunate circumstance in the history of the campaign; as the Indians and half-breeds had neither time nor opportunity to assemble in a large body to meet the sudden onslaught of the advancing troops. Notwithstanding this, the various tribes of Indians under Big Bear at Fort Pitt, and under Poundmaker at Battleford, accepted the issue of the Duck Lake fight as a signal to commence hostilities. Battleford at the time was defended only by a small body of Mounted Police, under Inspector Morris, supported by a local corps, The Battleford Rifles, under Captain Nash. The only other troops within a reasonable distance were twenty-five Mounted Police, under Inspector Dickens at Fort Pitt, the next post, a hundred miles distant. The Indians under Poundmaker commenced hostilities by the murder of Payne, whose duty among others was to serve out to them the Government rations. A small party went demanding an advance of rations, and because they were refused, he was shot, after a scuffle, by Ickta. The same day a party of four went to Tremont, who owned a large herd of cattle in the neighbourhood. They persuaded one of their number to shoot him, and there and then, without a moment's warning, the poor fellow was wantonly murdered, with the intent, probably, to take his cattle. The Indians continued pillaging and destroying property in the neighbourhood, advancing as far as that part of the village of Battleford which lies on the south side of the Battle River, and separated from the town which stands on the plateau to the north, as before described. In this part of the village was the Hudson's Bay post and other buildings, which were all pillaged and destroyed. The settlers congregated in the town, and great anxiety was felt for their safety in their isolated and defenceless position. The Indians, however, did not venture to attack the town, which is surrounded by open ground.

It was to the relief of this place that Colonel Otter was despatched with his column, with all speed, from Swift Current. On the 13th of April, Otter's column marched to Saskatchewan Landing, about thirty miles distant. He was delayed here at the crossing of the river a couple of days, awaiting supplies and transport. The troops and provisions were all conveyed across with despatch by the steamer *Northcote*, which had been made ready to convey supplies to General Middleton's force at Clarke's Crossing.

On the 18th of April, all was in readiness, and at one o'clock p.m. Colonel Otter commenced his march northward, with two hundred waggons laden with forage, supplies and men. He took one of the old trails, along which had been conveyed the supplies and stores in days gone by. His march differed little from that of the General's column to Clarke's Crossing, except that by means of the transport he was enabled to cover distances in a shorter time. His column took but five and a half days to cover the intervening distance of one hundred and eighty miles!

The country through which the column passed is a vast unoccupied prairie, covered with luxuriant vegetation and furrowed paths, known as "buffalo runs," and is now awaiting the industry of the settler to fill it with happy, industrious and contented homes. About ninety miles from Battleford the Eagle River had to be crossed, and pioneers were sent forward to construct a bridge for the passage of the troops and transport. This was speedily executed. After crossing this river into the Eagle Hills, greater caution had to be observed, as it was the neighbourhood of Indian reserves, where the disaffected tribes were on the war-path. By five p.m. on the last day's march, viz., 23rd of April, they reached within three miles of Battleford, Colonel Otter deeming it prudent to camp for the night and reconnoitre before proceeding, as traces of the Indians were met with. He sent forward some scouts who discovered that a band of Indians were surrounding the heights opposite Battleford, and were setting fire to the buildings which they had left standing in their former raid. Judge Rouleau's house, only lately built at considerable expense, was among the number to fall a prey to the flames. There is no doubt that the Indians were aware of the approach of the troops, and took the opportunity before their arrival to commit these additional outrages in their defiant and wanton spirit. The scouts opened fire and surprised them in their fiendish work, causing them to jump upon their horses and flee. Colonel Otter sent forward Colonel Herchmer with his Mounted Police to intercept them, but without avail. On the following morning, camp was struck at daybreak, and shortly after the troops reached Battleford, to the great relief and joy of the inhabitants. One of the principal citizens, Mr. Smart, had only two nights before been shot dead while on patrol, by Indians secreted in a gully between the two rivers, open in that direction to an attack. This was on the 25th of April, the day after the battle of Fish Creek.

After a few days' rest, Colonel Otter, fired with a sense of the wrongs committed upon the settlers and the murders perpetrated, determined to go out and punish Poundmaker and his Indians for their villainous acts. He gallantly organized a portion of his force to make an attack on Poundmaker, who was known to be in force at Cut Knife Hill, where his braves and people were feasting on the spoils they had lately taken. Poundmaker had selected this place as his stronghold, to protect the families in case of an attack, which he no doubt felt must soon come. Cut Knife Hill had been the scene of a fight between the Crees and Sarcees some fifteen years before, when the former came off victorious; so that on the present occasion they were well acquainted with all the advantageous points of the position, and the plans of defence had been thoroughly discussed and explained by the chief to his braves. From close enquiries made by Colonel Otter, it had been ascertained as nearly as possible that Poundmaker had three hundred and fifty braves in this strong position. However, it was determined to make them give an account of themselves, and so on Friday, the 1st of May, about three o'clock in the afternoon, the column of teams, nearly forty in number, carrying the force with their supplies and ammunition, were ready, and they marched out from Battleford.

The attacking column was composed of the Mounted Police and scouts, under Colonel Herchmer, with Captain Neil in advance, and the line of march was by the south side of the Battle River, going west in the direction of Poundmaker's reserve. Following the Police were the artillery, with two seven-pounders and the gatling under Major Short, with Captains Rutherford and Farley, and Lieutenants Pelletier and Prower. After them came "C" School of Infantry, under Lieutenant Wadmore and Lieutenant Cassels, Q.O.R., the half company of Ottawa Sharpshooters, under Lieutenant Gray; No. 1 Company of the Queen's Own Rifles, under Captains Brown and Hughes and Lieutenant Brock; the Battleford Rifles, under Captain Nash and Lieutenants Marigold and Baker, brought up the rear with the ammunition and forage transport. The staff consisted of Lieutenant Sears, Brigade-Major; Captain Mutton, Q.O.R., Brigade-Quartermaster; F.W. Strange, Brigade-Surgeon.

The troops, numbering in all about three hundred, rode in the waggons, and with a parting cheer, the little column moved off, determined upon a surprise at daybreak. Otter's plan was a rapid advance, a surprise, an attack and a retirement to Battleford. The distance to Cut Knife Hill was thirty-five miles, and about seven o'clock in the evening half the journey was completed, when a halt was made to await the rising of the moon. A day's rations were served out, and the men whiled away the time until eleven o'clock, talking over their probable fate should an engagement take place. At half-past eleven the column resumed its march, the men making themselves as comfortable as they could in the short time they had before reaching the scene of the action. The country in no way differed from the general aspect of the North-West prairies, being occasionally dotted with clumps of trees. Dawn soon appeared, which in this northern latitude is at an early hour, and as the sun rose in all its glory, the troops came upon the spot where the Indians, according to the reports of the scouts, were supposed to be encamped, but which showed evident signs of having been lately vacated. They advanced through a hollow which led them into a deep gully, two hundred yards wide, densely wooded with poplar and willow underbrush, through which ran the Cut Knife Creek, which gives its name to the locality. This gully differed in no way from that of Fish Creek or any of the numerous gullies with which the prairie is indented. But, unlike Fish Creek, the enemy, instead of being found in the gully, had taken up a position about a mile beyond, no doubt intending, had they not been surprised, to have contested the advance of the troops across it. The Indians, not anticipating this hastily conceived attack, were asleep in their tepees, unmindful of the fate that was about to overtake them.

The position Poundmaker had now taken up had to be approached from Battleford through this gully. The trail along which the troops had to march to reach the summit was flanked, a few yards to the right, by a smaller gully, and on their left flank the Indians were enabled to find protection in another one, running into the Cut Knife valley. Colonel Otter's force was thus placed with a gully on the right flank, a gully on the left flank, and the deep valley of Cut Knife Creek, which he had just crossed, was in his rear. Had the Indians been in this position, silently awaiting the approach of the troops, Colonel Otter would have found himself drawn into an ambuscade Indians are known to be successful in planning. With the exception of one Indian, who was up and looking after the ponies, the encampment was wrapt in slumber. But after the first alarm they were promptly in action, though not before Colonel Otter had placed his men to the best advantage. As the column crossed the creek before mentioned, and arrived at the prairie, they saw, about a mile to the left, the Indian tepees which marked their encampment; and the advanced scouts, as they reached the top of the hill, were observed to take shelter, thus denoting the presence of the enemy in position. Colonel Herchmer dismounted his men, and with a detachment of Police, who had come in waggons, extended in skirmishing order and advanced to the top of the hill. Major Short, with the guns and the gatling, followed, the remainder of the column still wending its way across the gully.

The rattle of musketry and fusilade of the gatling were soon heard, and the startled Indians opened fire upon the advancing line. The guns and the gatling were brought promptly into action; and, as in the battle of Batoche, the Indians made a determined charge to try to capture them, dreading the destructiveness of their fire, which they were powerless to silence. They advanced, holding their blankets in front of them, running in a zig-zag manner to puzzle our riflemen. Major Short called for volunteers to protect his guns, and made a gallant charge upon the advancing enemy, which caused them to fall back. In this charge, Corporal Sleigh, of the Mounted Police, who had passed safely through the Fort Pitt danger, was killed, and Lieutenant Pelletier and Sergeants Gaffney and Ward were wounded. Major Short received a bullet through his forage cap, coolly remarking, "It's a new one, too!" This charge was made before the remainder of the column had got into position.

The Indians, who now came pouring out of their encampment, were not long in taking up the positions they had thoroughly studied in anticipation of a fight. The remainder of the column had now reached the prairie level, having left the horses and waggons in a sheltered spot half way up the slope they had first ascended. The Queen's Own were extended along the crest of the gully to the left, to protect that flank; "C"

Company and the Ottawa Sharpshooters were extended to protect the right flank; the Battleford Rifles protected the rear, while the Mounted Police and the artillery attacked the front. Not many minutes had elapsed before Colonel Otter perceived he was being attacked on all sides, the enemy, under cover of the gully through which the column had approached, having even gone round and menaced his rear. Now was required all the steadiness and valour of the men to withstand the wily Indians.

The enemy outnumbered our troops, and were fighting for the safety of their families, who were close to the field of battle, and for the protection of the herds of cattle and ponies, which they prized so much, all of which tended to make their onslaughts more vicious and determined. This, with their thrilling war-cries, intermingled with the roar of the guns and the rattle of small arms, made the scene a peculiarly impressive one, and likely to strike terror into the hearts of raw and inexperienced troops. But in all the encounters throughout this campaign the men showed no want of either steadiness or discipline, but always a soldierly bearing and a laudable determination to succeed.

As soon as one flank was attacked and repulsed, another flank came under fire and the rear was menaced. But the Indians gained no advantage and got as good as they gave, although the clever way in which they are accustomed to take cover made it difficult for our troops to get a fair shot at them.

Colonel Otter, an hour after the action opened, finding that his rear was in danger, instructed the Battleford Rifles to clear the enemy from that position – a work which they admirably performed.

The artillery supported the various corps, from time to time, by shelling the enemy, occasionally dropping a shell into their encampment, some fifteen hundred yards away. The firing throughout of the two batteries ("A" and "B"), the one with the General's column, and the other with Colonel Otter's, was at all times excellent. At Fish Creek, Captain Drury, with the

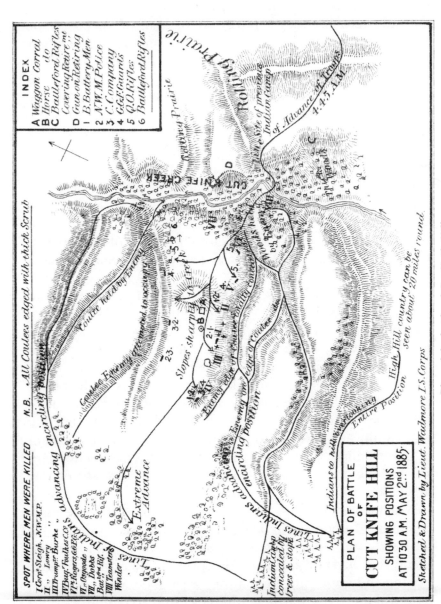

Plan of the battle of Cut Knife Hill

second shot, set fire to a house, at fifteen hundred yards' range, by throwing the shell through the thatched roof.

Until twelve o'clock the fight was maintained. As fast as the Indians were driven out of one position they made their appearance in another, and all efforts to dislodge them were without avail. Had Colonel Otter had a good support in his rear, there is no doubt he would have had sufficient confidence in his men to charge the enemy's encampment and take possession of it; but surrounded as he was by these precipitous gullies filled with savages, he did not change his original intention of coming out to make a reconnaissance, to punish the turbulent tribes, and then to retire. He maintained the fight, which may very properly be called an unequal one, until noon, when he determined to withdraw and return to Battleford with his tired troops. And now the most difficult movement of the day had to be performed, that of retreating across the deep gully with his entire force.

He ordered the scouts, the Battleford Rifles, and Captain Rutherford and his men, with one gun, to proceed through the gully and occupy the heights on the opposite side of Cut Knife Creek. By this movement the line of retirement could be commanded and protected. The waggons then made their way across the gully, the main body of the troops holding their position until they were safely across. And now began the difficult part – retiring the troops down the long incline leading to the gully and across it to the other side. It was a movement of great danger, but was well executed, the men retiring in skirmishing order, by alternate ranks, and holding the enemy in check.

When Colonel Otter's intentions were discovered, the Indians pressed upon the retiring troops with great vigour. But the steady and rapid firing maintained by every man restrained them: if it had not been for the precautionary measures in placing the guns and the gatling in so good a position, it is doubtful if the retirement could have been accomplished with so little loss of life. The guns dropped their shells into the advancing Indians, and the gatling swept the face of the hill down which they were following our troops, and soon the whole column was enabled to form upon the prairie level, to partake of a meagre meal and enjoy a short rest before returning to Battleford.

In summing up the casualties, it was found that there were eight dead and thirteen wounded, who were cared for by Brigade-Surgeon Strange, I.S.C., and Surgeon Lesslie, Q.O.R. The dead were all taken off the field, with the exception of Private Osgood of the Ottawa Sharpshooters, who was missing. A party was sent back for him, which met the ambulance corps with a body they said was Osgood's; this was not found to be incorrect until too late to again seek for it. Osgood, when shot, had, it appears, fallen in a coulée, and thus escaped the notice of those near him.

To praise too highly the conduct of the officers and men during the engagement is an impossibility, yet to underrate the strength of the Indians in their peculiar mode of warfare, on their own ground, I certainly think, is folly. While they have not the courage to face a foe in the open, their ability to protect themselves and to pick off their opponents from behind cover is certainly superior to ours. They are brought up to this from their youth, gaining their livelihood by stalking and shooting the game of the country.

After a short rest the column resumed its march and returned to Battleford, reaching there at ten o'clock at night, after an absence of thirty hours. Colonel Otter remained in Battleford until the arrival of General Middleton on the 25th of May, acting entirely on the defensive.

While Colonel Otter apparently acted upon his own responsibility in making his attack upon Poundmaker, the circumstances by which he was surrounded must be taken into consideration. On his arrival at Battleford, he found that several murders had been committed, settlers' property had been destroyed, and the owners were obliged to flee to Battleford for safety. A portion of Battleford itself was also burned and pillaged. These doings, no doubt, moved him to attempt to inflict some punishment upon Poundmaker's Indians. Moreover, an amalgamation between Big Bear's band (which had so recently captured Fort Pitt) and Poundmaker was to be feared, and Colonel Otter deemed it advisable for the safety of the country to inflict a blow on Poundmaker before this junction was effected. The reports that Big Bear's runners brought back to their chief about the fighting that had taken place and the loss the Indians had suffered at the battle of Cut Knife, no doubt led Big Bear and his tribe to feel that they were safer in the neighbourhood of Fort Pitt, and no junction was afterwards attempted. On the whole, then, this attack, it must be said, was well timed, and pluckily executed.

Poundmaker's attitude at this period may be gathered from the following letter to Riel from his camp, which throws considerable light upon Poundmaker's proceedings, and taken in connection with Colonel Otter's prompt action, is of interest here:

Cut Knife Hill,

April 29, 1885.

I want to hear news of the progress of God's work. If any event has occurred since your messenger came away, let me know of it. Tell me the date when the Americans will reach the Canadian Pacific Railway. Tell me all the news that you have heard from all the places where your work is in progress. Big Bear has finished his work. He has taken Fort Pitt. "If you want me to come to you, let me know at once," he said, "I will be four days on the road." Those who have gone to him will sleep twice on the road. They took twenty prisoners, including the master at Fort Pitt; they killed eleven men, including the agent, two priests and six white men. We are camped on the Creek, just below Cut Knife Hill, waiting Big Bear. The Blackfeet killed sixty Police at the Elbow. The half-breed who interpreted for the Police having survived the fight, though wounded, brought the news here. Here we have killed six white men. We have not taken the barracks yet, but this is the only entire building in Battleford. All the cattle and horses in the vicinity we have taken. We have lost one man, Nez Percé, killed, he being alone, and one wounded. Some soldiers have come from Swift Current, but we do not know the number. We have here guns and rifles of all sorts, but the ammunition for them is short. If it be possible we want you to send us ammunition of various kinds; we are weak only for want of that. You sent word that you would come to Battleford when you had finished your work at Duck Lake. We wait still for you, as we are unable to take the fort without help. If you send us news send only one messenger. We are impatient to reach you. It would give us courage as much to see you and make us work more heartily. Up to the present everything has gone well with us, but we are constantly expecting the soldiers to visit us here. We trust that God will be as kind to us in the future as in the past. We, the undersigned, send greeting to you all.

(Signed) Poundmaker,
Opin-o-Way-Win,
Met-tay-way-is,
Mus-sin-ass,
Pee-yay-chew.

When this reaches you, send us news immediately as we are anxious to hear the news. *If you send us news, send us as many men as possible.*

XIV

GENERAL STRANGE'S COLUMN

W e must now follow the fortunes of the third column, which was sent into the interior under General Strange, an old army officer. General Strange organized his forces at Calgary, and was directed to proceed to Edmonton, two hundred miles north of Calgary, and three hundred miles to the west of Battleford, on the North Saskatchewan. His force was composed of the 65th of Montreal, under Colonel Ouimet, three hundred and fifty strong; fifty-two Mounted Police, under Major Steele; forty-two scouts, under Major Hatton; twenty-five Mounted Police, under Captain Oswald; the Edmonton Volunteers; the Winnipeg Light Infantry, three hundred strong, under Colonel Osborne Smith, C.M.G.; and forty-six scouts under Major Perry, besides one gun. On his personal staff was Major Dale, who acted as Brigade-Major. The General had also attached to his staff the Reverend Canon McKay, of the Church of England, and the Reverend Mr. McDougall, a Methodist missionary, both of whom had resided a long time among the Indians in the Calgary and Edmonton districts, and knew the country well. General Strange placed great reliance on these local clergymen, and they became active assistants in the conduct of the column.

On the 20th of April General Strange moved out of Calgary for Edmonton, with Major Steel's scouts and the right wing of the 65th Battalion, under the command of Colonel Hughes. The left wing left on the 23rd with Major Hatton's corps, and was followed a day or two after by the Winnipeg Light Infantry, under Colonel Osborne Smith, with some Mounted Police, under Major Perry. Both detachments crossed the Bow River at the Government Ford, and arrived at Edmonton on the 2nd and 5th of May respectively. Edmonton is the centre of a prosperous settlement, and is surrounded by a number of Indian reserves.

General Strange stationed half a company of the 65th, under Lieutenant Normandeau, at Red Deer Crossing, and the other half, under Captain Ettieh, at the Government Ford about forty miles from Edmonton. Captain Ostell's company was sent to the Hudson's Bay post at Battle River, Colonel Ouimet remaining at Edmonton, his headquarters. The remainder of the 65th, under Colonel Hughes, with Colonel Smith's battalion and the mounted men, went to Victoria on their way to Fort Pitt, where they were delayed for some time, not leaving again until the 21st of May. They reached Moose Hill Creek on the 24th, and Fort Pitt on the 25th instant. General Strange had scows built to utilize the navigation and save his transport. They conveyed the 65th to Fort Pitt, keeping up communication with the remainder of the column, which marched by the trail. But we pause first to relate what occurred at Fort Pitt previous to this date, and to describe the most tragic incident of Riel's rebellion – the Frog Lake Massacre.

Frog Lake is a beautiful sheet of water, some ten miles north of the Saskatchewan and thirty miles from Fort Pitt. At this place a Hudson's Bay post and Roman Catholic mission is established, and it is the headquarters of an Indian agency. It is surrounded by numerous tribes of Indians, many of whom live there on their reserves and trade at Fort Pitt. Among the chiefs of these tribes, the most conspicuous was Big Bear, and his band was the most troublesome the Indian agents had to control. During the winter Corporal Sleigh with five constables was stationed at Frog Lake by Inspector Dickens, at the request of Mr. Quinn, the Indian agent. After news had been received of the engagement at Duck Lake, Inspector Dickens wrote to Quinn at Frog Lake, enquiring as to the state of the Indians there. He answered that the Indians on the reserves were quite peaceably inclined, that he could keep Big Bear quiet, and did not anticipate any trouble. As Inspector Dickens did not place much confidence in Big Bear and his band, he wrote to Quinn pointing out that it would be better that the Police should be all together; that in the event of an Indian rising the few Police at Frog Lake would all be massacred. He added that all the whites had better come into Fort Pitt, or if help were required, he would go out to them. Quinn and Delaney determined to remain at their posts, and the other whites elected to stay with them. Quinn ordered Corporal Sleigh to return to Fort Pitt with his men. Sleigh refused to leave without the ladies, but Quinn again ordered him to leave, saying that he would explain the matter to Mr. Dickens. Sleigh came in with his men and brought a letter from Quinn, in which he said that the presence of a few policemen only served to irritate the Indians, who had no animosity to the Indian Department officials, but only disliked the Police. He also asked Mr. Dickens not to send policemen as messengers, but to make use of the Hudson Bay Company's Indians and half-breeds. He also wrote that he would come in on the 2nd of April to see Mr. Dickens.

For some time Big Bear refused to take treaty, and had not yet selected a reserve, which the Government was anxious to locate him on in this district. It is worthy of remark here that when Lieutenant-Governor Morris first negotiated a treaty with Big Bear, one of the conditions the chief fought for was that none of his tribe should be hanged. Mr. Morris refused to entertain such a question, pointing out that if a white man should kill an Indian he would be hanged, and that if an Indian committed a murder he would have to suffer the same punishment. A number of the Indians who were hanged belonged to Big Bear's band. Big Bear had several times before this given the Mounted Police trouble, and he and his braves were the leaders of the rebellion at this point. When the news reached them of the Duck Lake fight, and that hostilities had commenced, they immediately went on the war-path, in accordance with the programme doubtless arranged by Big

Bear on his visit to Riel a few months before. In true Indian fashion his braves commenced by making excessive demands for rations, supplies and ammunition. When these demands were made, the people were taken as much by surprise as were those in the other parts of the country, for Quinn, the resident Indian agent, had sent down word only a few days before that everything was quiet and peaceable. But with a rapidity that could not be foreseen, the Indians lost not a moment in commencing trouble. A few who were in the secret were anxious to save some of the whites who had befriended them, and gave warning in time to enable them to leave for Fort Pitt. Mr. and Mrs. Gowanlock were apprised, and came up to the mission to the home of Delaney, the farm instructor, where they spent a few days, and where they were rudely taken prisoner by the Indians.

At daylight on the morning of the 2nd of April, the Indians became very excited, and visited the Hudson's Bay store, demanding provisions from Mr. Simpson. They also visited Mr. Quinn's with a like demand, and from taking stores they got to taking prisoners. It was the day before Good Friday, and the Reverend Fathers Farfard and Marchand were holding service in the church, where the people were assembled at the early morning service. All were rudely disturbed by the Indians. Father Farfard, seeing that mischief was brewing, warned the Indians against committing excesses, and the people, after leaving church, went to Delaney's house. The Indians followed and compelled them to leave there and go to their camp. While taking them to camp they, in the most wanton and cruel manner, shot down several, commencing with the Indian agent, Quinn. Mr. and Mrs. Gowanlock were walking together, and the former was shot, falling mortally wounded into his wife's arms. Delaney, who was also with his wife, was shot in like manner. The two courageous priests, seeing what was going on, interfered to try to save life, but both fell victims, Father Farfard being shot while leaning over the wounded Delaney, administering the last rites to him. Father Marchand was killed at the same time, and before the day was out, nine unfortunate people were massacred. The remainder of the party, with the tenderly reared ladies, were marched off as prisoners by these miscreants, the captive ladies fearing a worse fate.

Mr. Cameron was an eye-witness of the murderous scene; the following is an account of it:

Cameron had just finished breakfast and gone to the store, when Miserable Man entered with an order from Quinn, probably the last writing he ever penned. It read as follows:

"Dear Cameron, – Please give Miserable Man one blanket."

It was signed by Quinn.

Cameron said: "I have no blankets." Miserable Man looked hard at him but said nothing.

Yellow Bear said: "Don't you see he has no blankets." "Well," said Miserable Man, "I will take something else," and he took four or five dollars' worth of odds and ends. Just as they finished trading they heard the first shot. Miserable Man turned and rushed out. Cameron heard some one calling "Stop! stop!" This was Big Bear, who was in the Hudson's Bay Company's store, talking to Mr. Simpson. As Cameron went out of the store he locked the door, and while he was doing this an Indian ran up and said, "If you speak twice you are a dead man. One man spoke twice already and he is dead." This man, Cameron soon learned, was Quinn, who had been standing with Charles Gouin, the half-breed carpenter, in front of Pritchard's house.

Travelling Spirit said to Quinn, "You have a hard head. When you say no you mean no, and stick to it. Now, if you love your life, you will do as I say." "Why should I go?" said he. "Never mind," Quinn said quietly, "I will stay here." Travelling Spirit then levelled his gun at Quinn's head, saying, "I tell you go," and shot him dead. Gouin, who was an American half-breed, was shot by The Worm immediately after, on the road to the Indian Camp, a short distance from Pritchard's house.

Cameron asked Yellow Bear what all this meant. Yellow Bear caught him by the hand and said, "Come this way." Then seeing Mrs. Simpson about to leave her house, he said, "Go with her and leave here." Cameron walked away with Mrs. Simpson. When they had got a short distance from the house she stopped and called Mr. Cameron's attention to the priests, who were standing about a hundred yards away, expostulating with some Indians who were loading their guns. Delaney was close by. Suddenly the Indians raised their guns and rushed at Delaney. Father Farfard dashed up and placed himself in front of the menacing Indians, but was overpowered by numbers and thrown down, and Bare Neck shot Delaney, and then with the other barrel fired at the priests. Father Farfard and Delaney were badly wounded, and as they lay writhing, Man-Who-Wins walked up and fired at them, killing both.

Father Marchand was meanwhile attempting to keep the Indians from going after the women. When he saw that Father Farfard had been killed he attempted to push his way through the crowd of Indians to reach the body, but they resisted. He was a wiry man and fought hard. Travelling Spirit, however, rushed up and shot him in the chest and head, and he fell dead. In the rush that followed a moment after this, Gowanlock was killed by The Worm. Gilchrist and Dill were together, and Little Bear, who had previously killed Williscroft, fired on them. Gilchrist fell immediately, but Dill was not hurt, and started to run, but the Indians chased him on horseback, and he was finally killed by Man-Talking-to-Another. Cameron was horror-struck on seeing the killing of the priests and Delaney, but of course he could do nothing to save them.

Of all the disasters caused by this wicked rebellion, this was the most heart-rending. This cowardly tribe dignified the massacre by the title of a battle, as was disclosed in a letter sent to Lac la Biche to excite the half-breeds and Indians there to do likewise. They said they had had a glorious battle, thirteen were killed and not one of their number hurt. This disaster was another shock to the people of Canada, whose friends had been thus cruelly murdered, and it filled the minds of the little garrison at Fort Pitt with anxiety. Pitt, thirty miles distant, was defended by only twenty-five Mounted Police, under Inspector Dickens, a son of the celebrated novelist, and in their isolated position at that season of the year, before the ice had left the river, they had no means of escape. They did not know the moment these tribes would make their appearance before them. They, however, vigorously set to work to build two scows to float themselves away from the threatening danger the moment the river should open, and tried to put the fort, which was only a fort in name, in a better state of defence. They did not know the extent of the murders that had been committed, and anxiety for so many of their friends intensified their own. Their means of communication with the outside world was entirely cut off, so they had nothing to rely upon but their own exertions.

The little garrison was strengthened by the arrival of Mann, the farm instructor, and by the Reverend Mr. Quinney, the Church of England missionary, whose headquarters were at Onion Lake, not far from Frog Lake. They had received warning of approaching danger in a letter to Mr. Mann, and had come to Fort Pitt.

Mr. Quinn, the Indian agent, had confidence in these Indians, and had requested Mann, the instructor, to send some of them up to Big Bear on a council of peace, not, however, in time to prevent the attack. At daylight on the morning of the 3rd of April, Mann's house was invaded by Indians who brought news of the Frog Lake massacre, and some of them commenced to pillage his house. They counselled Mr. Quinney to leave with his wife, telling him of the departure of Mr. Mann with his family; in fact, Chief Cut Arm, with four of his men, escorted them to within sight of Fort Pitt, lending the missionary his own horse and buckboard, which the Indians had already appropriated for their own use, upon his promising to return it, and they then left to join Big Bear.

After the excitement of the massacre, the thirst for blood seemed to be appeased; for no more life was taken. The unfortunate ladies, who suffered such grief and terror in all this cruelty, were now forced to think of themselves and their safety, and had little time to indulge their grief. There were fortunately some kind-hearted half-breed prisoners with them, viz.: Pritchard, Adolphus Nolin, Peter Blondin, and André Nault. Pritchard's first thought was for the ladies; and in Indian fashion he purchased Mrs. Gowanlock from the Indian who had her in charge, giving one of his horses for her, and brought her to his own tent to camp with his family. He then went to the Indian who had Mrs. Delaney and offered to purchase her. The Indian replied, "I will take two good horses." Pritchard had only one good horse and one poor one left, and begged him to take them, but the man refused. So Pritchard told Nolin of his difficulty, and Nolin gave up his horse, and thus Pritchard was enabled to bring two good horses to the Indian, and took Mrs. Delaney away to stay with Mrs. Gowanlock, through the term of their imprisonment; both were carefully looked after by this humane half-breed and his family. By his promptitude and humanity he saved these ladies from harm. He and Panbrun, another half-breed prisoner, afterwards acted for me as guides for a short time. I found them to be trusty, deserving men, and I hope that they will be rewarded.

The Indians now gave themselves up to revelry and feasting upon the supplies and stores they had stolen. They burnt up the little village at Frog Lake, and threw the dead bodies into the cellars to cover up their deeds, mutilating one or two of them. When again getting short of provisions, they turned their steps towards the anxious little garrison, who, since they heard of the massacre, were in daily dread of an attack. It so happened that on the morning of the day they arrived, three scouts had left the fort to ascertain the whereabouts of the Indians, and while they were away, the Indians made their appearance by another trail.

The Hudson's Bay post, or Fort Pitt, as it is called, is situated in a valley of the Saskatchewan, close to the river bank. At this point, looking to the north, one sees a gradual ascent leading to a bench of the prairie, the brow of this bench being some six hundred yards off. It was beyond this brow that the Indians encamped, keeping themselves out of sight, and out of range of the rifles of the Police. From here Big Bear sent in a demand to the garrison to surrender, or, as he pertinently put it, "I cannot control my braves, so you had better surrender," which, of course, was repudiated by Inspector Dickens. At the same time Big Bear wrote a pathetic note to Mr. Maclean, asking him to put aside ten blankets for him, saying that he was old, and wanted to make sure of his share, for when the pillage commenced his young men would get everything. On his trial, it came out that this chief was treated by his people with scant consideration for his comfort or respect for his orders.

The Indians remained in position, showing no signs of leaving, and Mr. Maclean, the Hudson's Bay officer in charge of Fort Pitt, who has a large experience of the Indian character, felt no anxiety or fear in going out to speak to them. On the following morning he went to hold a parley on the brow of the hill, within sight of the fort. The object of this parley was to gain time, to allow the three scouts who were out to return in safety; Maclean himself returned to the fort. After dinner he went out once more, and this time the Indians persuaded him to go to their camp, which was out of sight of the fort. He did not like to refuse, lest it should show a want of confidence in them. He was taken to their camp to hold a council; and in pointing out to the Indians the danger they were incurring, and that the Government would surely punish them, a half-breed and an Indian jumped up and stood one on each side of him, and pointing their guns said, "We do not want to hear anything about the Government; that is not what we came to talk about," and forthwith made him a prisoner.

Mr. Maclean now entered into negotiations with them for the safety of the garrison; and Big Bear guaranteed that if the fort were given up to them, he would protect their families and take care of them. Maclean wrote a letter to his wife, telling her to bring the family and join him, and advising the others to do the same. He also warned the Police to leave, as the Indians were going to burn Fort Pitt that night.

While these negotiations were going on, the three scouts, Quinn (related to the Indian agent who was killed), Cowan, and Loasby, of the Police, who had been out to reconnoitre, returned and found the Indians encamped between them and the fort. Cowan and Loasby made a dash for the fort, galloping through the Indian encampment. Poor Cowan's horse was shot, and he at once fell victim, being killed after he was wounded by Louis Mongrain. Loasby was more fortunate; he got through the encampment, but when just at the brow of the hill his horse was shot. He jumped up and ran for it, but within about three hundred yards of the fort, he was shot down, receiving two severe wounds. The Indian who shot him ran up and took his revolver and rifle, thinking he was dead. The squaws and boys were going to take his body, but were fired upon by the Police from the fort, and to the joy of the garrison Loasby got up, and walked in. Quinn, the third scout, who was more accustomed to care for himself, instead of attempting to go through the encampment galloped off to the right, and secreted himself under the river bank about a mile away, and at night came up to join his comrades, but to his dismay, the fort was filled with Indians. An Indian from the upper story saw him, and ran down to get his rifle, but Quinn made good his retreat. He was seen and followed by a friendly Indian, who tracked him through the snow to his hiding-place, and brought him to camp under his protection, where he remained a prisoner with the rest.

The diary of Corporal R.B. Sleigh, North-West Mounted Police, who escaped from this difficulty only to be shot a short time after, gallantly fighting at the battle of Cut Knife, is interesting as an authentic record:

April 2. – Constable Roby left with train for Onion Lake, brought back lumber. Indians terribly excited out there. Mr. Mann, farm instructor, with wife and family, arrived at one a.m., with report all whites killed at Frog Lake. Assembled at twelve p.m. All hands working all night, blocking up windows and making loop-holes in the buildings. Double picket put on.

April 3. – Good Friday. Henry Quinn in from Frog Lake, reported all whites shot. They were led out for execution, when he ran for his life and managed to escape; poor fellow played out and showed good grit. The Indians the day before said they were going to remain quiet, and early next morning (Thursday) took all whites prisoners. Mr. and Mrs. Quinney in from Onion Lake. An Indian brought them in. All their goods and chattels stolen. The two priests, Pères Farfard and Marchand, were first beaten and then shot. Everybody busy pulling down outside buildings, and barricading the fort.

April 4. – Johnnie Saskatchewan in from Battleford with despatches. Indians down there turning loose, and several whites killed. Reported Little Poplar and nine lodges twenty-five miles off, and coming this way. Johnnie left again for Battleford with despatches. Men busy all day.

April 5. – Sunday. Men on fatigue most of the day. Mr. Quinney (Episcopal clergyman) held short service in barracks. Indians heard shouting on hill during night. Shots fired.

April 6. – Nothing exciting.

April 7. – Stockade being erected. Indians at Frog Lake looted all the stores at that place, also the barracks on the 2nd instant. Misses Maclean show great courage, and each one, rifle in hand, stands at a loop-hole. The men work like horses, and are cheerful. All civilians sworn in and armed. Bastion put up on left front of fort. Sentries put on in each house, four hours on duty.

April 9. – Another bastion put up near orderly-room corner.

April 14. – No relief, and things look blue. Everybody in good spirits. H. Quinn, D. Cowan, and C. Loasby, with three saddle horses, went out scouting to Frog Lake. Body of Indians at top of hill, 800 yards from fort. Two hundred and fifty Indians armed and mounted. Had Dufresne, sr., and Haplin, Hudson's Bay Company, prisoners. Big Bear sent letter down. Sent word for everybody to evacuate fort, and give up arms. Doors barricaded, and men in places. Indians had big war-dance on hill. Indians skulking through woods in every direction. Mr. Maclean, of Hudson's Bay Company, had parley with them on hill. Double sentries in barracks. Two hundred and fifty Indians on war-path surround us.

April 15. – Mr. Maclean at noon went on hill to parley. Three scouts came galloping through towards Pitt. Constable Cowan shot dead, Loasby badly wounded and horse killed. Shots fired from loop-holes; two Indians killed. Quinn missing, and two wounded. Mr. Maclean and François Dufresne taken prisoners. Mr. Maclean wrote down to his wife to come out and give herself up, and all the Hudson's Bay Company's employees to do the same. The Hudson's Bay employees, twenty-two in number, gave themselves up to Big Bear. Impossible to hold fort now, so we had to gracefully retire across the river in scow, and camped for night, not forgetting to bring colours along. Nearly swamped crossing, river being rough, and scow leaking badly. General idea prevailing that we would be attacked going down river. Took Loasby along. Thus ended the siege of Fort Pitt.

April 16. – Up at 4:30, after passing a wretched night. Snowing fast and very windy. Moving slow. Several men frost-bitten. Clothing frozen on our backs. Had some narrow escapes in ice jams. Camped at nine for dinner. Resumed trip at noon.

April 18. – Started at seven a.m. Day dull and cold. Much ice running.

April 19. – Sunday. Left Slap Jack Island at 7:13 a.m. Ran for five hours. Camped on Beaver Island, number 35. Ran on three hours, and camped on Pine Island for night.

April 20. – Here all day. Barricaded the scow. Inspected arms. Rough-looking parade. Wounded man better.

April 21. – Left island at seven a.m. Eleven a.m. hailed interpreter, Joseph Alexander, and two policemen on south bank. They had despatches for us. They reported Battleford safe, and troops expected daily. Ran all day, and stopped on Small Island for the night. River falling rapidly. Struck on sand-bars. All slept on board scow. Two men on picket.

April 22. – Started at 5:45 a.m., and reached Battleford at nine a.m. Garrison turned out and presented arms. Police band played us into fort. Enthusiastic greeting. Ladies gave us a grand dinner.

Mr. Maclean having now become a prisoner, his family, with the remainder of the people in the fort, who were all more or less acquainted with the Indians in their trading with them, determined, on the receipt of his letter, to go to join him. They resolved to throw themselves upon the mercy of Big Bear. Mann, it appears, had not been included in the surrender, and dreading the journey in the scow for his young family, sent word to Mr. Maclean that he too wished to take his chances; and thus the second move in Big Bear's proceedings was successful.

Inspector Dickens, having no further reason to protect the fort, which was now rendered more difficult, on account of the number of prisoners in the hands of Big Bear, determined upon retreating to Battleford in the scow. Taking Loasby, their wounded comrade, the Police moved across the river that night and camped on the opposite shore. The next morning they all set out for Battleford in the midst of ice, which was running in the river. The trip was most dangerous; but the little force successfully floated down in the cold and storm, reaching Battleford providentially without a mishap, in six days.

Mr. Maclean now did his best to conciliate the Indians. To meet Big Bear's views, he suggested that he should go down to deal out the stores in Fort Pitt, so that all might get an equal share; and as he further urged, it would have the appearance of their having been given, instead of being stolen, which would be in the Indians' favour. Mr. Maclean had twenty thousand dollars' worth of fur, and he hoped, by this stratagem, to save it by giving up the provisions. He also hoped to be able, by aid of his memory, to chalk down against individuals whatever was taken, for a future reckoning. This proposition struck the Indians as being a very equitable one, and would have been accepted; but some of the squaws, more eager than the rest to secure their share, had slipped down, under the cover of dusk, and were helping themselves, so that when it became known, there was a general rush, and the pillage and destruction that ensued was a sight to witness. Provisions were wasted most shamefully, and destruction was rampant. The prisoners looked on in dismay.

Big Bear and his tribes, having secured the booty, now moved about from one point to another, and being well stocked with provisions, they took it leisurely and did not move far. He sent emissaries down to Poundmaker, who arrived just after the battle of Cut Knife, and came back, describing what had occurred there, telling about the tepees they had seen, full of dead bodies, which Poundmaker had left in his camp at Cut Knife Creek. Poundmaker, in the meantime, had sent word to Big Bear to come down to join him, but Big Bear and his councillors thought they were well off where they were, and made no attempt to move from their own neighbourhood.

It is wonderful how these prisoners, thirty in number, most of them tender children, could have been dragged about from camp to camp, between the 16th of April and the 28th of May, without rousing the evil spirit of some of the Indians. The credit of this is entirely due to some friendly tribes of Wood Crees, who were not in sympathy with Big Bear, but who had been forced to join him or suffer themselves. Their presence was most opportune for the safety of the unfortunate prisoners. They were shrewd enough to know that by befriending them, it would tell in their favour when the day of reckoning came, and they were prepared to fight in their defence, should any attempt be made to harm them. I might here observe, that there is a difference between the Indians who gain their livelihood in the woods, and those who gain their livelihood on the plains. In our chase after Big Bear, we were struck with the beautiful reserves and the great resources at the disposal of these Wood Indians – lakes teeming with fish, woods filled with the most valuable fur and wild fowl and game of the greatest variety, with ample timber for building purposes and for fuel, and pasture for cattle, of which they had a herd. All these advantages, undoubtedly, made the Indians value the peacefulness of their homes much more highly than the Plains Indians, who wander far and wide on the boundless prairie, and who had been deprived of their main source of profit, support, and excitement, by the disappearance of the buffalo. To the friendly aid of these Wood Crees, who were equal in number to those from the Plains, Mr. Maclean attributes the safety of his people, and their ultimate release.

Until the appearance of General Strange's column, these Indians had received no check, and were no doubt lulled to a sense of security. On the 25th of April they camped in a pretty glade, a short distance from a strong position called Frenchman's Butte, which is one of those high hills, broken by precipitous gullies, on the side of the valley of the Little Red Deer River, and resembling the position of Cut Knife Hill. Here the Indians determined to hold a thirst or sundance, and for the purpose they put up a huge lodge, about a hundred feet in diameter, big enough to hold a respectably-sized circus audience. It was made of poles lashed together with shagannappi, with a railing across one side, where the chief men witnessed the performance and the initiation of the braves. The favourite mode of initiation is to make two parallel incisions, on each breast, or in the back, and then to work a hole beneath each with the fingers. To this is attached, after the manner of a seton, a lariat, or more familiarly, a lasso. The ends are then attached to the centre pole of the lodge, or held by others, and the brave commences his dance to the monotonous beat of the tom-tom, at the full stretch of the shagannappi, dancing wildly until from the excitement of the music and ecstasy of initiation he causes the flesh to give way, and so proves himself to be a brave. When the incisions are in the back, a buffalo or deer's head is attached, and the brave dances till it is torn off.

However, before these ceremonies had got well under way, they were rudely disturbed by the information that the Police were near, and such a skedaddling and skurrying as followed, the prisoners say, it is impossible to describe. But it raised an altogether opposite feeling in the breasts of the captives, as they felt that liberation was now close at hand. The prisoners and the families were at once moved off across the valley of the Little Red Deer, taking up a position in the gully leading into it on the opposite side, where the Indians spent the night in making rifle-pits, and throwing up defences for the morrow's battle. Some of the prisoners now determined to break away from their durance vile. Pritchard, with the ladies and a few other prisoners, besides a large party of half-breeds, made secret arrangements to take advantage of the first opportunity to gain their liberty. Mr. and Mrs. Quinney, with Mr. Cameron and a few others, had also arranged to slip off, as soon as the Indians were so engaged that they would not be missed. So the events of the morrow were awaited with anxiety, and hope. At daylight on the morning of the 28th, the main occupants of the camp were sent on, about four miles into the interior, to get out of the way. The prisoners heard the booming of the cannon and the volleys of musketry during the morning, and awaited anxiously the result; but the Indians came rushing into camp, abandoning their provisions, in fact abandoning everything, and fled north, carrying their prisoners with them. Pritchard's party, and the Reverend Mr. Quinney's party, were determined to make good their escape, but did not succeed until the following Monday, the day General Strange arrived on the scene.

The hardships the prisoners were forced to undergo can

hardly be imagined, but their joy at being released made them soon forget the past. They brought news of the safety of all the prisoners, about whom so much anxiety had been felt, and gave a detailed account of their adventures.

We must now transfer ourselves to General Strange's column. General Strange arrived at Fort Pitt on the 25th of May, having passed Frog Lake, the scene of the massacre, where he buried the dead he found there. Fort Pitt was still burning, having been lately set on fire; and on the evening of the 26th, Major Steele, preparatory to crossing the river, which General Strange purposed doing, was sent out scouting towards Onion Lake, to ascertain if the Indians were in the neighbourhood. At dawn, when about five miles east of Fort Pitt, Major Steele came across a few Indians, who fired upon his party, without doing any damage. He returned the fire, killing an Indian, who was recognized afterwards to be a chief from Saddle Lake. His name was Mamanook. He reported the result of his reconnaissance to General Strange, who now knew that Big Bear could not be far off, and he determined to advance that day. He marched, with one hundred and seventy-five men of Colonel Smith's battalion, the Mounted Police, the scouts, and the Alberta Mounted Rifles, under the command of Majors Steele and Hatton – about three hundred in all. He took with him a nine-pounder. About a hundred of the 65th, under Colonel Hughes, descended the river in a scow for some ten miles, leaving Captain Giroux with his company of the 65th to defend Fort Pitt. About mid-day, some Indians were encountered ten miles down the river. The 65th were now ordered to leave the scow to reinforce the General. This they promptly did, leaving behind them their blankets, greatcoats and everything, excepting their ammunition, which they carried with them, till they reached a waggon to load it on. A number of Indians now showed themselves and opened fire, shouting, with their usual bravado to come on, but they disappeared under the fire of the nine-pounder and upon the advance of the troops. The column advanced some two miles farther, and bivouacked for the night, where they were joined by the 65th, who had brought with them neither blanket nor greatcoat, and had to bivouac as best they could. The waggons arrived about eight o'clock in the evening. They again marched at daybreak in an easterly direction. The Police and scouts deployed as skirmishers, the 65th forming the advance guard about twenty yards behind, then followed the nine-pounder, and the waggons and the Winnipeg Light Infantry as rear guard.

About two miles farther on, they came upon the place where the Indians had been so hurriedly disturbed, in the thirst dance before described, which took place, it is supposed, the previous afternoon. Passing this, the column advanced about a mile farther to the edge of a deep ravine, which was the valley of the Little Red Deer River. This river winds through the bottom of a marshy valley, covered in places with willow scrub. Some Indians could be seen off to the left, retreating with their carts. The nine-pounder was brought to bear, and dropped a shell in their midst, which was answered by a volley of bullets from the ridge on the opposite side of the valley, at five or six hundred yards' range. The Police and scouts now advanced into the valley, in skirmishing order, followed by the 65th, and Colonel Smith's battalion, covered by the nine-pounder, which kept up a steady fire on the opposite ridge, where the Indians were in force. For about three hours this position was maintained, the troops receiving, and answering, the fire of the enemy.

Major Steele was now sent off to make a reconnaissance to the left, and Major Hatton to the right. They returned and reported the hills and gullies to be swarming with Indians, and General Strange feeling that with so small a force and no supports nearer than Battleford, it was useless to go on, determined to retire and await reinforcements. So the troops were withdrawn and retired up the hill, covered by the Winnipeg Light Infantry.

General Strange retired to Fort Pitt, arriving there on the following day. He at once sent two men off in a canoe down the river, to report the engagement to General Middleton.

In this engagement the troops behaved admirably, and not

only would they have held their own all day, but were anxious to advance. General Strange, however, had brought his waggons and transport on to the scene of action, and remembering he had no supports, he became cautious, and ordered a retirement, without having inflicted that chastisement on Big Bear's tribe which they so richly deserved. When he advanced once more the wily Indian was well away through the swamps and woods to the north. On the 2nd of June General Strange marched his column to the Red Deer, and once more took up a position near the scene of the late engagement.

XV

THE PURSUIT OF BIG BEAR

Prince Albert is a stirring place, with a number of important interests, including good educational facilities. It is situated on the north branch of the Saskatchewan River, and is a point of call for steamboats plying between Lake Winnipeg and the west. The surrounding country is very picturesque; the land is of excellent quality, and well settled. The advantages of the district are evident, from having drawn so large a population from the outer world, including men of wealth, birth and education, to find a field for their industry in so remote a region. There had been a good deal of discontent among the people, which caused some of them to mix themselves up with Riel. This discontent arose chiefly from the want of railway facilities and from continued isolation from the markets of the world. The people began to be impatient, looking year after year for the long-expected railway facilities so necessary to their material prosperity, and their discontent found vent in agitation. Beyond a few turbulent spirits, however, there is not a more loyal or more industrious class in the country.

Our two days in Prince Albert were much enjoyed by the troops, but the General was impatient to be off, to join Colonel Otter at Battleford, and to push on to Fort Pitt and complete the task of restoring peace and protection to the country. He took with him the Midland Battalion, "A" Battery, and my two troops on one steamer, leaving the other two steamers to bring the 90th and the Grenadiers. The transport, under the escort of the Intelligence Corps, and Captain Brittlebank's men (Captain Brittlebank had been appointed to the command of the late Captain French's Scouts) were ordered to march by land, crossing the river at Fort Carlton, by the north trail. We arrived at Fort Carlton at 7 o'clock the following morning, and visited the ruins of this now historic place. After leaving Carlton, a deputation from Poundmaker awaiting the arrival of General Middleton was met on the bank of the river. Poundmaker had received the news of Riel's defeat and capture, and wishing to make peace, immediately despatched a letter to the General; of which the following is a copy:

> Sir, – I am camped with my people at the east end of Eagle Hills, where I am reached by the news of the surrender of Riel. No letter came with the news, so I cannot tell how far it may be true. I send some of my men to you to learn the truth and terms of peace, and hope you will deal kindly with us. I and my people wish you to send us the terms in writing, so that we may be under no misunderstanding, from which so much trouble arises. We have twenty-one prisoners, whom we have tried to treat well in every respect. With greeting.
>
> (Signed) Poundmaker. His
X
Mark.

General Middleton was on the steamer *Northcote, en route* for Battleford, when he received the message, and sent back Poundmaker's runner with the following reply:

> Poundmaker, – I have utterly defeated the half-breeds and Indians, and have made a prisoner of Riel and most of his council. I have made no terms with them, neither will I make terms with you. I have men enough to defeat you and your people, or at least drive you away to starve in the woods, and will do so unless you bring in the teams you took. Yourself and your councillors to meet me with your arms at Battleford on Tuesday, the 26th. I am glad to hear that you treated the prisoners well, and have released them.
>
> (Signed) Fred. Middleton, *Major-General*.

When Poundmaker's deputation had been dismissed with this reply, we proceeded on our way to Battleford, arriving there the same night. Here we found that a similar commu-

nication had been sent by Poundmaker to Colonel Otter, showing that he was very anxious to come to terms.

After disembarking, we pitched our camp alongside Colonel
Otter's, on the plateau near the town, where the General
awaited the arrival of the remainder of his column, and the
expected surrender of Poundmaker and his braves.

After the battle of Cut Knife, an event occurred which
threatened to interfere with our movements; namely, the
capture of a transport train by Poundmaker. Feeling no longer
safe in his proximity to Battleford, Poundmaker determined
to move east to join Riel, who, after the battle of Fish Creek,
had sent him urgent appeals to hasten to his standard. He was
on his way thither, when, crossing the main trail from Swift
Current, a transport train of bullock teams, with forage and
supplies, had the misfortune to be passing. The opportunity
was too good to be lost. The teamsters were surprised and
surrounded, but they immediately formed a corral with their
waggons, which brought on a parley. The Indians sent forward
a half-breed to negotiate, and the safety of the teamsters was
guaranteed, on condition of their quietly surrendering. This
they did, and were at once conducted in triumph to Poundmaker's camp. A portion of their experiences may be gathered
from the following account given to the correspondent of the
Montreal *Star*:

> About nine o'clock on Thursday, the 14th instant, the forage-
> trains were passing through a piece of open, surrounded by
> wooded bluffs, about eight miles from Battleford, when the
> teamster in front observed mounted men closing in upon them
> from all sides. At first they were inclined to think that the
> newcomers were friends, but a few piercing war-whoops, uttered
> from a place of cover, convinced them that they had been
> ambushed. Notwithstanding the utter suddenness of the attack,
> many of the drivers did not lose their wits, but made a hastily
> improvised laager. By this time the Indians, who numbered about
> a hundred, led by paint-bedaubed half-breeds, approached,
> gesticulating and shouting at the same moment, without firing
> a single shot. The rear was not well guarded, and while the excite-
> ment continued in front, six or seven teamsters who owned horses

cut loose and made their escape amid a heavy fusilade. Meantime, the Indians approached nearer and nearer the laager, while twenty of their number went in pursuit of the retreating horsemen. The enemy finally sent a half-breed towards the waggons. Throwing down his weapon, to show his good intentions, the man advanced within fifty yards and called for one of the teamsters' number. The head teamster responded and walked toward him. A brief discussion followed, the half-breed promising that their lives would be spared if they would quietly surrender. The teamsters immediately gave up their arms, consisting of sixteen Winchesters, two Sniders, and three shot-guns. After robbing each prisoner of every valuable, the Indians, who were overjoyed at their success, began to examine the contents of the various waggons, and in a few minutes a start was made for the Indian camp, which was pitched in a ravine about four miles west of the Swift Current trail. The prisoner teamsters were compelled to drive the oxen. Soon the warlike Stonys, who had not been present at the capture, galloped up and attempted to shoot the prisoners. The half-breeds, however, proved themselves to be endowed with some redeeming traits, and frustrated this cruel design. Rifles were levelled by both parties, and the determined stand taken by the half-breeds alone saved the teamsters from a cruel death.

As the train approached the Indian camp, squaws and toddling papooses poured out from every tepee, and advanced with cheers of joy to greet the returning braves. The females, at sight of the prisoners, were especially boisterous, and shouted to the braves to put them to death. Through the jeering, howling, yelling mass, the frightened drivers were hustled, every moment expecting to be struck down from behind. Finally they were conducted to a ravine close to the camp, and after receiving a parting shout from the ugly squaws, they were left to their own reflections. A strong guard surrounded them, precluding all possibility of escape. The Indians held a formal council to discuss the propriety of shooting the teamsters, but decided not to do so. Shortly afterwards Poundmaker put in an appearance in the ravine. After shaking hands with each man in turn, the redoubtable chief assured them, through a half-breed interpreter, that their lives would be spared. He added that he was aware there was a Manitou above, and that he could not permit them to be slain without cause. Poundmaker then left, and shortly afterwards the Indians struck camp.

Tepee-poles were thrown down in a twinkling by the squaws, who, assisted by young boys and girls, rapidly packed everything away in carts and waggons already in line for the start. Bucks lolled around, whiffing "kineekinick" (tobacco) from long-stemmed pipes, or attended to the trappings of their horses, while youngsters, scarcely able to crawl about, drove in the cattle. Finally a start was made, and preceded by twenty-five or thirty scouts riding a mile ahead, the disorganized mob moved east-wards on their way to reinforce Riel. Instead of proceeding in column, the Indians moved along in extended order, leaving a trail behind them over two miles wide. First came about three hundred and sixty war-painted braves, mounted on wiry ponies, or on the more powerful animals stolen in the early raids. Next came Red River carts, waggons and every other variety of vehicle ever manufactured. Each was loaded with plunder or tepee-poles, while perched on top were seated old men, armed with bows and arrows. Behind followed a chaotic mass of waggons and carts, surrounded by lowing cattle and little boys on foot. Other Indian lads added to the grotesqueness of the scene, and mounted on young colts kept up to the moving outfit. Further in rear, at a distance of half a mile, came other herds of cattle, while bring-ing up the whole came another herd of horses. Young girls and squaws were mounted, several of the females riding along on oxen. In this manner, the followers of Poundmaker covered three miles an hour with ease.

These teamsters were released as soon as Poundmaker made up his mind to surrender, and to the relief of their friends they came into Battleford.

While awaiting the arrival of the transport from Prince Albert, the General celebrated the Queen's birthday by a divi-sional parade of the two columns. A salvo of artillery and a *feu-de-joie* were fired, and three hearty cheers given in honour of her Majesty, followed by a march past. This imposing cere-mony, performed by so large a number of troops, could not fail to impress the half-breeds and Indians, who were now flocking in to surrender themselves. The first detachment to arrive was a camp of French half-breeds, who had been with Poundmaker all this time, but, as they claimed, in the position of prisoners. They approached with a long string of horses, carts and waggons, with their families and all their household goods, and had every appearance of being a prosperous community. On the following day, to the great interest of the troops, came Poundmaker, with a number of his councillors and braves, having left their camp some ten miles out. (The teamster prisoners had before marched in.) They brought with them two hundred and seven stands of arms in waggons.

General Middleton arranged to have a pow-wow with Poundmaker in the afternoon, to hear what he had to say for himself, and this was one of the most interesting features of the campaign. The grim old soldier was seated in front of his tent, surrounded by his officers, in the midst of the largest camp of soldiers that had ever visited the North-West territories. Arraigned before him were the various chiefs, councillors, and braves, to answer for their conduct during the outbreak. Similar pow-wows had often been held in treaty-making, and on other occasions, when there was only the moral force of the country behind its officers; but here, the Indians could see a portion of the physical force of the Dominion, with which they had to contend – a force that had been successful in overcoming their leader at Batoche, and had in a short time penetrated the fastnesses of these tribes, no doubt deemed by them an impossibility for soldiers to accomplish.

The Indians squatted themselves in a semi-circle in front of the General, to the number of sixty or seventy. They were well dressed in their fashion, being painted up in war costume. Some of the men were adorned with kid gloves, others had on ladies' hats and feathers, and all presented a most picturesque group. The talking commenced through Hourie, the chief interpreter. The General, in his matter-of-fact way, desired them to keep to plain facts, and to leave the flowery embellishments of their Indian tongue to one side for the present. It was impossible, however, to prevent them commencing with the earth, the sky, the grass, the sun, etc., one and all, young and old, seeming to be imbued with the allegorical style of oratory, and unable to express themselves without this verbiage. Poundmaker knew nothing. He claimed that he had done his best to keep his braves in order, and seemed to think that having come to make terms of peace was quite sufficient merit to entitle him to every consideration. He is a fine-looking Indian, and one cannot help being interested in him. He is undoubtedly clever, and had the honour of accompanying the Marquis of Lorne on his trip through the country in 1881, who enjoyed nothing better than listening to his tales, over the camp-fire, through an interpreter. One brave after another told his story, commencing with a desire to shake hands with the General, who, however, steadily refused, telling them that he never would shake hands with bad Indians. They must first prove themselves good. After several had spoken, a squaw came forward, and was anxious to have her say, but the General said he never listened to women. The statement was pertinently made that the Queen was a woman, and that she ruled the country; but the General readily answered that the Queen, though ruler, only spoke through her councillors, and with that the indignant squaw had to be satisfied. After hearing all they had to say, the General made them the following address:

> After many years of peace, when the half-breeds rose in rebellion, these Indians rose to join them. The Indians all around here, like Poundmaker's band, rose, thinking the white man would be beaten. They did not hesitate to murder. All round they attacked the stores of the Hudson's Bay Company and others, and killed men and women, and thought they were going to have their own way. Instead of saying when you heard of the half-breeds' rebellion, "now is the time to show how we value the kindness of the white man to us," you turned upon us. This very band of Poundmaker's was going to join the enemy, and if we had been beaten they would have done more murder. And now when you find the head rebel-chief, Riel, and the other warriors are beaten, you come in and tell all sorts of lies, and beg for peace. You thought the Government had no more men; you thought you were better fighters; that you could lie in ambush in the bluffs and shoot us down. Now we have shown you there is no use of lying in the bluffs and pits, that we can drive you out and kill you.
>
> *Poundmaker* – True.

Middleton – Up to this time you Indians have been in the habit of going to the settlers' houses, saying you were hungry and wanted food, and frightening the women. Let the Indians understand that they must do so no more, and that if one more white man is killed ten Indians will suffer in consequence. If any disturbance takes place, and if any of the young men think they can go and rob and pillage, they will find themselves much mistaken, and all the men will suffer. More soldiers are now coming here, and if Poundmaker had not come in, I would have followed him and killed every one of his men if necessary. We want to live in peace with the red man, but we can't allow you to go on in this way, and the sooner you understand that the better. I am only a soldier, and I do not know what the Government will do in the matter, but I have no doubt you will be helped to live in the future by the cultivation of the land as in the past. If Big Bear doesn't do the same as you have, I will take my troops and go after him and his men. I have received orders from the Government at Ottawa to detain as prisoners Poundmaker, Lean-Man, Mud-Blanket, Breaking-Through-the-Ice, and White Bear. The rest of you and your people had better return quietly to your reserves, giving up the men who did the murders. No agent at present will live among you, after the way you have behaved, so that you will have to come and get your rations here, once a week.

After the General's demand for the murderers to be given up, one of the braves, called Wa-Wa-Nitch (the Man Without Blood), came forward and sat himself down cross-legged immediately in front of the General. Taking his feet in his hands, he confessed to the murder of Tremont, as I have before described. When that scene was over, another Indian, named Ickta, who had stripped himself to the waist, came forward, and made a similar confession of having murdered Payne, the farm instructor. The General ordered four of the leading chiefs whom he named, with these two murderers, to be made prisoners, and the remainder were allowed to return to their reserves. Wa-Wa-Nitch, on his way up to the fort, made signs to Poundmaker indicative of hanging, which was intended to convey, "I am going to be hanged; I am a brave man, and I don't care." The Mounted Police were now instructed to ascertain who were guilty of the minor crimes, of stealing, committing depredations, etc., and made several arrests. The remainder of the Indians and half-breeds returned to their respective camps.

Cut Knife Hill was visited, where tepees with dead bodies in them were found, as reported by Big Bear's emissaries. The Indians, now deprived of their means of subsistence, which had been so plentiful for the past two months, had a hard time of it. Proverbially thriftless, the Indian will feast inordinately, upon whatever he many have at the time, taking no thought for the morrow; hence the plentiful supplies they had feloniously gathered were about consumed. The General told them to come to Battleford, in order to get rations; but the dread of showing themselves in the country, filled with soldiers and scouts, prevented them from taking advantage of the offer for some time.

The next day the General went down on a visit to Moosomin's reserve, about eighteen miles to the west of Battleford, taking my men as escort. We found comfortable houses, ploughed fields, and everything that denotes industry and comfort. Moosomin was a loyal Indian, and proud of his loyalty. He had gone off with his tribe to the north of the Saskatchewan, to get out of the way of Poundmaker and his tribe, that he might not be drawn in to commit disloyal acts. He was still absent from his reserve, but on the following day, he came into Battleford to visit the General, and was warmly thanked for his steadfastness and loyalty, which pleased the old man greatly.

Being cut off by several hundred miles from all telegraph communications, nothing for some time had been heard of General Strange's movements. Scouts were sent out to ascertain if any trace of Big Bear could be found between Fort Pitt and Battleford, as it was suspected he was on his way to join Poundmaker. On Friday, Major Perry, of the police force, marched down with his men from Fort Pitt, on the south side of the river, and though he had left before General Strange's encounter with Big Bear, he was able to give a detailed account of General Strange's movements up to that time. The steamboat was at once sent, in charge of Mr. Bedson, with Captain Forrest and one company of the 90th as an escort, laden with supplies and forage for General Strange at Fort Pitt. Major Perry, with his men, returned on board the steamer, and when half way to Fort Pitt, a canoe was met, bringing news of General Strange's engagement with Big Bear. Mr. Bedson landed Major Perry, to continue his march, and returned with the steamer for further orders.

At eight o'clock p.m., orders were issued for the troops to hold themselves in readiness to embark early the next morning. The General took the infantry, and went in the steamboats to Fort Pitt. The mounted men he ordered to march by the south trail.

On a bright Sunday morning we started, and made the ninety miles in two days, reaching Fort Pitt almost simultaneously with the infantry. On Tuesday morning, we crossed the river to the encampment, where we met Captain Leacock, the provincial member for our district. He had been left here with a small detachment, to advise General Middleton that General Strange had left that day to return and take up his position at Frenchman's Butte, the scene of the late engagement.

Now commenced a fresh campaign after Big Bear, for General Middleton was determined not to leave the country until every insurgent tribe had been brought into subjection. Before General Middleton disembarked, General Strange despatched Major Steele, with seventy-five mounted men, upon Big Bear's trail. On Wednesday morning, the day after our arrival at our new encampment, the General ordered his mounted men, consisting of fifty Mounted Police, under Colonel Herchmer; forty Intelligence Corps, under Captain Dennis; sixty of my corps, and twenty of Captain Brittlebank's men to advance to General Strange's position. After giving orders to Colonel Van Straubenzie to form up the infantry brigade at Fort Pitt, he followed in the afternoon with fifty of the Grenadiers, fifty of the Midland, and fifty of the 90th, under the command of Major Hughes, of the Midland. "B" Battery, under

Major Short, with the gatling under Lieutenant Rivers, also accompanied the General, while Captain Peters, of "A" Battery, acted as transport officer.

I was accompanied by two or three other officers who wished to survey the scene of General Strange's engagement, and after a march of twelve miles we reached the place. We passed through the camp where the sundance had been held, which showed traces of about one hundred and seventy-five tepees, and evident signs of a hurried flight; all the tepee-poles were left strewn about. These poles are made of light spruce sticks, and take about twelve to each tepee, the tepee itself being composed of dressed moose or deer skins, sewn together to cover the poles. Two miles farther on, we came upon the camp and the rifle-pits, where bacon, flour, carts and waggons of every description – a heterogeneous collection of savage and civilized articles – were found. The position was a strong one, but had been hurriedly selected. The careful preparations which Poundmaker had made, for the protection of his position, were wanting. As we rode round the heights, a dog which had been left behind sprang out of the bush, challenging our intrusion. We looked in and discovered a pup being suckled by its mother, both having been left behind by the Indians. Colonel Williams jumped off his horse and secured the pup, intending to bring it home to his little boy as a memento of Big Bear's camp. He carried it all the way back to Fort Pitt in a birch-bark basket, which he picked up at the sundance camp. I mention the circumstance, for Little Bear, as Colonel Williams called the pup, was an object of great interest, and was brought carefully home to Port Hope. We arrived about twelve o'clock, and camped beside General Strange, who had just struck tents preparatory to moving off to Onion Lake on a more westerly trail towards Beaver River. General Middleton, with the three infantry companies, arrived at three o'clock in the afternoon.

That night, at twelve o'clock, a messenger came back from Major Steele, to say that he had caught up to Big Bear's band, forty-five miles from this point, and had had an engagement with him. Major Steele had left Frenchman's Butte at ten o'clock on Tuesday morning, and picked up Big Bear's trail a few miles from there; following it up he came upon a portion of Big Bear's band the next morning at seven o'clock, having had one man wounded on the march. He surprised the Indians on this side of a ford leading across a small bay in Loon Lake and had an engagement lasting two hours, during which time two of his men were wounded. This was a plucky, well-executed march and attack. We found out afterwards that Major Steele had killed four Indians, thereby inflicting some punishment on this tribe, although unfortunately one of the killed was Chief Cut Arm, who had befriended the missionary, Mr. Quinney. Major Steele pushed on, with only three days' rations, through the dense woods which Big Bear had traversed, and gallantly followed by his little body of men, he finally reached Big Bear's camp. Had he sent for supports when he struck Big Bear's trail, he would no doubt have brought the Indians to bay, but for want of rations and support he could pursue the attack no further, and retired with his three wounded men. General Middleton having now ascertained that Big Bear had escaped to the north, through the forests and muskegs with which that part of the country abounds, this district had to be penetrated.

With that object in view, the General sent orders to Colonel Otter to march north, parallel to him, from Battleford to Turtle Lake, to endeavour to intercept any Indian tribes escaping east, leaving Major Dawson, of the Grenadiers, who had recovered from his wound, in command at Battleford. Orders were also sent to Colonel Irvine, at Prince Albert, to march north from there to Green Lake, the General himself intending to follow Big Bear's trail, as General Strange had expressed a wish to move to Beaver River by a more westerly trail. In the meantime we had received news of the prisoners and Big Bear's movements. The Reverend Mr. Quinney and his wife, who had made their escape and wandered back to try to find the troops, were attracted by the whistle of the steamboat, and in Mrs. Quinney's own words, I give her account of their escape:

The Indian, Longfellow, was friendly, and we owe our escape
to him. He never slept that night, watching lest any of Big Bear's
braves should come. The first we knew of the presence of troops
was when entrenched in the ravine, where we heard firing, and
we also heard it the next day. This was the occasion of General
Strange's engagement, but none of us knew anything about it,
except that we heard the firing. We made a further march of
about eight miles through the thick bush. We continued marching until Sunday, on which day we rested in the woods, and Mr.
Quinney held service. Previous to this, Mr. Quinney wished
Longfellow to let him and me go, as I was not able to tramp
through the bush. But the answer was, "Yes, but if you go we
must send you to Big Bear's camp." On Saturday Mr. Quinney
told me that when the order to start was given I was to refuse
to go any farther north, and I did so, and my husband also
refused; but we learned afterwards that had we gone back that
morning, Mr. Quinney would have been killed, as an Indian had
gone back and was in waiting to shoot him as he passed. Fortunately my husband decided to go on with the Indians, and it was
not until Monday that my husband finally made up his mind to
escape. On that day when the order was given to go on, my
husband, Halpin, Cameron, Dufresne (father and son) and family,
myself and others, started back. Longfellow made no resistance
to our going, but was willing that we should escape. I asked him
if he was sure the Indians were willing also, as I feared some of
them might come after us, and he said they were all willing. We
were a strange lot; some of the women were carrying children
and some of the children were walking, and all of us suffering
from the hardships of the march. The first day, we got about
twelve miles away from the Indians, when we camped. Mr. Quinney, Mr. Dufresne, and Cameron left us in charge of three men,
and went to find General Strange's column. We remained where
we had been left, and all night the men left with us watched.
Early the next morning, we heard three shots fired, which was
the signal that our party had returned. They had found the
soldiers, and a few minutes afterwards about twelve mounted
men rode up with eatables and other necessaries, and I need not
say we were all rejoiced and happy. When we finally reached the
soldier's camp, our party were welcomed by the men, who all
turned out to greet us with three hearty British cheers.

General Middleton, on the following morning, after the arrival of Steele's courier, ordered the mounted men, one gun of "A" Battery, and the gatling, with the three infantry companies, under Major Hughes, to march to the support of Major Steele. Our little column had now to cross swamps and bogs, and through brush, which made our progress slow; but we kept strictly to the trail which Big Bear had taken. The great interest of the march was inspecting his camps as we passed them, which always contained something hurriedly abandoned. At one camp we found a quantity of fur hid in the woods. We found unmistakable evidences of the recent presence of the prisoners in the locality, with an occasional message dropped by Mr. Maclean. At the first camp we picked up a silver mug, engraved on it, "Presented by General Rosser to Katie Maclean," which the General took possession of afterwards to return to its lawful owner. Also at the first of Big Bear's camps from Frenchman's Butte, we found a grave containing the body of Man-Who-Talks-Like-Another. He had been killed by a shell, and was said to be one of the murderers of Dill at Frog Lake. After a march of about twelve miles we met Major Steele on his return. The General halted for the day, and sent down to Fort Pitt to have pack-saddles made so that he might push on without his waggons, and the men were set to work to make travoies. A travoie is two long poles crossed and attached to the neck of the horse, the ends dragging on the ground, the load being bound on behind the horse. This is the Indian mode of transport over these roads. The General determined upon advancing without the infantry, and sent them back to Fort Pitt, taking with him only the artillery and the mounted men, with the gatling. And I might here say that our Canadian artillery proved themselves a most useful arm of the service, penetrating the most remote districts, and whether acting as infantry or gunners were always ready for work.

On the 6th of June we marched once more, leaving our tents and baggage behind. The Intelligence Corps rendered the greatest services, by brushing the swampy spots in advance of the column, and making roads. On the night of the 7th we reached the scene of Major Steele's engagement, and camped in view of Loon Lake, a beautiful sheet of water surrounded by hills. Here we remained for the night, and the General sent on two half-breed scouts to ascertain what difficulties were ahead of us. They had to cross the ford which lay beneath our camp, and after going five miles the trail turned north to another crossing, where the water was too deep to allow them to ford. Big Bear evidently was cunning enough to put all possible obstacles in our way. However, the General pushed on, and next morning we crossed this ford, and by noon had reached the other crossing, where it was necessary to make a raft. It was an inspiriting sight to see the men swimming their horses across and rafting their saddlery and equipment over on a few logs tied together, and the General watched it with great interest. By nightfall he had all of his mounted men on the other side, leaving the artillery and transport behind.

On the following morning it was discovered that there lay a broad deep muskeg a short distance ahead, and before proceeding the General sent his half-breed scouts across. The General told me to send an officer and men with them. I sent Lieutenant Pigott and Sergeant Selby, and they were accompanied by Mr. Reid, the Assistant Indian Commissioner. They crossed the slough, and went as far as Big Bear's next encampment, which was on the north shore of the lake. It took them half an hour to cross, only the strong horses being able to plunge through with their riders on their backs. Some of the party had to get off and wade a portion of the way; I ventured in for about two hundred yards, but was glad to turn back.

When the Indians went over three days before, the ice was not out of the bottom, leaving hard footing, but the heavy traffic, caused by their crossing, made the mud much deeper, and the Indians told Mr. Maclean that when the ice was all out of the bottom it was impassable even to them. However, the General determined to push on, and ordered my corps and Major Steele's to take three days' rations and make a reconnaissance in advance, and to leave at six o'clock the following morning.

In the morning at five o'clock the General sent word that he had changed his mind, not caring to place such a deep swamp barrier between his troops and his supplies. I afterwards found out, upon conversing with Mr. Maclean and with Big Bear after he was taken, that Big Bear and his tribe had started for Turtle Lake and had separated from the Wood Crees on the 7th of the month, so that by the time we crossed the slough he would have been closer to Colonel Otter's column, which arrived at Turtle Lake on the 14th, and on which date Colonel Otter's scouts picked up the trail of Big Bear still going east. The General was criticized for having allowed this muskeg to balk him, but he, unquestionably, saved his men and his horseflesh from a most severe undertaking, and as it turned out, used good judgment.

At this encampment, near the slough, we found a dead squaw who had committed suicide by hanging herself. We were afterwards informed that she was a cripple, and had been left behind by the Indians (as they could not take a cart across the slough), who intended coming back for her with a horse; but feeling lonely and overcome with fear she put an end to herself.

We suffered here greatly from mosquitoes and flies, and were glad when the order was issued to retrace our steps. The men put out the nets, of which they found a number, and caught a good supply of fresh fish – white fish and pickerel. We re-crossed the creek and the other ford on the 10th. At Loon Lake we found a number of rifle-pits dug, the Indians no doubt anticipating a further advance on the part of Major Steele, when he attacked them at the ford, five miles back. We returned to Fort Pitt on the 12th, having spent nine days in the bush. On arriving at Fort Pitt we found that Mrs. Gowanlock and Mrs. Delaney, with Pritchard and his party, had come in. They had managed to escape from the Indians, and were traced by the Reverend Mr. McKay and some of Major Hatton's men, and brought back to Fort Pitt, to the relief of the poor ladies, who, for nearly two months, had been dragged about from place to place by their captors.

On the 14th the General determined to march with the mounted men to Beaver River, to try to reach Lac des Iles and Cold Lake from that point, where he suspected the Indians had retreated with their prisoners. On the 16th we reached Beaver River, where General Strange was encamped, having sent a hundred men on to Cold Lake, under Colonel Smith. This was the centre of the Chipewayan reserve.

Beaver River is a beautiful, deep-running stream, flowing east and north to lake "Ile à la Crosse," which empties into the Churchill River. The latter flows north-east into Hudson's Bay. At Beaver River the Chipewayans, who have their reserve there, surrendered themselves with Father Legoff, their faithful missionary, who had been taken prisoner on the 12th of May; these Chipewayans left Big Bear before the battle with General Strange. They had for some time been endeavouring to get away, and were closely watched. On this occasion they purchased their release by a gift of forty head of cattle which they gave to Big Bear, and of which they raised a large number on their reserves. Father Legoff, like all the other missionaries in the North-West, rendered valuable services during the rebellion; he remained with his tribe, and by his efforts and counsel, no doubt lessened the dangers to which the settlements were exposed, and restrained the excitement of the Indians.

General Strange sent two scouts belonging to this Chipewayan tribe to endeavour to find some traces of Big Bear; and Captain Constantine, with a small escort, accompanied by Mr. Ham, the able correspondent of the Toronto *Mail*, undertook to go through the woods with a small party in the direction of Loon Lake, where they had a most fatiguing and tiring journey, finally reaching Fort Pitt. The Indian scouts returned and brought news that they had met an Indian, who told them that the Wood Crees had separated from Big Bear's band and had gone north with the prisoners. It was also said that their intention after getting well away from Big Bear was to allow the prisoners to return to Fort Pitt by the trail they had come upon, which was good news to all of us.

The previous day, General Middleton had gone on a fishing excursion to Cold Lake and to visit Colonel Smith's detachment camped there. The Reverend Canon McKay, he found, had taken two Indians in a canoe to visit Lac des Iles, to endeavour to get some word from the Indians at that point. Upon the General's return in the evening, the Indian scouts had brought the information about the prisoners. On the following morning, General Middleton ordered us back to Fort Pitt, leaving General Strange to collect his forces and to follow, sending word at the same time to the Indians who had released the prisoners to come in and surrender themselves at Fort Pitt. As he passed by Frog Lake, he instructed Colonel Williams to bring in his battalion, also to Fort Pitt. On arriving at the post, the General sent Mr. Bedson off with teams to meet the returning prisoners at Loon Lake, which he reached at the same time as they did, to their great joy and relief. The Indians, it seems, had sent them off to make this journey of a hundred miles without provisions, and they had to rely upon what game they could catch to feed themselves. Mr. Maclean with his family, and Mr. Mann with his family, and about fifteen others, returned to Fort Pitt, thus completing the release of every prisoner that had been taken during the rebellion.

Colonel Otter had left Battleford with his column, a few of my men, under Corporal Marriott, accompanying him as scouts. At their head was Mr. Ross, one of the most daring and enterprising of scouts. They arrived at Turtle Lake on the 14th, just as Big Bear had passed by the north end; but his band had now become so small that by separating up they left no distinct trail behind them. The scouts captured a few of Big Bear's ponies, loaded with pack-saddles, but their drivers escaped. Colonel Otter pushed on east to Birch Lake, where he captured a band of Indians under chief Yellow Sky, who had a large herd of cattle belonging to a settler and a considerable stock of store goods, which they had obtained at Green Lake.

The account this band gave of themselves was that they had remained loyal, and that the cattle they held they had taken charge of lest they might be stolen by other bands; but hearing that the Indians were plundering and destroying, and fearing that there would be nothing left for their use and support, they had provided against that exigency by helping themselves at Green Lake. At this post, property belonging to the Hudson's Bay Company had been pillaged and destroyed to the value of one hundred and fifty thousand dollars; the history of this post is contained in the interesting account given by Father Paquette, which I here insert.

On the 18th of March I was staying at St. Laurent, four miles from here. About fifteen minutes before midnight, just as I was going to sleep, someone knocked at the door. It was Louis Riel. Two men were with him, Dumas and Moise Ouellette; Jackson, who I think was insane, was also at the mission at the time. When Riel got in, he began to say, in a loud voice: "The provisoire is declared, and we have got five prisoners already, I have already destroyed the old *Romain*, and have a new Pope, Archbishop Bourget." And to me he said: "You are to obey me." I said I would never obey him. "If you will not," he replied, "the churches will stand, but they will stand empty." Among other outrageous things, he said: "You are in danger here; I have got an affidavit against you, and will get some Indians to fix you." Riel stayed there two hours, at one time kneeling and calling on the Holy Spirit, and then crying out, "To-morrow morning I will go and destroy the soldiers, and at night, I will go and destroy Fort Carlton." His eyes were like the devil's. He is not mad this Riel; he has a very good mind, but he is extremely wicked.

Some hours after he left – before daylight, in fact – I left and escaped to Carlton to give the news that Riel had declared a new government, so as to prevent a surprise and massacre. The fort was full of half-breeds, so I said nothing except to the clerk, and told him to tell Major Crozier after I had left. In consequence of this action of mine, which was some way told to Riel, I was afterwards informed that I had been condemned to death by the council. Crossing the river and arriving at my mission, I found all quiet there. On the same night five half-breed families – including that of François Primeau – crossed the river from near

Carlton and followed me to my mission, where I hid them from the 19th March till the 7th of April.

Twice during that time, half-breeds came to my place from Riel to get government cattle. On the first occasion, March 31st, Joseph Delorme and Baptiste Ouellette came to my room with loaded guns, saying that they were sent by "the government" – meaning the rebel government – for animals, and asking me if I thought the Indians would give them up. I said I did not know, but I would see the chief. "If they give the animals," one of the envoys said, "I promise that we will leave the people quiet." On the same day, seeing these two half-breeds coming in the distance, I had rung the church bell; it had been agreed that on hearing that signal at any time, the Indians would make off to the woods. They did so, but I knew where to find them, and leaving Delorme and Ouellette, I sought out the chief and told him, "Riel says that if you don't give up your cattle, he will come with many men and fetch both oxen and Indians." To which he replied that he did not want to go to Riel, even if he died for it. I advised him to go to the hills with all his best cattle, leaving only nine head. He did so, and I told the two half-breeds that the nine were all that were there now, so they took the nine and went away.

The Indians then came back, but merely to get their property, and immediately went away again to the hills – three days' journey. Only my hired man stopped at the mission. On the 7th of April, early in the morning, an Indian from Battleford passed and told me that I had better run, as five other Indians on horseback were coming from Battleford, and two priests had been killed already. The half-breed families, with me, also thought it best to go; and I was the more afraid because some Battleford Indians had demanded provisions of me last summer and threatened to break into my store, saying that when they were numerous they would come and fix me. Taking the most precious articles with me, and locking all the doors, I set off for Shell River, where there is a half-breed settlement. On my explaining the situation to the half-breeds, they all turned against Riel, whom they had ignorantly imagined to be a great benefactor. Then, knowing that Riel intended to pillage the stores at Green Lake, and hearing that the Indians were disposed to take his side, I went there to persuade them all, as good Catholics, that they would be wrong to do so. At a meeting there, I found that all the people were in Riel's favour, thinking that he wanted to get the half-breeds their rights. They did not know that rebellion had actually been begun. I told them, "You deceive yourselves; Riel wants to put down the Pope and the priests, and to make a new religion." An old chief, or headman, of the half-breeds, called Vieux Payette, then spoke with great indignation, saying, "If Riel is against religion, let us take our guns and fight him." Then they ran to hide in the woods.

Arriving at the Hudson's Bay Fort, I advised the clerk to load up in four boats with gunpowder and provisions, and take them to Ile à la Crosse, putting all lead ammunition into the lake. He did so, sending the boats to Beaver River, ten miles distant, and thereby keeping two hundred and forty-six kegs of powder from the Indians. In the morning, when one boat was following with the families, twenty-seven Indians from Loon Lake appeared and caught us. When the people had got ashore, the Indians forced Mr. Sinclair, the clerk, to go back with them to the fort. There, as they were very hungry, they began by getting something to eat, after which they destroyed all the goods, including the property of both Protestant and Catholic missions. They wanted to take Mr. Sinclair prisoner, saying that they had Riel's order to catch him or kill him; but he managed to escape with two Carlton half-breeds, and made his way down the river in the boat. An Indian, named Makasis, aimed at him; but a chief, to whom Mr. Sinclair had just given his gloves, pulled the gun aside.

The journey to the Ile à la Crosse took four days. It was a terrible journey. It was extremely cold – snowing and raining – and we got very wet. We camped on the shore each night. On the third day, Mrs. Sinclair became a mother, and I was chosen godfather of the little child. The Indians, in honour of the event, fired off about three hundred shots. I had sent a letter to La Crosse saying that we were on our way, and the people of the fort, when they heard the shots, fancied that the Indians were killing us. The next day, when we got to the fort, we found only the clerk, Mr. Franklin, and one pig. The chief factor, Mr. Ross, the sisters, and all the half-breeds had gone off to an island about sixty miles north-west. Our boats had stopped where Beaver River enters the lake, as the lake ice had not yet broken up, so I had to walk nearly the whole of one day across the ice, accompanied by an Indian boy and a carpenter. I was very hungry when I got to the fort, and my clothing was very ragged. Mr. Franklin not only gave me plenty to eat but gave me his own clothes, and these are his boots and pants I am wearing now. The other people waited until we sent back dogs, and pulled the boats over the ice. The provisions were hidden in every direction through the woods.

I told the clerk to get all the half-breeds together, so he sent off for them without delay, and the next afternoon, 30th April, they all assembled at the fort. About sixty-five or seventy, all men, were there; half-breeds and Indians, including Chipeway-ans and Wood Crees, some of whom had come a good day's journey, from Canoe Lake. I spoke first, and said that though they were poor, I knew that they were good and honest. A half-breed then declared that he had an order from Mr. Lawrence Clarke and Mr. Ross to take whatever he wanted in the store for his own use. Mr. Sinclair and Mr. Franklin both said it was not true, and I asked who had brought the letter. The man said, "Angus Mackay." Then I said, "You lie, because I read the letter, and there was not a word about such a thing." To that he made no reply. Then I spoke very strongly to them for nearly an hour. I said to them, "Those who will not listen to me, I will excom-municate, because Riel is a heretic and an apostate." And I told everyone who was for me to put up his hand. All put up their hands except one, who explained to me that he had only a stick and consequently could not fight. The one who had spoken was a very good Catholic, and held up his hand like the rest. From that time all were against Riel and all lived quietly.

Two days after, three boats were sent to Green Lake, escorted by about fifty armed men. They travelled for two days and then met Indians, who told them that Big Bear was coming through the woods to burn Fort La Crosse. The boats turned back and brought the news that perhaps Big Bear would be at the fort that very night. On the people's advice I then went over to the island, where the others were. The chief of the Chipewayans brought two hundred men, with three families, to protect us, and we took advantage of this to carry on a mission among them. After three weeks on the island, we returned to the fort – where Franklin and Sinclair had remained – and about four hundred men, Indians and half-breeds, stayed there to protect the mission and the fort. Only when news came, about May the 27th, of Riel's capture, did they allow me to return to my mission. On arriving, after three days' travelling, at Green Lake, I found everything destroyed; even my harness had been cut to pieces with a knife.

Colonel Otter, through Lieutenant Seers, his Brigade-Major, and my scouts, opened up communication with Colonel Irvine, who was scouring the country in the neighbourhood of Pelican and Green Lakes. Big Bear, finding that he was pursued on all sides by troops, turned south between Colonel Otter and Colonel Irvine's men and crossed the Saskatchewan a little west of Fort Carlton. There he camped in the settlements in the neighbourhood, and reported himself to the Hudson's Bay officer at Fort Carlton, and eventually gave himself up to Sergeant Butlin, under Inspector Gagnon, of the Mounted Police.

The news of this was telegraphed at once to General Middleton, who was now enabled to announce to the Government, while Parliament was still in session, that the campaign was over, resulting in the complete occupation of the country and the surrender of all the insurgent tribes.

XVI

THE EXECUTIONS

I now come to the last event of the campaign – the imprisonment, trial, and execution of Riel for the crime of high treason. He was taken to the gaol in Regina, closely guarded, in the charge of Captain Young, of the Winnipeg Field Battery, and handed over to the care of the Mounted Police. A discussion arose as to the mode of trial and the locality in which he should be tried. According to the laws of the country it was found necessary to try him in the North-West Territory, the scene of his crimes.

In proceeding against Riel for leading the new rebellion, the Government placed the case for the Crown in the hands of Mr. Christopher Robinson, son of the late Sir John Beverley Robinson, in his lifetime Chief Justice of Upper Canada, and Mr. B. B. Osler, assisted by Mr. Burbidge, Deputy Minister of Justice, Mr. Casgrain, of Quebec, and Mr. Scott, of Regina. Riel's friends in Quebec raised a fund for his defence, and Mr. Fitzpatrick and Mr. Lemieux, of Quebec, were employed to defend him. The presiding judge was Colonel Richardson, Stipendiary Magistrate for the district. The charges were formulated and proven. The trial was fair and open, every opportunity being given to the prisoner's counsel to defend him. The proofs of his criminality were so overwhelming that his counsel did not attempt to refute them, but relied entirely upon the plea that insanity, which it was sought to prove, existed in their client's case. Riel, being endowed with a vain, egotistical disposition, and feeling that his counsel were not adopting the best methods for obtaining his acquittal, took the ground, as he cleverly expressed it at the trial, that "the Government was trying to prove him guilty, and that his friends were trying to prove him insane." "Life, without the dignity of an intelligent being," as he phrased it, "was not worth having." He attempted to defend himself upon the plea that he was right in what he did, and this interference almost led his counsel to abandon his case. He made a most eloquent and pathetic appeal to the jury, lasting several hours, and when the jury retired and appeared in court, they returned a verdict of "Guilty." In consequence of his pathetic appeal, the verdict was accompanied with a recommendation to mercy. The sentence of death was pronounced upon him by Colonel Richardson, and he was condemned to be executed on the 18th of September.

After sentence had been passed on Riel, Mr. Fitzpatrick, one of the prisoner's counsel, gave notice of appeal for a new trial to the Court of Queen's Bench of Manitoba, upon the question of the jurisdiction of the Court. The trial and sentence was upheld by the Court of Queen's Bench at the sitting of the full Court in Winnipeg, on the 9th of September. After judgment had been delivered by the Court of Queen's Bench, Riel's counsel notified the Executive that they would appeal to the Privy Council in England. In order to give the prisoner's counsel an opportunity to test fully the legality of the proceedings, a respite was granted until the 10th of November. The appeal was heard before the Privy Council in England and was dismissed, and the sentence of the Court was confirmed.

No doubt to give Riel due notice that the sentence of the Court would be carried into execution, a further respite was granted from the 10th of November until the 16th, and on the 16th of November his execution took place. Father André, his spiritual adviser, spent much time with him to prepare him for his end, and Riel was allowed the privilege of having writing materials, that he might employ his time while in prison to write a book, giving the history of his life. Latterly, Riel began to realize that it would have been wiser if he had yielded to the legal advice of his friends, and accepted the position they adopted to get him off upon the plea of insanity. For some time previous to his execution he therefore attempted to give evidence by his acts that he was not sane; but it was too late now to avail himself of this, for the evidence of experts, who watched him carefully throughout his trial and afterwards, showed that he was perfectly cognizant of, and responsible for, the crimes he had committed. Riel played for a big stake, in the hope that he would get a large pecuniary benefit out of the agitation and that the Government would accede to his demands rather than go to the labour and expense of upholding the laws of the country, in so remote a portion of it. In this he was mistaken, for the Government were bound to show the people, as well as the Indians and half-breeds, that they were able and determined to uphold the laws of the country, and to protect the people throughout the North-West, and that neither expense nor distance was too great to prevent the dignity and power of the country being expressed.

On the morning of the 16th of November, the time came when Riel had to undergo the same ordeal he had put Scott through fifteen years previously, and the similarity of proceedings in both cases is a coincidence. Riel for some time had had the benefit of the constant attendance of Père André, who was with him during the whole of his last night on earth. About eight o'clock in the morning, the deputy sheriff, Mr. Gibson, went to Riel's cell and told him that his time had come. Riel at the moment turned pale, realizing his position, but braced himself up and a procession was formed. Father McWilliams, who was also in attendance on Riel, went first, Riel next, and Father André followed, the deputy sheriff leading the way. After them came the orderly officer of the Mounted Police, Captain White-Frazer, with ten men who had been on guard all night. They were followed by Colonel Irvine, four or five officers of the Mounted Police, Dr. Jukes, as medical officer, and four correspondents. They all marched up some steps to the room above the guard-room, and through this barrack-room to a small building which had been erected to contain the gallows. As they passed through the barrack-room, Riel exclaimed, "Courage, mon Père!" The gallows was entered by a window, temporarily used as a door, where the hangman awaited them.

Before stepping through the window the priests knelt down with the prisoner. The remainder, with the exception of the guards, removed their hats, and Father André prayed, Riel making the responses in a firm voice and praying also. His demeanour betokened suppressed excitement; his brow was covered with drops of sweat. Contrary to popular expectation, Riel met his death like a man, all the while holding a candle in one hand and a crucifix, which had been lent to him by Madame Forget, in the other. After the praying had continued for some time, at twenty-five minutes past eight o'clock the deputy sheriff touched Father McWilliams on the shoulder and told him the time was up. Père André saw this, and notified Riel that they must cease. They then all rose up and Père André, after explaining to Riel that the end was at hand, asked him if he was at peace with all men. Riel answered "Yes." The next question was, "Do you forgive all your enemies?" "Yes." Riel then asked him if he might speak. Father André advised him not to do so. Riel then received the kiss of peace from both the priests, and Father André exclaimed in French, "*Alors, allez au ciel!*"

While this conversation was taking place, the hangman was engaged in pinioning the prisoner's arms. The procession then went through the window, preceded by the hangman, who happened to be one of the men whom Riel had held in prison in 1869. Dr. Jukes and Colonel Irvine went on to the platform with Father McWilliams and Père André and two correspondents. The prisoner got on to the drop, his legs were pinioned and the rope adjusted. His last words were to say good-bye to Dr. Jukes and thank him for his kindness, and just before the white cap was pulled over his face he said, "Remerciez, Madame Forget." The cap was pulled down, and while he was praying the trap was pulled. Death was instantaneous. His pulse ceased beating four minutes after the trap-door fell. The body was to have been interred inside the gallows' enclosure, and the grave was commenced, but an order came from the Lieutenant-Governor to hand the body over to Sheriff Chapleau, which was accordingly done that night. Previously, however, to handing it over, Colonel Irvine, in presence of Dr. Jukes, Colonel McLeod and others, had the coffin opened to inspect the body, in consequence of reports which had spread, and which had even got into the papers, that Riel's body had been mutilated. The mutilations consisted in Father McWilliams' having cut off a lock of his hair and beard, and in taking off his left moccasin. The other moccasin and other locks of his hair had been distributed among some of his friends. Next day he was interred beneath the Roman Catholic Church in Regina. Subsequently his body was removed to his mother's house, near Winnipeg, and there in presence of a large number of people was interred at St. Boniface.

In addition to the trial of Riel in Regina, a number of half-breeds were tried on the charge of treason-felony. These men composed Riel's council. They pleaded guilty to the charge and were sentenced to various terms of imprisonment in the Manitoba Penitentiary.

In addition to these half-breeds, One Arrow, the chief of his tribe, White Cap, chief of his tribe, Poundmaker and Big Bear, chiefs of their tribes, were all tried at the same time at Regina, before Judge Richardson and Colonel McLeod. They were defended by Mr. Beverley Robertson, who was instructed by the Crown to do so. With the exception of White Cap, these chiefs were likewise sentenced to undergo an imprisonment in the Manitoba Penitentiary. At Battleford, the Indians who had committed the murders around that region and the massacre at Frog Lake were arraigned before Judge Rouleau, upon the charge of murder. Other Indians were also arraigned upon minor charges. Eleven of them were sentenced to be hanged upon the 27th of November. Two of them had been convicted of murdering a squaw, who was accused by the Indians of the crime of "wittigo" or cannibalism; they were reprieved, and their sentences commuted to imprisonment for life. Louis Mongrain, who shot Cowan at Fort Pitt, also had his sentence commuted to imprisonment for life. This clemency was in consequence of his having notified the farm instructor, Mr. Mann, and his family, in time to save their lives at Onion Lake.

The following are the names of those who were tried before Judge Rouleau, and sentenced to be hanged: Pa-pa-mah-cha-kaw-yo (Wandering Spirit), for murdering Thomas Quinn, Indian agent; Ickta, for the murder of Payne, the farm instructor at Battleford; Louis Mongrain, who killed Cowan, shooting him dead after he was wounded, sentenced to be hanged, sentence commuted; Apistaskous (Little Bear), and Napase, *alias* Iron Body, were sentenced for the murder of George Dill; Pa-pa-mek-sick (Round the Sky), was sentenced for the murder of the Reverend François Xavier Farfard, who was killed by him when wounded; Wa-Wa-Nitch (the Man Without Blood), was sentenced for the murder of Bernard Tremont; Manetchus (Bad Arrow) and Kitiemakyin (Miserable Man) were sentenced to be hanged for the murder of Charles Gouin. The Indian who killed the Reverend Father Marchand escaped to the United States with Little Poplar.

On the morning of the 27th of November, at Battleford, the day broke dark and cloudy, with a frosty air, upon the execution of the eight Indians who had been sentenced to be hanged for murder. The hangings were conducted publicly, and were witnessed by a large number of whites and a few Indians. The Government authorities had permitted Indians from reserves distant ten or fifteen miles from Battleford to be present at the execution, and all night groups of the braves hung about the stores and camped upon the open ground in the vicinity of the barracks of the Mounted Police. Camp-fires lit up the prairies, and the comrades of the warriors to be executed could be heard chanting the death-songs of their tribes. Fathers Bigonnesse and Cochin remained with the condemned Indians all night. At 7:30 in the morning, each man was pinioned and marched to the scaffold, around which a strong guard was thrown. The scaffold was so arranged that each man took his place on the trap, side by side. When they were asked if they had anything to say, Wandering Spirit, in his native tongue, acknowledged that he deserved death. He warned his people not to make war on the whites, as they were their friends. He told of the Frog Lake massacre, and took the burden of the crime upon himself. He was followed by Miserable Man, who spoke in the same strain. When he had concluded, the condemned Indians, who had remained quiet through the speeches, except to exclaim "how" at various periods during Wandering Spirit's address, to signify their acquiescence in what he said, began to chant their death-song. All the while the priests could be heard reciting prayers. The chant of the savages continued even after the white caps had been adjusted, and in the midst of their song the bolt was drawn and all fell together, each one apparently dying instantly. Dr. Rolph examined the bodies and pronounced life extinct, and in fifteen minutes they were cut down and placed in coffins, and handed over to the coroner and jury. The executions occurred without any mishap. The Indians who stood at a distance and witnessed the affair were quiet, and immediately after the executions most of them set out for their reserves. Those who remained behind showed no special signs of excitement. Though all must deplore the necessity that arose for setting so severe an example, it was done in the cause of humanity. The lesson which the Indians have been taught has been a severe one and most judicial in its character, but it will do them good in the long run, and render the peace of the country more secure – and now having asserted the majesty of the law, Canadians will realize that clemency to those misguided men who are undergoing their sentence would be magnanimous and humane.

OTHER BOOKS OF INTEREST FROM JAMES LORIMER & COMPANY

STRANGE EMPIRE
Louis Riel and the Métis People

Joseph Howard

Both a biography of Louis Riel and a history of the Métis, *Strange Empire* has long been considered a classic of Canadian History. First published in the United States in 1952, *Strange Empire* in its new edition includes an introduction by Martin Robin.

SALT OF THE EARTH
Heather Robertson

This collection of photographs and text tells the story of the homesteaders who streamed to the Canadian West from 1880 to 1914. It is the settlers themselves who describe their experiences in letters, diaries, autobiographies and reminiscences. From these accounts emerges a rich portrait of the West's pioneering past.

JOURNEYS TO THE FAR WEST
Accounts of the Adventurers in Western Canada, 1858 to 1885

Edward Cavell

Through a combination of handsome historical photographs and excerpts from explorers' own accounts, Edward Cavell brings to life the period that saw the West opened up for colonization.

PEASANTS IN THE PROMISED LAND
Canada and the Ukrainians, 1891-1914

Jaroslav Petryshyn

For the peasants of the Ukraine, Canada was the promised land. Here is a rich, detailed account of their struggle – against the toil and heartbreak of homesteading on the unforgiving prairie, and against the prejudice and exploitation with which many Canadians welcomed them to the new land.

THE WEST
The History of a Region in Confederation

J.F. Conway

Here is the history of Confederation – from the point of view of the four western provinces. John Conway shows that although the focus of western dissatisfaction may have changed in recent years, the root cause – having to "buy dear and sell cheap" – remains.

THE NORTH-WEST IN 1885

CHURCHILL

Ile à la Crosse

Canoe Lake

Beaver River

Loon Lake

Green Lake

SASKA

North

Turtle Lake

Fort Pitt

Saskatchewan

Birch Lake

Prince Albert

SASKATCHEW

Battle

River

Fort Carlton

St. Laurent

River

CUT KNIFE HILL

Battleford

EAGLE HILLS

Duck Lake

Batoche

BIRCH HILLS

ALTA.

Clarke's Crossing

SASKATOON

Humboldt

MANITOBA AND

Eagle River

TOUCHWOOD HILLS

NORTHWE

South

Saskatchewan

River

Long Lake

Qu'Appelle

Fort Qu'Ap

Swift Current

REGINA

Troy (Qu'Appelle)

ASSINIBOIA

0   50   100 Miles

UNITED STATE